THE ETTRICK SHEPHERD

THE
ETTRICK SHEPHERD

BY

EDITH C. BATHO

CAMBRIDGE
AT THE UNIVERSITY PRESS
1927

CAMBRIDGE
UNIVERSITY PRESS

University Printing House, Cambridge CB2 8BS, United Kingdom

Published in the United States of America by Cambridge University Press, New York

Cambridge University Press is part of the University of Cambridge.

It furthers the University's mission by disseminating knowledge in the pursuit of education, learning and research at the highest international levels of excellence.

www.cambridge.org
Information on this title: www.cambridge.org/9781107638433

First published 1927
First paperback edition 2014

A catalogue record for this publication is available from the British Library

ISBN 978-1-107-63843-3 Paperback

To

W. P. KER

CONTENTS

PREFATORY NOTE

To most of us the Ettrick Shepherd is scarcely more than a name: we have all read how "Bonny Kilmeny gaed up the glen," and wondered at that delicate piece of magic, and we think vaguely of the author as a protégé of Scott and the hero of certain laughable anecdotes told by Lockhart and others. It is not always realised that besides *Kilmeny* Hogg produced a formidably large quantity of prose and poetry, of which little is worthless, much of good second-class quality, and some among the best of its kind; and that he himself is a figure of unusual interest. He stood between two worlds, a belated minstrel making his living, for the greater part of his life, by journalism. He was an almost uneducated peasant, not, like Burns, in the true line of Scottish poets, but far more original and racy and, in a sense, cultured than the purely peasant poets with whom it might seem natural to compare him, and the second-rate literary men with whom some of his work would associate him. He knew nearly all his great and most of his lesser contemporaries, and was liked and laughed at by all of them. Scott comes with justice first on the list, unfailing in kindness and generosity from their earliest meeting over *The Minstrelsy of the Scottish Border*; Wordsworth displays a degree of humorous appreciation of character of which he might not have been suspected, and is moved by the news of the Shepherd's death to write one of the tenderest of his poems—his lament for the makers; Byron writes him friendly letters—afterwards stolen, he tells us indignantly, by a conscienceless visitor. He moves through the literary and polite society of his day, sometimes outraging conventions but more often escaping happily from unseen difficulties by his observance of what is, after all, the fundamental rule of good breeding, that of having only one set of manners for all companies. Some aspects of his character are glorified by Wilson in his portrait of the Ettrick Shepherd in the *Noctes Ambrosianae*, but not the whole truth is there. The sketches by Mrs Oliphant, Mrs MacCunn and Sir George Douglas give an impression whose truth is confirmed by reading Hogg's works, but these, like the recent biographical study by Professor H. T. Stephenson, deal almost exclusively with one side of the question, that of personality. There has been no general critical study, except the essay by Professor Saintsbury, and that does not cover the whole ground.

Hogg's literary relations contain several points of interest which have not been fully investigated: though Lang vindicated the honesty of both Scott and Hogg in the matter of the *Border Minstrelsy*, there is other evidence to be given; and no one has, to my knowledge, dealt with the curious incident of Hogg's adaptation of some of Moore's *Irish Melodies*, or, by telling the full history of the publication of *The Domestic Manners of Sir Walter Scott*, disproved the charges sometimes brought against Lockhart on Hogg's behalf. And no one has considered the voluminous works of the Shepherd in detail from the critical standpoint. That is the chief object of this study, but biography has not been and could not be altogether excluded.

There is no complete edition of Hogg, just as there is no authoritative detailed biography, Thomson's edition and memoir of 1865 being the nearest to both but not entirely trustworthy in either respect. Delightful as Hogg is at his best, both in life and in literature, he hardly deserves to have his life fully written or his works fully edited, but anyone who wishes to undertake either task will, I hope, find the Bibliography and List of Authorities appended to this study useful. It is probable that in spite of efforts at completeness in the Bibliography, some things have escaped my notice, and in the List I have not included references to books and articles which appear to be purely derivative or to unimportant contemporary reviews.

This study in its original form was accepted as a thesis for the M.A. degree of the University of London, and was awarded the Rose Mary Crawshay Prize of the British Academy in 1922. It has since been considerably revised and enlarged, and is now published with the assistance of a grant from the Publications Board of the University of London. One correction on p. 25—from "tower" to "bower"—I owe to the courtesy of Mr Hugh Walpole and the kindness of Mr A. D. Chander, who verified the passage in Hogg's original letter now among the Abbotsford MSS. In the general work of revision I have to thank Professor R. W. Chambers and Professor J. G. Robertson for criticism and help; to W. P. Ker my thanks cannot now be expressed, but it is good to remember that it is with his permission that the book is dedicated to him.

E. C. B.

University College, London
March, 1927

THE ETTRICK SHEPHERD

1. *EARLY STRUGGLES*

JAMES HOGG, more euphoniously known as the Ettrick Shepherd, was born towards the end of 1770, the oldest as he was the latest survivor of the poets commemorated by Wordsworth in the *Extempore Effusion.* He came of good country stock on both sides. His father, Robert Hogg, could claim descent from the Hoggs of Fauldshope, a connection of which the son was proud, chiefly, one suspects, because "several of the wives of Fauldshope were supposed to be rank witches," and one of them, though she subsequently had reason to regret her triumph, even had the better of Michael Scott himself. Margaret Laidlaw, the Shepherd's mother, was the daughter of William Laidlaw of Fawhope or Phawhope, commonly called Will o' Phaup, whose feats of strength and dealings with the Good Folk and other less pleasant people his grandson has saved from oblivion. It is not difficult to see some of Hogg's own nature in this description:

> Will o' Phaup, one of the genuine Laidlaws of Craik, was born at that place in 1691. He was shepherd in Phaup for fifty-five years. For feats of frolic, strength, and agility, he had no equal in his day. In the hall of the laird, at the farmer's ingle, and in the shepherd's cot, Will was alike a welcome guest; and in whatever company he was, he kept the whole in one roar of merriment. . . .He was the last man of this wild region, who heard, saw, and conversed with the fairies; and that not once, or twice, but at sundry times and seasons.

It was from the Laidlaws, not the Hoggs, that James Hogg inherited the unearthly imagination which inspired his best work, the lightness of heart and love of frolic which carried him through all his troubles, and the touch of personal charm which makes it difficult for the most severe moralist to frown very heavily on his sins.

Robert Hogg was originally a shepherd but prospered sufficiently to take the two farms of Ettrickhall and Ettrickhouse. He was a man of some ability and note, a ruling elder in the parish, and at the time of the birth of James, his second son, his fortunes were at their highest. There were three other sons, all of whom became shepherds: William, who also tried his hand at writing and was the father of a poetical son, Robert; David, afterwards in the service of Sir Walter Scott; and Robert, who emigrated to the United States about 1830 but died either on the voyage or shortly after landing[1].

When James was six years old, his father was ruined by falling prices and a defaulting debtor, everything had to be sold, and it was only through the kindness of Brydon of Crosslee, who took the farm of Ettrickhouse and let Robert Hogg live on there as his shepherd, that the family was not left without shelter. Little Jamie was sent to herd cows for wages of a ewe-lamb and a pair of shoes for the half-year. Next winter he went to school—he could already read a little—and was there until the spring, when his schooling stopped for ever, so that at the most he had only six months of it. Then came long years of herding, first of cows and later of sheep, never an easy life, and a very hard one for the child who began it so young. There is one pretty story of those early days:

That summer, when only eight years of age, I was sent out to a height called Broad-heads with a rosy-cheeked maiden to herd a flock of new-weaned lambs, and I had my mischievous cows to

[1] His wife and children settled at Silver Lake, Susquehanna; I do not know whether they founded an American line.

herd besides. But, as she had no dog and I had an excellent one, I was ordered to keep close by her. Never was a master's order better obeyed. Day after day I herded the cows and the lambs both, and Betty had nothing to do but to sit and sew. Then we dined together every day at a well near to the Shiel-sike head, and after dinner I laid my head down on her lap, covered her bare feet with my plaid, and pretended to fall sound asleep. One day I heard her say to herself, "Poor little laddie! he's juist tired to death," and then I wept till I was afraid she would feel the warm tears trickling on her knee. I wished my master, who was a handsome young man, would fall in love with her and marry her, wondering how he could be so blind and stupid as not to do it. But I thought if I were he, I would know well what to do.

But he rarely had more company than his own, and he found amusement partly in running races against himself and partly in dreaming.

Very early in Hogg's life it is possible to trace the two most marked sides of his character, the physical vigour and high animal spirits, and the quick imagination and sensibility. Both found sufficient nourishment in the circumstances of his childhood and youth. The long days spent in the open air hardened a constitution originally not strong, and the absence of regular schooling was compensated for by that education through tradition which is now almost unknown. He was fortunate in the place of his birth, in the midst of that Border country which rings with history and romance, where every stream and hill has a tale to tell even to us whose knowledge comes too much from books; where in Hogg's childhood the Covenanters were a memory of yesterday, and Border raids of the day before; and those were alive who had witnessed the strivings of the great and worthy Mr Boston, minister of Ettrick, and his spiritual brother, Mr Davieson of Galashiels, with unhappy ghosts. In those remote districts, almost cut off for much of the year from the outer world, there were still strange beasts and apparitions about. Old Andrew Moore, Mr Boston's servant, whom Margaret Laidlaw knew well, had himself seen the water-cow of St Mary's Loch come swimming towards him and his comrades in the evening twilight; and a farmer of Bowerhope once got a breed of her, who throve well until one pleasant March evening she appeared and summoned them with such a roar that all the hills shook again, "upon which her progeny, nineteen in number, followed her all quietly into the loch and were never more seen." The devil himself and the witches his creatures went about openly after dark, and even in broad daylight there was no safety from their malice except by taking many precautions. As for less harmful beings such as brownies, though they had not been seen very recently, it might be supposed that they had not vanished entirely and for ever. Then Hogg's mother and her brother had between them an almost inexhaustible collection of old songs and stories, which united with the living legend and beliefs of the countryside to give him a complete education of one kind; and for the moment it was of comparatively small importance that he had forgotten how to write and could only read with great pains. At fourteen, when he was with Scott of Singlee—the last of a dozen masters who had succeeded each other as he grew stronger and fit to receive higher wages—a new and keen pleasure came to him. With five shillings which he had saved he bought a fiddle and, though he does not tell us how he learnt to play it, he seems afterwards to have had some skill and some knowledge of music.

A year later he passed into the service of his distant cousins the Laidlaws, first at Elibank, then at Willanslee, and finally at Blackhouse. One of the sons at Blackhouse was that William Laidlaw who was later Scott's friend and amanuensis, and he has left us a pleasant picture of Hogg as he was at Whitsuntide 1790:

> His face was fair, round and ruddy, with big blue eyes that beamed with humour, gaiety, and glee.... His height was a little above the average size, his form at that period was of faultless symmetry, which nature had endowed with almost unequalled agility and swiftness of foot. His head was covered with a singular profusion of light brown hair, which he usually wore coiled up under his hat. When he used to enter church on Sunday (of which he was at all times a regular attendant), after lifting his hat, he used to raise his right hand to his hair to assist a shake of his head, when his long hair fell over his loins, and every female eye at least was turned upon him as with a light step he ascended to the gallery.

This description needs some correction, for the hair had a strong tinge of the sandy and the eyes were rather blue-grey than the much more unusual blue, but the hints of character in it are supplemented and strengthened by the remarks of a shrewd American observer forty years later[1]:

> His face is very pleasing, and shows much good nature and self-complacency. His light grey eye, when at rest, would not be distinguished for either quickness or brilliancy; his lips rather large, and not firm, seem to lack decision—if it were not for his noble forehead he might pass in a crowd for an ordinary man—a respectable farmer—but his is a broad and lofty brow, denoting both judgment and imagination.... There is indeed much resemblance in the face of Hogg to that of Scott: the head of the latter from the eyebrows to the crown is much higher, the lips firmer and more compressed; and the arch of the eye more prominent, but still there is a striking resemblance between them.

---

[1] *A Visit to the Ettrick Shepherd* (*American Monthly Magazine*, vol. III, pp. 85–91).

The mouth not too firmly set might have been suspected, but both pictures are attractive in their lines of good humour, innocent vanity and sensibility. "I have liked the women a great deal better than the men ever since I remember," Hogg himself remarks with charming simplicity; he seems to have fallen in love frequently and easily but never, as far as can be judged, at that period very seriously—he adored rather Lovely Woman in general than, at least with any depth of feeling, a succession of particular women.

Owing to the encouragement of the Laidlaws, Hogg began to read seriously and taught himself to write by copying Italic printing. They lent him books, and his knowledge of literature, which had hitherto been confined to the Bible and the Metrical Psalms, grew more general, but though his reading was curiously mixed, it was never very great. He used to read to his father James Hervey's *Meditations among the Tombs*; he knew also John Harvey's *Life of Bruce* and Hamilton of Gilbertfield's *Wallace*; he knew almost by heart Ramsay's *Gentle Shepherd*, whose influence can be seen in his own pastorals; and another book which influenced him and is probably responsible for some of his wild cosmogony was Burnet's *Conflagration of the Earth*. "I cannot think of such a treasure as Burns possessed in the days of his youthful ardour, without envying him," he wrote long afterwards. In reading poetry he found curious and unexpected difficulty in getting used to the forms of verse. He was, he tells us, "immoderately fond" of *Wallace* and *The Gentle Shepherd*, but he wished that they had been in prose or in the metre of the Psalms. The Scots of Ramsay was another distress, as any deviation from normal spelling always is to those who read with effort. "Before I got to the end of a line," he explains, "I had commonly lost the rhyme of the preceding one; and if I came to a triplet, a thing of which I had no conception, I commonly read to the foot of the page without perceiving that I had lost the rhyme altogether. I thought the author had been straitened for rhymes, and had just made a part of it do as well as he could without them." The younger Laidlaws helped him out of these and similar difficulties, and before he was twenty-five he was not only composing verses on his own account—he had done that by ear, imitating the songs with which he was familiar, from his childhood—but writing them down and publishing them.

The Shepherd was fond of writing about himself, as he himself confessed, and he did it most fully in the Memoir which was published with the first edition of *The Mountain Bard* and again, with additions and omissions, whenever he felt that public interest in him needed stimulating. From this, checked by contemporary articles by Z[1]—who, if he was not actually Hogg himself, wrote under his close supervision—it is possible to trace his career with some certainty from 1793 onwards. He himself afterwards told how in 1797 he heard for the first time of Burns and wept because he could not write and therefore could not be a poet—a pretty and touching story, the end of which will not bear examination. Not only could he write in 1797, but he was writing poetry four years earlier and published his first poem in 1794. The story, which, however, is very likely true in part and only exaggerated for artistic reasons, does not occur in the first, the 1807, edition of the Memoir,

[1] In the *Scots Magazine* for 1805; v. *List of Authorities*.

where Hogg states that he began to write in the spring of 1793 and gives the titles of some poems written between 1793 and 1797. The first thing which he attempted was a poetical epistle to a friend, a student of divinity, "a piece of most fulsome flattery," he tells us, "mostly composed of borrowed lines and sentences from Dryden's *Virgil* and Hervey's *Life of Bruce*." Then came *An Address to the Duke of Buccleuch, in beha'f o' mysel', an' ither poor folk*; a song called *The Way that the World goes on*; an eclogue, *Wattie and Geordie's Foreign Intelligence*; and, arising out of a conversation with an old woman called Cameron from Lochaber—probably Mrs Betty Cameron, who had, or had not, some hand in the *Jacobite Relics*[1]—*Glengyle*, a ballad[2], and *The Happy Swains*, a pastoral in four parts which seems to have had its scene laid in the year 1746.

Besides these acknowledged poems of 1793–4, we have the credible evidence of Z that Hogg wrote an unsigned poem which appeared in the *Scots Magazine* for October 1794. It is however possible that this, *The Mistakes of a Night*, is the song that Hogg calls *The Way that the World goes on*, with its title altered by the editor so as to have some obvious connection with the plot. It is in the *Hallowe'en* stanza:

Tak my advice, ye airy lads,
That gang to see the lasses,
Keep weel your mind, for troth, the jads
Tell ilka thing that passes.

[1] *Vide* p. 41.

[2] This ballad, like most of the other poems mentioned here, is lost, but it is referred to in the 1803 *Tour*: "Query. Was it not remarkable that both you and I should each of us have made Glen-Gyle a party in a ballad in imitation of the ancients, and that before we had either seen or heard of each other? Answer. The poetical sound of the name, sir."

Anither thing I wad advise,
  To gang on moonlight weather;
A friend o' mine, he was sae wise,
  He kiss't his lass's mither,
        Ae Friday's night.

The poem is a rather clumsy affair, fumbling for words as Hogg did much later than this, and giving away the point of the story in the first stanza. Judging by its form, it seems possible that Hogg had heard some of Burns's poetry before 1797[1], though the name of its author may have been unknown to him. Hearing something of Burns's story may have fired his ambition, but that is another matter. He was quite sure that he could do as well: "I have much more time to read and compose than any ploughman could have, and can sing more old songs than any ploughman could in the world."

It may be noticed in passing that the Shepherd's honest admiration of Burns had the odd effect of confusing his mind about the date of his own birth. Accuracy, especially with regard to dates, was not his strong point, and though he was in fact baptized on December 9th, 1770, until nearly the end of his life he declared that he was born on January 25th, 1772. He may have reasoned that, as he was a shepherd poet, he must have had the same birthday as a ploughman poet, but the mistake in the year is less easy to explain. Dr Russell of Yarrow says that he was at last undeceived by the parish register and mourned over having two years less to live. But as late as 1834 he still believed that he was born on January 25th, and in a letter of that year[2] he tells how he had further

[1] He may however have learnt the stanza from *The Justing and Debate up at the Doun* in Ramsay's *Evergreen*, or from Ramsay's refashioning of *Christ's Kirk on the Green*.

[2] *Notes and Queries*, Fifth Series, XI, pp. 432–3; communicated by J. Manuel.

expected to die at the same age and on the same day as Burns—he had made another mistake and expected his death on August 21st instead of a month earlier—and he very nearly did die, as far as one can make out, from pure nervousness. "What would I give," he exclaims with that want of logic which is one of his charms, "to have a son on the 25th of Jan., for I am sure he would turn out the greatest poet of us all."

In 1795 he began a comedy in five acts, *The Scotch Gentleman*, which he only abandoned with reluctance in 1801. He had, indeed, always a hankering after the drama. In 1800 he made another attempt, the first two acts of a tragedy called *The Castle in the Wood*, but Laidlaw's comments on it were so unfavourable that Hogg "cursed his stupidity, threw it away, and began no more plays for some years." A romantic piece, *The Hunting of Badlewe*, was published in 1814 and again, with its title changed to *The Profligate Princes*, in the *Dramatic Tales* of 1817, which also included *All-Hallow Eve*, *Sir Anthony Moore*, and *The Haunted Glen*. Besides these, there is a pastoral play, *The Bush aboon Traquhair*, in the 1837 *Tales and Sketches*, and in 1822 Hogg produced in an access of loyal fury a disjointed kind of masque, *The Royal Jubilee*. Thomson includes *The Haunted Glen* in his large edition of Hogg, and some songs have been rescued from the other plays, but the Shepherd had no dramatic gifts, and his plays are only interesting as examples of the way in which he persisted in trying to do things which he could not do. Though his other early verses are bad they are not as bad as his plays. Z preserves two fragments which have not been reprinted; both are also mentioned in the Memoir. The first is part of a paraphrase of the 117th Psalm, as far from the original as any paraphrase:

Ye straggling sons of Greenland's rigid wilds,
Y' inhabitants of Asia's distant isles,
With all between, make this your final aim,
Your great Creator's goodness to proclaim.

Hogg had evidently read with attention the Paraphrases and Hymns at the end of his Bible, for there is a clear note here of "The spacious firmament on high." He was, he confesses, early introduced to Addison. The second, in much the same style, is the beginning of a poem entitled *Reflections on a view of the Nocturnal Heavens*, written in competition with his brother William and Alexander Laidlaw[1]. William Hogg's poem was considered the best, and that of James has only the merit—absent, he tells us, from his brother's—of being metrical:

'Tis solemn silence all, and not a breath
In this sequestered solitude, I hear;
Save where the bird of night his mournful scream
Sends from the ruins of yon lofty dome

—and so on. These are too much like the epistle to the divinity student, but Hogg was doing better work in his songs.

The 1831 volume of *Songs* contains some of these "songs of my youth," with annotations — *Donald MacDonald*, *By a Bush*, *Scotia's Glens*, *The Gloamin'*, and perhaps half-a-dozen more. Of *The Gloamin'* Hogg remarks that "the futile efforts of an untutored muse to reach the true pathetic are quite palpable, and bordering on the ridiculous"—a self-criticism true of

[1] In the 1807 Memoir this competition is dated 1796, but after 1821 it, like all Hogg's early work, is shifted some years further on. There can be hardly any doubt that Hogg told the truth in 1807 and afterwards tried to make himself more interesting by extending the period of his illiteracy. The dates of early poems are omitted or put later in later editions of the Memoir, and the competition is moved to 1798.

some of his verses but rather harsh in this instance. *Donald MacDonald* is however a much better song. It was composed about 1800, sung at a masonic meeting in Edinburgh with deserved applause, and received by General M'Donald, according to Hogg, as being made in his honour; but no one troubled about the author's name, and the Shepherd laments that he got neither credit nor profit from it. The odd thing is that he should have put two songs and no more into his first published volume, and neither of them *Donald MacDonald.* A possible explanation is that his visit to the Edinburgh publisher of this volume late in 1800 or early in 1801 was not so unpremeditated as he afterwards asserted, and that he had with him copies of what he then thought to be his most imposing work. Certainly his own account of the affair is not quite self-consistent:

> In 1801, believing that I was then become a grand poet, I most sapiently determined on publishing a pamphlet, and appealing to the world at once. This noble resolution was no sooner taken than executed....Having attended the Edinburgh market one Monday, with a number of sheep for sale, and being unable to dispose of them all, I put the remainder into a park until the market on Wednesday. Not knowing how to pass the interim, it came into my head that I would write a poem or two from my memory, and get them printed....I was obliged to select, not the best poems, but those that I remembered best.

It requires a great effort of faith to believe that Hogg really remembered the *Dialogue in a country Church Yard* and *The Death of Sir Niel Stuart and Donald M'Vane, Esq.* better than his songs.

Scottish Pastorals, Poems, Songs, etc., was published by John Taylor in the Grassmarket in January 1801 at the price of one shilling. It was not very successful, and success was hardly to be expected. The *Scots Magazine* of January 1801 was the only periodical to notice it, probably with the same kindly intention of encouraging a young poet as in its publication of *The Mistakes of a Night* seven years earlier, and the advice given to him then was still and always applicable: "to make his rhymes answer, and to attend more to grammatical accuracy." The rhymes in this volume are extraordinarily bad, and it is strange that he, who had a good ear for music, should at this time have had so little sense of the sounds of words. It is however possible that the easy rhyming of the ballads led him astray.

The *Scottish Pastorals* still survive, in spite of the bad paper and print which vexed their author. There is a copy in the British Museum, bound up with a guide to Birmingham and the *Miscellaneous Productions* of Thomas Dawson Lawrance, who was a friend of Goldsmith and bold enough to write a sequel to *The Deserted Village*. The *Pastorals* are neither so elegant nor so consistently amusing as *The Fair Auburnian*, but though Hogg was honestly ashamed of them and never reprinted any, they are not all as bad as he pretended. The first, *Geordie Fa's Dirge*, has a pleasant flow and half-refrain:

Baith auld an' young come join wi' me;
Come greet as if ye'd lost a plea;
Come shake your head, an' whinge, an' claw,
And murn the death of Geordie Fa.
Auld 'onest, hearty, jocun' carle!
Without a grane he left the warl'.
Death in a twinklin' quite bereft us
O' a' our joy, whan Geordie left us.
He was mair true than ony Roman;
Was lov'd by all—and fear'd by no man.

(Not so bold a rhyme as Pet Marjorie's)

The rich did woo, the poor did bless him;
But now he's dead, and fair we'll miss him.

. . . .

Ye poachers now scour up your guns;
Ye fishers try wha fastest runs;
The muirs and streams will sport afford ye,
Their harmless tenants live for Geordie.
On days whan he was young an' keen,
In vain ye watch'd the curlin' stream;
In spite o' ye a', wi' muckle pride,
He haul'd his sa'mon to the side.
Oft hae I stood hale days to see him,
But now he's dead, an' peace be wi' him.

The next poem, *Dusty; or Watie and Geordie's Review of Politics*, seems to be the same as that mentioned in the Memoir as *Watie and Geordie's Foreign Intelligence*; Geordie's dog Dusty has been hanged because his master could not pay the tax, and Geordie takes a gloomy view of public affairs in consequence. The description of Dusty's death is more pathetic than a good many of Hogg's pathetic verses. There is a curious point at the end: Geordie says that he must meet his Nelly "up on Annan's treat," a place which, according to Veitch in his remarks on the *Minstrelsy* version of *Yarrow*, does not exist; "it is a pure misnomer, a reading of Scott's own, which has no foundation either in tradition or fact." Scott had it from Hogg, who seems to use it here without guile.

Next comes *Willie an' Keatie*, which was quoted in full by the *Scots Magazine* as "no unfavourable specimen of the work." Hogg hints that it was founded on an affair of his own. The record of this "amour," as he coyly names it, is very long and tedious, though a few of the verses are pretty. He himself thought it not as good as the next poem, *A Dialogue in a country Church Yard*, which, written in memory of that Brydon of Crosslee who had shown so much kindness to the Hoggs, is not as excellent as its sentiments. A narrative follows, perhaps the very worst of all Hogg's stories in prose or verse, and last come two songs which are more like the Shepherd whom we know. They are not particularly good and the second at least is not as elegant in its nature as it tries to be in its language:

O Shepherd, the weather is misty and changing,
  Will you show me over the hills to Traquair?
I will, gentle stranger, but where are you ranging?
  So brisk a young gentleman walking is rare.
I came to the Forest to see the fine lasses,
  And sing wi' the shepherds on ilka green hill;
And now I am leaving this modern Parnassus,
  Of ilka thing in it I have got my fill.

The other song is more singable, but the Shepherd could do better than that. He needed some outside impulse to set him going in the right direction, and that was provided by his introduction to Scott.

2. *COMPILER AND EDITOR*

It was *The Minstrelsy of the Scottish Border* that roused Hogg and decided that the chief business of his life was to be poetry and not herding sheep. His share in it has been the cause of more confusion and misunderstanding than any of his later undertakings, but the facts can be made out.

In 1801 Laidlaw, who had not yet made Scott's acquaintance, heard from Mr Andrew Mercer, a Selkirk man in Edinburgh, that Scott was collecting ballads, and was asked to help in the work. He began to collect them himself and, knowing that Hogg's relations had preserved many old songs and traditions, enlisted him. The first reference by Scott to Hogg's labours is in a letter to Ellis dated April 20th, 1801: "One of our best reciters has turned religious in his later days, and finds out that old songs are unlawful." The pious reciter was Hogg's uncle, and in a letter of Hogg's to be quoted presently[1] there is a glorious description of the difficulties of dealing with him. He had his more worldly moments, however, and Hogg made the most of them. Some of the results are shown in a letter from Hogg to Laidlaw, preserved by Carruthers in the *Abbotsford Notanda*[2]:

> Dear Sir, I received yours, with the transcript, on the day before St Boswell's Fair, and am sorry to say it will not be in my power to procure you manuscripts of the two old ballads, especially as they which Mr Scott hath already collected are so near being published. I was talking to my uncle concerning them, and he tells me they are mostly escaped his memory, and they really are so—in so much, that of the whole long trans-

[1] Pp. 24–27, esp. the end. This uncle evidently gave Scott hints for Davie Deans.

[2] Pp. 115–7.

actions betwixt the Scottish king and Murray, he cannot make above half-a-dozen of stanzas to metre, and these are wretched. He attributed it to James V, but as he can mention no part of the song or tale from whence this is proven, I apprehend from some expressions it is much ancienter. Upon the whole, I think the thing worthy of investigation—the more so as he was the progenitor of a very respectable family, and seems to have been a man of the utmost boldness and magnanimity. What way he became possessed of Ettrick Forest, or from whom he conquered it, remains to me a mystery. When taken prisoner by the king at Permanscore, above Hanginshaw, where the traces of the encampments are still visible, and pleading the justice of his claim to Ettrick Forest, he hath this remarkable expression:

"I took it from the Soudan Turk
When you and your men durstna come see."

Who the devil was this Soudan Turk?...I imagine the whole manuscript might be procured from some of the connections of the family. Is it not in the library at Philiphaugh?

It may be noted here that Hogg took down the expression "Soudan Turk" quite fairly although he had not the faintest idea of the meaning. It was nonsense to him, and very possibly to his uncle too, but he left it without any attempt at emendation because he had heard it so. There are other instances of the same conscientiousness in his versions of other ballads, one of the most remarkable being in *Erlinton*[1].

[1] In Hogg's version, which Scott used:

"In my bower there is a wake,
And in that wake there is a wane."

Scott gave a satisfactory explanation of *wake* and *wane*. But in *Kilmeny*, ten years later, Hogg introduced the lines in a way that shows he did not understand them, but used them simply because he thought they sounded well:

"In yon green wood there is a waik,
And in that waik there is a wene,
And in that wene there is a maike....
In that green wene Kilmeny lay."

The place-name "Annan's treat" in Hogg's version of *Yarrow* (v. p. 16) seems to be another example of conscientiousness.

Scott used a version of *The Outlaw Murray* in which the words came in a different context, and altered them to make sense—"From Soudron I this forest wan." But the version which Aytoun found at Philiphaugh read "Soldan Turk," and so confirmed Hogg's honesty.

Hogg then proceeds to the second of the "two old ballads":

> As to the death of the Baron of Oakwood and his brother-in-law on Yarrow, if Mr Mercer or Mr Scott, or either of them, wisheth to see it poetically described, they might wait until my tragedy is performed at the Theatre-royal; and if that shall never take place, they must sit in darkness and the shadow of death for what light the poets of Bruce's time can afford them!
>
> I believe I could get as much from these traditions as to make good songs out of them myself. But without Mr Scott's permission this would be an imposition; neither would I undertake it without an order from him in his own handwriting, as I could not bring my language to bear with my date. As a supplement to his songs, if you please, you may send him the one I sent last to you: it will satisfy him, yea or nay, as to my abilities.

Hogg's later attempts at imitating old ballads show that his self-distrust at this time was well-founded. The last sentence is rather obscure, but possibly refers to an original ballad sent for the "imitation" section of the *Minstrelsy*, though none of Hogg's is there. The letter concludes:

> Haste; communicate this to him, and ask him if, in his researches, he hath lighted on that of John Armstrong of Gilnockie Hall[1] as I can procure him a copy of that. My uncle says it happened in the same reign with that of Murray, and if so, I am certain it has been written by the same bard. I could procure Mercer some stories—such as the tragical, though well-authenticated one of the unnatural murder of the son and heir of Sir Robert Scott of Thirlestane, the downfall of the family of Tushilaw, and the

[1] "Johnny Armstrong of Gilnockie is another song altogether" (than the *Johnny Armstrong* of the *Minstrelsy*); Hogg to Scott, June 30th, 1802.

horrid spirit that still haunts the Alders. And we might give him that of John Thomson's Aumrie, and the Bogle of Bell's Lakes.

My muse still lies dormant, and with me must sleep for ever, since a liberal public hath not given me what my sins and mine iniquities deserved.

I am yours for ever,

July 20th, 1801. JAMES HOGG.

This is clear enough so far; neither Laidlaw nor Hogg knew Scott personally, but Hogg was supplying Laidlaw with ballads and Laidlaw was sending them on to Scott, apparently through Mercer.

Scott does not seem to have made much use in his first two volumes—in the first edition at least—of the material supplied by Hogg, chiefly because he already had good versions, partly also because Hogg's stuff arrived too late to be easily fitted in and was reserved for the second edition. But with the third volume and the second edition of the two earlier volumes the case was altered. Some of Hogg's contributions call for little or no remark, but the authenticity of two ballads in the third volume—*Auld Maitland* and *The Lament of the Border Widow*—has been questioned, and there are interesting points in the history of *Otterburn*. The question of *Auld Maitland* has been, I think, settled entirely in Hogg's favour for sound reasons, philological and other: he told the truth[1]. Not the weakest of the arguments in its favour is that old Mrs Hogg knew it, long as it is, by heart, and Hogg's account of its effect on Scott, as she sang it, is worth giving. The two men had met for the first time the night before, not, as Hogg says, on the same day[2]: the Shepherd was summoned to Ramseycleuch, where Scott and

[1] For a summary of the evidence with regard to *Auld Maitland* and *Otterburn*, v. Appendix.

[2] *Vide* Carruthers, *Abbotsford Notanda*, pp. 129–31.

Laidlaw were spending the evening, and came "to tea," bringing with him sheaves of ballads and ballad fragments. Scott liked him at once and soon put him at his ease—not, one would imagine, a very difficult task. "The best proof of Jamie's enjoyment," writes Laidlaw, "was that he never sung a song that blessed night, and it was between two and three o'clock before we parted." Hogg was not often thus musically self-denying.

On the next morning Scott visited the Hoggs' cottage and heard old Mrs Hogg sing *Auld Maitland*, as the Shepherd reminded him in the *Lines to Sir Walter Scott*:

> Scarce grew thy lurking dread the less,
> Till she, the ancient minstreless,
> With fervid voice, and kindling eye,
> And withered arms waving on high,
> Sung forth these words in eldritch shriek,
> While tears stood on thy nut-brown cheek—
>
> "Na, we are nane o' the lads o' France,
> Nor e'er pretend to be;
> We be three lads of fair Scotland,
> Auld Maitland's sons, a' three!"
>
> Thy fist made all the table ring—
> "By —, sir, but that is the thing!"

She scolded him for printing the ballads "nouther richt spelled nor richt setten down"; and, indeed, for printing them at all. "They were made for singin' an' no' for readin', but ye hae broken the charm noo, an' they'll never be sung mair."

The rest of the chronicle may be read in the *Autobiography* and the *Domestic Manners*: including the argument about long and short sheep which afterwards betrayed the author of *The Black Dwarf* to Hogg, and—celebrated also in verse—the *Antiquary*-like incident at the chapel, where Scott found a tar-pot which he tried to prove was an ancient consecrated helmet.

I cherish still
Mirth at the scene, and ever will,
When o'er the fells we took our way;
('Tis twenty years, even to a day,
Since we two sought the fabled urn
Of marble blue by Rankleburn)[1];
No tomb appeared; but oft we traced
Towns, camps, and battle-lines effaced
Which never were, nor could remain,
Save in the bold enthusiast's brain:
The same to us—it turned our lays
To chiefs and tales of ancient days.
One broken pot alone was found
Deep in the rubbish under ground,
In middle of the ancient fane—
"A gallant helmet split in twain!"
The truth was obvious; but in faith
On you all words were waste of breath;
You only looked demure and sly,
And sore the brow fell o'er the eye;
You could not bear that you should ride
O'er pathless waste and forest wide,
Only to say that you had been
To see that nought was to be seen.

In the *Autobiography* Hogg refers to "a better version" of *Auld Maitland* which he afterwards obtained from a Laidlaw. I do not know whether he wrote this down, and if so what happened to the manuscript; his own quotations from the ballad in the *Lines to Sir Walter Scott* and *The Three Perils of Man* do not agree exactly with the Abbotsford MS or the *Minstrelsy*, but his uncertain memory may have caused the differences. His last words on *Auld Maitland* at that time are to be found in his letter to Scott of June 30th, 1802, already mentioned. This letter has been printed incompletely by Douglas in the *Familiar Letters* and

[1] It was eighteen years at most, but that is a detail.

also incompletely by Lang in *Sir Walter Scott and the Border Minstrelsy*; through the kindness of Professor W. P. Ker I am able to give it here in full:

Ettrick House, June 30, 1802.

Dear Sir, I have been perusing your Minstrelsy very diligently for a while past, and it being the first book I ever perused which was written by a person I had seen and conversed with, the consequence hath been to me a most sensible pleasure; for in fact it is the remarks and modern pieces that I have delighted most in, being as it were personally acquainted with many of the modern[1] pieces formerly.

My mother is actually a living miscellany of old songs. I never believed that she had half so many until I came to a trial. There are none[2] in your collection of which she hath not a part, and I should by this time[3] have had a great number written for your amusement,—thinking them all of great antiquity and lost to posterity—had I not luckily lighted upon a collection of songs, in two volumes, published by I know not who, in which I recognised about half a score of my mother's best songs almost word for word. No doubt I was piqued, but it saved me much trouble, paper, and ink; for I am carefully avoiding everything which I have seen or heard of being in print, although I have no doubt that I shall err, being acquainted with almost no collections of that sort; but I am not afraid that you too will mistake. I am still at a loss with respect to some[4]: such as the Battle of Flodden beginning "From Spey to the Border," a long poetical piece on the battle of Bannockburn, I fear modern: The Battle of the Boyne, Young Bateman's Ghost, all of which, and others which I cannot mind, I could mostly recover for a few miles' travel were I certain that they could be of any use concerning the above; and I might have mentioned May Colin and a duel between two friends, Graham and Bewick, undoubtedly very old. You must give me information in your answer. I have already scraped together a considerable quantity. Suspend your curiosity, Mr Scott. You will see them when I see you, of which I am as impatient as you can be to see the songs for your life. But as I suppose you have no personal acquaintance in this parish, it

[1] Corrected to *antient* by Douglas.

[2] some, Lang. [3] omitted, Lang.

[4] such...quantity, omitted, Douglas.

would be presumption in me to expect that you will visit my cottage, but I will attend you in any part of the Forest if you will send me word. I am far from supposing that a person of your discernment—d–n it, I'll blot out that word, 'tis so like flattery—I say I don't think that you would despise a shepherd's "humble cot an' hamely fare" as Burns hath it; yet though I would be extremely proud of a[1] visit, yet[2] hang me if I would know what I would do wi' ye[3].

I am surprised to find that the songs in your collection differ so widely from my mother's. Is[4] Mr Herd's MS genuine? I suspect it. Jamie Telfer differs in many particulars[5]. Johnny Armstrong of Gilnockie is another song altogether. I have seen a verse of my mother's way called Johnny[6] Armstrong's last goodnight cited in the *Spectator* and another in *Boswell's Journal*. It begins, "Is there ne'er a man in fair Scotland?" Do you know if this is in print, Mr Scott? In the Tale of Tomlin the whole of the interlude about the horse and the hawk is a distinct song altogether. Clerk Saunders is nearly the same with my mother's, until that stanza which ends, "was in the bower[7] last night wi' me," then with another verse or two which are not in yours, ends Clerk Saunders. All the rest of the song in your edition is another song altogether[8], which my mother hath mostly likewise, and I am persuaded from the change in the stile that she is right, for it is scarce consistent with the forepart of the ballad. I have made several additions and variations out, to the printed songs, for your inspection, but only when they could be inserted without disjointing the songs as they are at present; to have written all the variations would scarcely be possible, and I thought would embarrass you exceedingly. I have recovered another half verse of Old Maitlan, and have rhymed it thus—

Remember Piercy of the Scot
Hath cowr'd aneath thy hand;
For ilka drap o' Maitlen's blood
I'll gie thee rigs o' land.

---

[1] the, Douglas. [2] yet, omitted, Douglas.

[3] w'ye, Douglas. [4] Is...heart, omitted, Douglas.

[5] Hogg seems to have known the "Elliot" version, cf. Colonel Fitzwilliam Elliot, *Further Essays*, pp. 180–84. But this letter seems to show that Scott did not know the Elliot, or at least Mrs Hogg's, version before the first publication of the *Minstrelsy*.

[6] Johny, Lang. [7] tower, Lang and Ker transcript.

[8] Hogg was, of course, right here.

The two last lines only are original; you will easily perceive that they occur in the very place where we suspected a want. I am surprised to hear that this song is suspected by some to be a modern forgery; this will be best proved by most of the old people having a great part of it by heart. Many indeed are not aware of the manners of this place; it is but lately emerged from barbarity, and till this present age the poor illiterate people in these glens knew of no other entertainment in the long winter nights than in repeating and listening to those feats of their ancestors which I believe to be handed down inviolate from father to son for many generations, although no doubt, had a copy been taken of them at the end of every fifty years, there must have been some difference which the repeaters would have insensibly[1] fallen into, merely by the change of terms in that period. I believe it is thus that many very antient songs have been modernised, which yet to a connoisseur will bear visible marks of antiquity. The Maitlen, for instance[2], exclusive of its mode of description, is all composed of words which would, mostly every one, spell[3] and pronounce in the very same dialect that was spoken some centuries ago.

[4]I formed a project of collecting all the tenors of the tunes to which these old songs were sung, and having them set to music . . . ; but I find it impossible. I might compose kind of tunes to some of them, and adapt others, but can in no wise learn the original ones. I find it was only the subject matter which the old people concerned themselves about; and any kind of tunes that they had, they always make one to serve a great many songs.

My uncle hath never had any tune whatsoever saving that which he saith his prayer to: and my mother's is quite gone, by reason of age and frailty, and they have had a strong struggle with the world ever since I was born, in all which time, having seldom or never repeated many of the songs, her memory of them is much impaired. My uncle, said I! He is, Mr Scott, the most incorrigible man alive. I cannot help telling you this: he came one night professedly to see me and crack with me, as he said. Thinking this a fair opportunity I treated him with the best the house could afford, gave him a hearty glass, and to humour him, talked

[1] have insensibly have, Douglas.
[2] for instance, omitted, Douglas.
[3] both spell, Douglas.
[4] This paragraph and the next are omitted by Lang.

a little of religion. Thus I set him on, but good L–d, had you heard him, it was impossible to get him off again. In the course of his remarks he had occasion to cite Ralph Erskine. Sundry times he'd run to the dale where the books lay, get the sermons and read near every one of them from which he had a citation. What a deluge was poured on me of errors, sins, lusts, covenants broken, burned and buried, legal teachers, patronage, and what not! In short, my dram was lost to my purpose. The mentioning a song put him in a passion.

Pardon, my dear Sir, the freedom I have taken in addressing you,—it is my nature, and I could not resist the impulse or writing to you any longer. Let me hear from you as soon as this comes to your hand, and tell me when you will be in Ettrick Forest, and suffer me to subscribe myself, Sir, your most humble and affectionate servant,

JAMES HOGG.

For the *Border Widow* the evidence is not so conclusive as for *Auld Maitland*, but I think it falls into the same category as the Hogg version of *Otterburn*: "These [lines] I have been obliged to arrange somewhat myself...but so mixed are they with original lines and sentiments that I think, if you pleased, they might pass without any acknowledgement. Sure no man will like an old song the worse of being somewhat harmonious[1]."

The accusation against Hogg is that he made the ballad out of the song *Oh onochrie* in the first volume of Johnson's *Scots Musical Museum*, this song again being like *The Famous Flower of Serving Men* in Percy's *Reliques*. There is a close resemblance among the three, chiefly of situation, but also of phraseology. The general effect is not the same: the *Border Widow*, genuine or not, is poetry, and the others are only poetry in the lines which they share with it.

[1] Hogg to Scott, Sept. 10, 1802. *Vide* Appendix, p. 182.

Here, for convenience of comparison, is the *Border Widow*:

My love he built me a bonny bower,
And clad it a' wi' lilye flour,
A brawer bower ye ne'er did see,
Than my true love he built for me.

There came a man, by middle day,
He spied his sport, and went away;
And brought the king that very night,
Who brake my bower and slew my knight.

He slew my knight, to me sae dear,
He slew my knight and poin'd his gear;
My servants all for life did flee,
And left me in extremity.

I sew'd his sheet, making my mane;
I watch'd the corpse myself alane;
I watch'd his body night and day;
No living creature came that way.

I took his body on my back,
And whiles I gaed, and whiles I sat;
I digged a grave and laid him in,
And happ'd him with the sod sae green.

But think na ye my heart was sair,
When I laid the moul' on his yellow hair?
O think na ye my heart was wae,
When I turn'd about away to gae?

Nae living man I'll love again,
Since that my lovely knight is slain;
(Wi' ae lock of his yellow hair
I'll chain my heart for evermair).

Dr Blacklock told Burns[1] that *Oh onochrie* was composed on the massacre of Glencoe, and most of it was certainly composed in the 18th century and is intolerably elegant. The situation is the same as in the *Border Widow*, and one couplet is like it:

Even at the dead time of the night
They broke my Bower and slew my Knight.

[1] Note at end of vol. II of Johnson's *Scots Musical Museum*.

The next couplet is like the final couplet of the *Border Widow* in the *Minstrelsy*, but this, which I have bracketed above, was not in Hogg's version; it was added to that by Scott. In both poems it seems to be taken over from *Helen of Kirkconnel.*

The *Famous Flower* is much closer:

And there my love built me a bower,
Bedeck'd with many a fragrant flower;
A braver bower you ne'er did see
Than my true love did build for mee.

And there I livde a ladye gay,
Till fortune wrought our loves decay;
For there came foes so fierce a band,
That soon they overrun the land.

They came upon us in the night,
And brent my bower, and slew my knight;
And trembling hid in mans array
I scant with life escap'd away.

In the midst of this extremitie,
My servants all did from me flee:
Thus was I left myself alone,
With heart more cold than any stone.

After which the Famous Flower goes on with her story and ruins the tragedy.

The *Border Widow* is undeniably very like this, stanza 5 is very like *The Three Ravens*, and the last stanza and a half in Hogg's MS are so like *Helen of Kirkconnel* that it is not surprising that Scott added the final couplet from that poem. The tradition which Hogg gave with the lines is quite unhistorical, but he may not have invented it or them. Henderson points out[1] that the story is not true, and also that Scott makes no reference to *Oh onochrie* or the *Famous Flower*, but this may have been only an oversight or Scott may not have thought it worth while. If that

[1] In his edition of the *Minstrelsy*, vol. III, pp. 109–11.

be all, the *Famous Flower* is not the best kind of ballad and is just as likely to have borrowed from the *Border Widow* as that from it; in fact, it would seem that there was an old song remarkably like the *Border Widow* from which both *Oh onochrie* and the *Famous Flower* derived something. Whether anything of the last four stanzas of the *Widow* is original, whether they were attracted from the other ballads, whether Hogg added them to make the old song more harmonious, or whether the much-suspected man made a cento and sent it to Scott, cannot be decided. I think that Hogg made an old song more harmonious.

One thing may be noted, which leads on to some evidence which has been overlooked by critics. Henderson considers the art of the *Border Widow* "much more refined and faultless than that of the rude Border balladists"; that is a sweeping criticism of the Border ballads, and does not touch the fact that the *Border Widow* is not really a peculiarly Border ballad. It has been arbitrarily assigned to the Border, but it belongs to the kind of thing that might have happened and been sung of anywhere in this world or in faery. Except that it has a tradition attached to it without any right, it is more like another poem which came through Hogg than like anything else—a poem which is not in the *Minstrelsy* and may never have been sent to Scott, and which Hogg certainly did not forge. It is ancient, but after first admitting fairly that it was not his own, Hogg some years later worked it into a poem of his own without acknowledgement.

One of the best poems in Hogg's *Mountain Bard* is *Sir David Graeme*, but the most interesting thing in it has nothing to do with Sir David himself. The first line is this:

> The dow flew east, the dow flew west

and then Hogg has a footnote:

> I borrowed the above line from a beautiful old rhyme which I have often heard my mother repeat, but of which she knew no tradition, and from this introduction the part of the dove naturally arose. The rhyme runs thus:
>
> "The heron flew east, the heron flew west,
> The heron flew to the fair forest;
> She flew o'er streams and meadows green,
> And a' to see what could be seen;
> And when she saw the faithful pair
> Her breast grew sick, her head grew sair[1];
> For there she saw a lovely bower,
> Was a' clad o'er wi' lilly-flower[2];
> And in the bower there was a bed
> With[3] silken sheets, and weel down spread;
> And in the bed there lay a knight,
> Whose wounds did bleed both day and night;
> And by the bed there stood a stane,
> And there was set a leal maiden,
> With silver needle and silken thread,
> Stemming the wounds when they did bleed."

The lines must have haunted Hogg, for he brought them in again, without the doubtful four and this time without acknowledgement, in the poem which the shepherd William recited to the King and court in the eleventh chapter of *The Bridal of Polmood.* If Hogg were not so careless and disjointed a romancer that it is dangerous to suggest a reason for anything he did, it might be supposed that William, who died

[1] There are two versions of *Sir David Graeme,* and ll. 3–6 do not appear in the note to the revised version. Nor are they in the other Hogg version, v. p. 32. They are obviously not of the same date as the rest.

[2] Child, in his remarks on the *Border Widow,* asks whether the ballad-lily is a climbing plant; Henderson suggests that 'lily' is a colour-term. The simplest explanation is that the inside, not the outside, of the bower is referred to, as in the parallel verses (v. p. 33): "That was hanged with purple and pall."

[3] wi', in the revised version.

towards the end of the preceding chapter, was raised to life again simply for the sake of the verses, and, being alive, was made to play a bigger part in the story than was originally intended for him. The poem is good in spite of the mock-antique spelling which Hogg sometimes affected, but the best lines are these which follow and which are not of his making.

The *Herone* flewe eist, the *Herone* flewe weste,
The *Herone* flewe to the fayir foryste.
And ther scho sawe ane gudelye bouir,
Was all kledde ouir with the lille flouir:
And in that bouir ther was ane bedde,
With silkine scheitis, and welle dune spredde;
And in thilke bed ther laye ane knichte,
Hos oundis did bleide beth day and nicghte:
And by the bedde-syde ther stude ane stene,
And thereon sate ane leil maydene,
Withe silvere nedil, and silkene threde,
Stemmynge the oundis quhan they did blede.

The differences from the *Mountain Bard* version are very small and are probably due to Hogg's uncertain memory.

The real question is this: what is the relation between these verses, twice used by Hogg and apparently noticed by no one else before or since, and the verses on f. 165 of *The Commonplace Book of Richard Hill* (Balliol MS 354) which was not even described until by Coxe in 1852[1], and not printed even in part until Flügel published his *Neuenglisches Lesebuch* in 1895? I give them here from Flügel's later transcription in *Anglia*[2],

[1] Coxe, H. O., Catalogus Codicum MSS qui in collegiis aulisque Oxoniensibus hodie adservantur.

[2] *Anglia*, XXVI (Neue Folge XIV), 1903, pp. 175–6. In the *Lesebuch* they are on p. 142. Also in *Early English Lyrics*, ed. Chambers and Sidgwick, 1907, p. 148; and in *Songs, Carols, and other miscellaneous Poems from the Balliol MS* 352, *Richard Hill's*

merely modernising the spelling. "Make" in the refrain is "mate."

Lully, lulley, lully, lulley,
The falcon hath borne my make away.

He bare him up, he bare him down,
He bare him in to an orchard brown.
(*Refrain.*)

In that orchard there was an hall,
That was hanged with purple and pall.

And in that hall there was a bed,
It was hanged with gold so red.

And in that bed there lieth a knight,
His woundès bleeding day and night.

By that bed side kneeleth a may,
And she weepeth both night and day.

And by that bed side there standeth a stone,
Corpus Christi written thereon.

It is obvious that these verses are the same as Hogg's dove or heron verses, though neither their editors nor the editors of other versions make any reference to Hogg.

There are two other traditional versions, recovered within the last seventy years. One[1] was sent to *Notes and Queries* in 1862 by "ε.τ.κ.," who had taken it down some years earlier from a boy in a troupe of Christmas morris-dancers in North Staffordshire; he "had learnt it from his father, but had never seen it written or printed." The other version was taken

Commonplace Book, ed. Roman Dyboski, Ph.D. (E.E.T.S., 1907), p. 86. The text of the last agrees with Flügel's in *Anglia*, except that it reads be*dis* and bed*dis* in stanzas 6 and 7 respectively, and *Chris*ti in stanza 7, where Flügel has bede, bedde, and Xristi.

[1] *Notes and Queries*, Third Series, II. 103, Aug. 9, 1862; compared with Hill's version in *Notes and Queries*, Tenth Series, IV. 181, Sept. 2, 1905, by Mr Frank Sidgwick, who also prints it in the notes to *Early English Lyrics*, p. 357.

down in Derbyshire in 1908[1]. The earlier, Staffordshire, version may be quoted here for the sake of comparison:

> Over yonder's a park which is newly begun,
> *All bells in Paradise I heard them a-ring,*
> Which is silver on the outside and gold within,
> *And I love sweet Jesus above all thing.*
>
> And in that park there stands a hall,
> Which is covered all over with purple and pall,
>
> And in that hall there stands a bed,
> Which is hung all round with silk curtains red.
>
> And in that bed there lies a knight,
> Whose wounds they do bleed by day and by night.
>
> At that bedside there lies a stone,
> Which is our blessed Virgin Mary then kneeling on.
>
> At that bed's foot there lies a hound,
> Which is licking the blood as it daily runs down.
>
> At that bed's head there grows a thorn,
> Which was never so blossomed since Christ was born.

Except for the different refrain, this is an elaborated—one might fairly say corrupted—version of the poem in Hill's manuscript, but like Hogg's in running the "stone" and "maiden" stanzas together. The Derbyshire version is much more corrupt, indeed incoherent through the omission of the knight, but otherwise nearest the Staffordshire version. The only important difference between Hogg's version and Hill's is in the sudden turn of the last stanza of Hill's—the lifting of it into another and rarer atmosphere. Flügel at first considered *Lulley* the ordinary love-song which Hogg's version really is, but changed his

[1] Both versions are given in the *Journal of the Folk-Song Society*, IV, pp. 52–66, June 1910, and a cento of these two is given in *The English Carol Book*, ed. by Dr Percy Dearmer.—Again none of the editors of these later versions refers to Hogg's lines, which do not seem to have attracted their attention.

mind when he reprinted the lines in *Anglia*. His second view is certainly correct: "dieses lied ist eine geistliche allegorie." But what were the verses originally—sacred or profane?

Miss Annie Gilchrist, in an article[1] on the three "religious" versions, argues that the poem refers to (*a*) the Eucharist, (*b*) the Graal legend, varying the interpretation with each version and taking the Amfortas story "or perhaps even the Celtic legend of Arthur lying wounded in Avalon," as the original. This seems to me very doubtful. The title *Corpus Christi Carol*, which has been taken from the last stanza and lately been attached to the verses, has done some harm; it naturally suggests the Feast of Corpus Christi, which again suggests the Eucharist and the Graal; but the reference in the oldest version is obviously and simply to the Passion, and *Passion Carol* would be a better name. The view of Christ as the wounded knight is one of the commonplaces of mediaeval literature; the poem falls easily into an allegory of the Passion, lifted out of conditions of time and space into eternity[2], and so indirectly into an allegory of the Eucharist; but any detailed Eucharistical interpretation, and still more the interpretation which would fix every line into a description of Glastonbury and the sanctuary of the Graal, is too ingeniously complicated to be convincing. One cannot cram so much allegory into twelve lines and keep the poetry, and here the poetry is kept.

It is to be noted that the poem grows more elaborate

[1] With additional notes by Mr Frank Sidgwick and Mr G. R. S. Mead, *Journal of the Folk-Song Society*, IV, pp. 52–66, June 1910.

[2] There seems to be a touch of the same thought in the Danish ballad *Jesus og Jomfru Maria* (D.g.F., No. 97), where the Virgin finds her lost Son in his "Urtegaard."

and less pointed as it comes down. The hound is found only in the 1862 version, the thorn in 1862 and 1908; this 1908, Derbyshire, version has also a final stanza, turning it into a Christmas carol:

> Over that bed the moon shines bright,
> Denoting our Saviour was born this night:

and a peculiar stanza which is almost certainly a late addition is worth quoting for its hint of a memory of the *Passion* idea:

> Under that bed there runs a river,
> The one half runs water, the other runs blood.

The thorn, in 1862 perhaps still due to a confused memory that the verses were somehow connected with Joseph of Arimathea, may itself have caused the final development into a Christmas carol, and the hound may so well have come in from what may be called the *Three Ravens* tradition that it cannot fairly be used to press an argument one way or the other. Miss Gilchrist considers that the poem was originally secular, or at most concerned the wounded King Amfortas. But though the ballad type is older than the allegorising carol type, it does not follow that the particular *Passion Carol* was originally a secular ballad. The allegory there is not an ornament added by a pious transmitter, but of the essence of the poem, and Hogg's version falls short of the highest beauty by its lack of the religious element. Mrs Hogg "knew no tradition" of the rhyme; the stanza which explained it had been confused with the preceding stanza by the time it reached her, and I should guess that the merely pretty ending of "silver needle and silken thread" is due to her feeling or her son's that something was wanted to round off the sense.

Hogg's secular version is interesting not only in itself but for the witness it gives to his character at the beginning of his career and in 1820. In 1807 he adapted the first line to his purpose and almost unnecessarily gave his authority; in 1820 he embedded the whole poem among his own verses with no indication that the resulting mixture was not all of one piece; more than that, he told a tall story of his finding the "ancient song"—a story which his readers probably took and were intended to take as a commonplace method of introducing his own verses. In fact his actual crime in 1820 was the reverse of that of which he is accused in 1801. All the evidence we have points to his innocence in 1801, but he was certainly less scrupulous twenty years later.

Twice again in his life Hogg had to do with the collection and publication of other men's works, and though a good many years separated the three undertakings, it is convenient to consider them together. In the *Minstrelsy* he was at most a collaborator, but twenty years afterwards he appeared as a responsible editor. In consequence of a suggestion made at a dinner of the Highland Society of London, he was asked to collect and edit the Jacobite songs and ballads, and accordingly he produced the first volume of the *Jacobite Relics* in 1819, the second following in 1821. He had some of the qualities necessary in their editor: he knew the Highlands well and could make a Highlander talk, he had a good deal of traditional information—his father remembered the battle of Prestonpans—and though he had very little book-learning, he could, when confronted with great problems, apply to Scott for enlightenment.

"Hogg is here busy with his Jacobite Songs," Scott wrote to Lord Montagu (March 4th, 1819). "I wish he may get handsomely through, for he is profoundly ignorant of history, and it is an awkward thing to read in order that you may write. I give him all the help I can, but he sometimes poses me. For instance he came yesterday, open mouth, enquiring what great dignified clergyman had distinguished himself at Killiecrankie—not exactly the scene where one would have expected a churchman to shine—and I found with some difficulty, that he had mistaken Major-General Canon, called, in Kennedy's Latin Song, *Canonicus Gallovidiensis*, for the canon of a cathedral. *Ex ungue leonem*[1]."

But this want of learning prevented Hogg from being a really good editor or anything more than a collector, and he would have made a better book if he had let the historical annotations go and merely published the songs with a note on how he got them. Even so there would have been one question to ask, and that a serious question for his honesty. How much of the two volumes is not traditional but Hogg's own? He speaks with condemnation of the "modern manufacture" of most of the ballads in Cromek's collection, but his own conscience ought not to have been quite easy, though I do not think he was as guilty as some would make him.

In the first volume *Donald M'Gillavry* was inserted with intent to deceive, and Hogg owned it joyfully as soon as it had achieved its purpose. "That we may not close this article without a specimen of the good

[1] Lockhart, VI, 36–7. It is amusing to notice that Hogg took care that no one else should fall into his mistake. In his annotations to the song (*Jacobite Relics*, I, pp. 200–6) he observes that the phrase, "by many readers supposed to mean some great Galloway priest who had made a figure in the battle, refers to Colonel Cannon, who was a native of that country."

songs which the book contains," wrote the reviewer in the *Edinburgh* at the end of a not too favourable criticism[1], "we shall extract the one which, for sly characteristic Scotch humour, seems to us the best"; and he quotes *Donald M'Gillavry* in full. Hogg answered the criticism as a whole in a letter published in *Blackwood's* of October 1820 (pp. 67–75), but oddly kept his best stroke for his covering letter to "Christopher North": "After all, between ourselves, 'Donald Macgillavry,' which he has selected as the 'best specimen of the true old Jacobite Song,' and as remarkable above its fellows for 'sly characteristic Scotch humour,' is no other than a trifle of my own, which I put in to fill up a page." These two letters have never been reprinted as Hogg's[2], and have certainly been worked over by someone else, but there can be no doubt that they are his in essence and that *Donald M'Gillavry* is also his. He claimed it on other occasions, and it bears his stamp, not the stamp of the traditional Jacobite ballad.

Of the other songs in this volume, No. IX—*Hey, then up go we*—was included as Hogg's by Thomson, but it is taken from *Eglogue* XI in Quarles's *Shepheards Oracles*, published in 1646, and Hogg rightly and persistently disclaimed it. Thomson may have been misled by a copy in Hogg's hand-writing[3]. No. XXXIII—*I hae nae kith*—is a little doubtful, and so is No. XXI—*Willie the Wag*—but he never reprinted them as he did others no better. No. LXIV—*The Thistle of Scotland*—reads like his and had, according to him, been published as his, but he disclaims it.

In the second volume there is certainly much more

[1] *Edinburgh Review*, vol. XXXIV, pp. 148–60.

[2] *Vide* pp. 97–8.

[3] As with other songs, *v.* pp. 102–3.

of Hogg's, but most of it is covered by his note on pp. 300–1:

> I may here mention, once for all, that these songs from the Gaelic were mostly sent to me by different hands, translated simply into English prose, and have all been versified by me.

The additional note to No. LXXXV probably also applies more or less to all:

> I must beg pardon of the Highlanders for adding so much to the original ideas in this song.

There are other "translations from the Gaelic" signed "T. G.," whom Hogg professed, probably with truth, not to know; they do not read as if composed by himself, and his other ascriptions, to Willison Glass, William Nicholson, "a Mr William Glen about Glasgow," and Miss Blamire of Carlisle, can be checked. "M. L." stands or falls with "T. G." and I think they both stand. Hogg may of course have revised their work. Thus, *Culloden* is found in the works of both Glass and Nicholson, with considerable variations; the *Relics* version does not agree exactly with either, but is nearer Glass than Nicholson—Hogg shows some doubt over the authorship of their songs.

All the translations from the Gaelic, except those by "T. G." and *The Lament of Flora Macdonald*, were reprinted by Hogg as his own, perhaps on the ground that he had added so much to the original ideas that he had some claim to them. The *Lament* he professed to have revised from a "rude" version given to him by Niel Gow, "without altering one sentence." There are three others which I think belong to him although he did not reprint them. Two of these, Nos. LI and LVII, he almost explicitly owned. Of LI—*Turn the blue bonnets wha can*—he wrote, "Neither this beautiful air nor song have ever before been published. The name is ancient. I dare not take it upon me to say so much for either the words or the music." No. LVII—*Turnimspike*—"is an excellent and very popular song"—it is also very like Hogg—"but is rather one against the modern encroachments on the Highlander's liberty than any dynasty." The third is No. LXXXVIII—*Prince Charles and Flora Macdonald's Welcome to Skye*—which "was copied verbatim from the mouth of Mrs Betty Cameron from Lochaber....She said it was from the Gaelic, but if it is, I think it is likely to have been translated by herself. There is scarcely any song or air that I like better."

Now there probably was a Mrs Betty Cameron from Lochaber; at least Hogg referred to her in the 1807 Memoir, when he was still innocent; but that last sentence, and the whole song, make it very doubtful whether she had anything to do with *Prince Charles and Flora Macdonald's Welcome to Skye*.

There is no very serious attempt to deceive and keep up the deception here, but in a sequel to the *Jacobite Relics* Hogg is not to be acquitted of deliberate deception, unless it be argued that he told a story so elaborate that he thought it would betray itself. He sent half-a-dozen songs to the *Scots Magazine*, where they appeared in November 1821 and January and April 1822: some he said he had received from a gentleman in London, the others came from a collection made by a Cumberland schoolmaster. He afterwards acknowledged the second set as his own, and indeed they bear marks of their maker; they are *Red Clan-Ranald's Men*, *The Two Men of Colston*, which had when first printed an additional verse, and *Up an' Rin Awa, Geordie*. The London set are not like Hogg's, were never owned by him, and may possibly be genuine; he may have added his own, with the unlikely explanation of their origin, in order to swell the bulk of his contribution to the Magazine. But the affair inevitably raises a suspicion that he may have made similar additions to swell the bulk of the *Relics* themselves.

The edition of Burns which appeared in 1838 and the following years, though it bears the names of the Ettrick Shepherd and Motherwell, has comparatively little of Hogg in it. The publisher seems to have thought that there was a certain suitability in issuing the works of Burns edited by Hogg—one peasant poet on another; but the likeness between Burns and Hogg is barely superficial and hardly worth discussion, though it has frequently been discussed. The great difference between them, which comes out in nearly every line they wrote, was that Burns was a man of education and knowledge of all the traditions of Scottish verse, conscious of his own powers and able to use them, whereas Hogg had no education to speak of, no tradition except the ballad tradition—which, good as it is, will not carry a man far—and mixed with real genius a large vanity which was continually driving him to attempt things beyond his strength. A good song-writer himself, he might have edited Burns's songs, but nothing more.

In this edition, with one or two exceptions the notes are by Motherwell, and the Shepherd is responsible for the Memoir in the fifth volume[1]. It is very like Hogg—even with scraps of autobiography and verses of his own[2] inserted when his enthusiasm for his subject overpowered him. There are a few anecdotes which Hogg himself collected from those who knew Burns,

[1] None of it was published during Hogg's life, but he was engaged on it at least as early as 1832.

[2] The songs on pp. 28–9 and 287–8 of vol. v.

but the greater part of the Memoir is made up of quotations—not always acknowledged—from earlier biographers, especially Currie and Lockhart.

The conclusion of all this is that Hogg was a bad editor but an excellent "source" for a collector or editor. He knew a good many ballads and songs himself, he knew where to get more, and in his youth he was even slavishly faithful to his tradition. If he heard "Soudan Turk" where it made nonsense, he wrote it down and hoped for the best; if he heard "With springs: wall stanes and good of ern," he calmly wrote down that amazing nonsense and again hoped for the best. Now and then an incomplete stanza roused him to suggest a wooden couplet to fill the gap, but he claimed his own, and when he wrote a complete ballad in the manner of the ancients it was not intended to deceive and would not have deceived anyone. But by the time he came to the *Jacobite Relics* he had learned the lesson of forging for fun, with or without intent to deceive, and he had immediately before him the bad example of Allan Cunningham. It is at least possible that he wrote the doubtful songs in the *Relics* out of a spirit of emulation: if Cunningham could write Jacobite songs which would take in Cromek and others, Hogg was sure he himself could, and *Donald M'Gillavry* proved that he could. In the edition of Burns he attempted nothing shady and merely pointed out with verses of his own that he too could write songs. On the whole we are safe in considering him innocent in his youth and not so black as he has been painted in his later years.

3. *PICTURESQUE TOURS AND* THE MOUNTAIN BARD

To the *Scots Magazine*, which printed Hogg's first published poem and noticed his first volume, Hogg contributed frequently between 1803 and 1806, again in 1807–8, and sometimes between 1810 and 1822. His first direct introduction to the magazine was made in October 1802 by Scott, who sent some letters which Hogg had addressed to him, and explained in a covering letter that the author really was a shepherd of Ettrick[1]. These letters were published from October 1802 to June 1803 under the title of *A Journey through the Highlands of Scotland in the months of July and August* 1802, *in a Series of Letters to* ——, *Esq.*, and as they were the first of several chronicles of Hogg's Highland expeditions, and in some ways the most amusing, they deserve attention.

This seems to have been a holiday journey, unlike Hogg's earlier and one at least of his later visits to the Highlands; he had been as far as Breadalbane and Glenorchy about 1792, to look at sheep, and in 1801 "took another journey through the eastern parts of the Grampian Hills, penetrating as far as the sources of the Dee," and again looking about him with a

[1] The covering letter is signed S.W., but its writer was certainly Scott. The *Scots Magazine* had a tradition of kindliness towards young writers, and a fondness for printing letters of travel. Compare Darsie Latimer in the first chapter of *Redgauntlet*: "All I stipulate is, that you do not communicate (my letters) to the *Scots Magazine*; for . . . I am not yet audacious enough to enter the portal which the learned Ruddiman so kindly opened for the acolytes of the Muses."

professional eye. But sheep were not his business in 1802, and he takes some time in these letters to get even as far as Perth. He begins by describing Ettrick and Yarrow and their inhabitants, with stories of magic and spells, and after this introduction, travels to Edinburgh and takes up his lodgings in the Candlemaker Row, perhaps in the same house where he used in later years to give the suppers described by Robert Chambers[1]. He goes to see *The Heir at Law*, which he criticises, and attends the races at Leith, where the crowds remind him of bad dreams and so of his own *Dialogue in a country Church Yard*, "which in case you have not the opportunity of perusing, I will here transcribe the passage,"—and he accordingly does so. After seeing *Hamlet* and enjoying small adventures, he at last, in the fourth letter, reaches Perth and goes on by way of Dunkeld to Athol through wooded country—"I wished several times that Dr Johnson had passed that way." He goes on to Pitlochrie, Killiecrankie and the Garry, where he almost decides to go home, but dreaming that Scott comes to him angry at such faintness of heart, proceeds to Rannoch. Here the letters end, though the last is followed by "To be continued"; whether the editor, who had already shown signs of impatience and begun to publish the letters monthly instead of in alternate numbers, declined any more, or whether the Shepherd sent none, must be uncertain.

Hogg was by this time, June 1803, on the point of setting out on another journey, to the Western Highlands and the Isles, and of this also he wrote a lively account to Scott in letters which were not published until 1888. As a contrast to his adventures among the

[1] *Vide* pp. 107–8.

Great at Inverary—marred in his story by rather too strong a sense of himself as a comic figure—there is the less lucky adventure in Glenshiel:

Before it was quite dark I reached the inn of Invershiel, or Shiel-house, held by a Mr Johnston from Annandale. It is a large, slated house, but quite out of repair, and the accommodations are intolerably bad. The lower apartments are in utter confusion, and the family resides in the dining-room above. Consequently, they have only one room into which they thrust promiscuously every one that comes. The plaister of this being all discoloured, and full of chinks, the eye is continually tracing the outlines of monstrous animals and hobgoblins upon it. I got the best bed, but it was extremely hard, and the clothes had not the smell of roses. It was also inhabited by a number of little insects common enough in such places, and no sooner had I made a lodgement in their hereditary domains than I was attacked by a thousand strong. But what disturbed me much worse than all, I was awaked during the night by a whole band of Highlanders, both male and female, who entered my room and fell to drinking whisky with great freedom. They had much the appearance of a parcel of vagabonds, which they certainly were, but as the whole discourse was in Gaelic I knew nothing of what it was concerning, but it arose by degrees as the whisky operated, to an insufferable noise. I had by good fortune used more precaution that night than usual, having put my watch and all my money into my waistcoat and hid it beneath my head. I also took my thorn-staff into the bed with me, thereby manifesting a suspicion that I had never shewed before. I bore all this uproar with patience for nearly two hours in the middle of the night, until, either by accident or design, the candle was extinguished, when every one getting up, a great stir commenced, and I heard one distinctly ransacking my coat which was hanging upon a chair at a little distance from the bed. I cared not much for that, thinking that he could get nothing there, but not knowing where this might end I sprung to my feet in the bed, laid hold of my thorn-staff, and bellowed aloud for light. It was a good while ere this could be procured, and when it came the company were all gone but three men, who were making ready to lie down in another bed in the same room. I reprimanded the landlord with great bitterness for suffering such a disturbance in the room where I slept, and received for answer that all would be quiet now. They were all gone before I got up next morning, and it was not until next night that I perceived I had lost a packet of six letters which I carried, to as many gentlemen in Sutherland, and which prevented me effectually from making the tour of that large and little-frequented county. These being rolled up in a piece of paper by themselves and lodged in my breast pocket, some one of the gang had certainly carried off in expectation that it was something of more value.

Hogg was horrified by the complicated system of land tenure in Lewis, and still more by the method of ploughing usual there:

I could venture a wager that Cain himself had a more favourable method of tilling the ground. The man was walking by the side of the plough, and guiding it with his right hand. With the left he carried a plough-pattle over his shoulder, which he frequently heaved in a threatening manner at such of the horses as lagged behind; but as it had the same effect on them all, and rather caused the most fiery ones to rush on, he was obliged sometimes to throw it at the lazy ones. The coulter is very slender, points straight down, and is so placed that if it at all rip the ground it hath no effect in keeping the plough steady. The horses, impatient in their nature, go very fast, and the plough being so ticklish, the man is in a perpetual struggle, using every exertion to keep the plough in the ground, and after all, the furrow is in many places a mere scrape. The four ponies go all abreast, and such a long way before the plough, that at a little distance I could not imagine they had any connection with the man or it. They were all four tied to one pole, and a man, to whom the *puller* is a much more applicable name than the *driver*, keeps hold of it with both hands, and walking backwards as fast as he can, pulls them on. Those of them that walk too fast he claps the pole to their nose, which checks them. He finds means also to carry a small goad, with which he strikes the lazy ones on the face, asserting that that makes them spring forward. I had once an old brown mare, if he had struck her on the face he would have got her no farther in that direction. A man can scarcely conceive a more disagreeable employment than that of this "driver" as he is called. The ploughman's post being such a very troublesome one he is mostly in a bad humour, and if the line of horses angle, the plough in spite of his teeth is pulled out of the land to the side on which the line is advanced. This puts him into a rage, and he immediately throws the pattle, or a stone at the hindmost. Now, although the man may be a tolerable good archer, yet passion may make him miss, and the driver runs a risk of meeting with the fate of Goliath of Gath. But granting this should never happen, and the ploughman's aim should always hold good, yet "I own 'tis past my comprehension" how a man can walk so fast the whole day in a retrograde direction without falling, when he must that moment be trodden under foot by the horses. In fact I have seen many people who would be often missing their feet on such land although walking with their face foremost; and it is a fact that many of these drivers are hurt by accidents of the above nature.

In 1804 Hogg made yet another visit to the Highlands; his lease of Ettrickhouse had expired and he was thinking of emigrating to Harris, and on this visit he, with two friends who had decided to join him in his venture[1], intended to make the final arrangements. He was so confident of success that he had already written his poetical farewell to Ettrick, but it proved to be a luckless expedition:

We never, in our way out, walked an hour without being drenched to the skin, and mudded to the knees. . . . We never went on the sea, though but for a few miles, without encountering storms, accidents and dangers: nor ever, after leaving Greenock, proceeded one day by the route we intended, but either lost our way by land, or were thwarted by the winds and the sea.

Most of the time was spent in trying to reach Harris in stormy weather, and in the end Hogg failed to see the man he most needed to see. He wrote another series of letters to Scott and published them in the *Scots Magazine* in 1808 and 1809; they are more cheerful reading than might be expected, but the Shepherd was never depressed for long. One of the

[1] He calls them at first by their Christian names: "Mr William" and "Mr John." The surname of the first began with L. (v. Letter II), and from Hogg's description, he would seem to be Laidlaw; "Mr John" was a townsman, his surname (v. Letter II) began with G., and he was very probably John Grieve (v. p. 62).

best passages is this in which he hurries over some of his adventures, in the manner of Grumio:

> You would lose all patience, were I to detail the whole of our adventures in Uist, which are nevertheless well worthy of a place; and if you had not found fault with me in this respect, you should have heard such a story! What should I have heard, James? You should have heard what a curious waiter we had;—how he clasped his hands above his head whenever he could not comprehend our meaning;—how much we were at a loss for want of Gaelic;—how we hunted the rabbits;—tired of waiting at Kersaig, and set out to traverse the country on foot to its northern extremity, and there procure a passage for Harries. You should have heard of our unparalleled embarrassments and difficulties, and how we fell out with the natives and were obliged to return;—how we arrived again at the place where we set out in the morning, both completely drenched and fatigued;—how the house, and every part about it, was crowded with some hundreds of Lord Macdonald's people, who were assembled to pay their rents;—what an interesting group they were, and how surprised my two friends were at seeing such numbers in a place which they had judged a savage desert, and unfit for the nourishment of intellectual life. You should likewise have heard how our crew fell asleep on board, and could not be awaked;—of Donald's despair: and many other interesting particulars, of which you must now live and die in ignorance.

According to Z, after the Harris fiasco Hogg prepared for the press his first, second and third journeys through the Highlands, but with the exception of the 1803 journey they do not seem to have been published in volume form either during his life or after his death.

Hogg's later Highland adventures have not been chronicled so minutely, or at least the chronicles have not been published. There is one exception, the tour which he made about "the Trossacks and Loch Ketturin" in March 1811, and described in *The Spy* under the title of *Malise's Tour*; it was afterwards included in the *Winter Evening Tales* as *Highland Adventures*. He had an eye for the humour of the preparations which were being made for the benefit of visitors to the scene of *The Lady of the Lake*; there was to be a bower on the island, and a pretty girl in tartans to ferry tourists over; and a certain Duncan, having rashly pledged his credit that the Goblin of Correi Uriskin was frequently seen, had provided himself with the skin of "a monstrous shaggy black goat" so as to play the part and prevent any unfortunate disappointment. Hogg tells a story of the goblin which is told of other trolls who have deer under their protection, and one of the Shepherd's hosts told him a tale which he promptly turned into rhyme and afterwards utilised as the eleventh bard's song in *The Queen's Wake—The Fate of Macgregor*. It is a pity that no more of these letter-journals have been preserved, for the Shepherd's letters are always good reading, and one would like to know more of his adventures a few years later, when he was collecting the materials for the *Jacobite Relics*.

The gap between Hogg's first and second volumes of poetry was larger than any other interval between his publications; *The Mountain Bard* did not appear until 1807, though Hogg had contemplated issuing it at least as early as 1803. On one of his visits to Edinburgh in that year he called on Scott to ask his advice and was invited to dinner in Castle Street, and the story of that evening, though it has been frequently quoted from Lockhart's account, is too good not to be repeated here:

When Hogg entered the drawing-room, Mrs Scott, being at the time in a delicate state of health, was reclining on a sofa. The Shepherd, after being presented, and making his best bow, forthwith took possession of another sofa placed opposite to hers, and stretched himself thereupon at all his length; for, as he said afterwards, "I thought I could never do wrong to copy the lady of the house." As his dress at this period was precisely that in which any ordinary herdsman attends cattle to the market, and as his hands, moreover, bore most legible marks of a recent sheep-smearing, the lady of the house did not observe with perfect equanimity the novel usage to which her chintz was exposed. The Shepherd, however, remarked nothing of all this—dined heartily and drank freely, and, by jest, anecdote, and song, afforded plentiful merriment to the more civilized part of the company. As the liquor operated, his familiarity increased and strengthened; from "Mr Scott," he advanced to "Sherra," and thence to "Scott," "Walter," and "Wattie,"—until, at supper, he fairly convulsed the whole party by addressing Mrs Scott as "Charlotte."

Mrs Scott's polite silence seems to have had the unfortunate effect of assuring Hogg that the sofa was the right place for him, for he once shocked Mrs William Laidlaw by taking up the same position. His hostess received the reward of her patient endurance of an always unwelcome guest in the *Domestic Manners*, where Hogg exclaims enthusiastically:

I must say this of Lady Scott, though it was well known how jealous she was of the rank of Sir Walter's visitors, yet I was all my life received with the same kindness as if I had been a relation or one of the family....She is cradled in my remembrance, and ever shall be, as a sweet, kind, affectionate creature.

His only complaint against her was that for a long time she could not understand what he said to her.

A few days after that first dinner Hogg wrote to Scott, beginning with an apology and proceeding to business:

Dear Mr Scott, Ettrick-House, December 24, 1803.

I have been very impatient to hear from you. There is a certain affair of which you and I talked a little in private, and which must now be concluded, that naturally increaseth this.

I am afraid that I was at least half-seas over the night I was with you, for I cannot, for my life, recollect what passed when it was late; and, there being certainly a small vacuum in my brain, which, when empty, is quite empty, but is sometimes supplied with a small distillation of intellectual matter—this must have been empty that night, or it never could have been taken possession of by the fumes of the liquor so easily. If I was in the state in which I suspect that I was, I must have spoke a very great deal of nonsense, for which I beg ten thousand pardons. I have the consolation, however, of remembering that Mrs Scott kept in company all or most of the time, which she certainly could not have done, had I been very rude. I remember, too, of the filial injunction you gave at parting, cautioning me against being ensnared by the loose women in town. I am sure I had not reason enough left at that time to express either the half of my gratitude for the kind hint, or the utter abhorrence I inherit at those seminaries of lewdness.

You once promised me your best advice in the first lawsuit in which I had the particular happiness of being engaged. I am now going to ask it seriously in an affair, in which, I am sure, we will both take as much pleasure. It is this:—I have as many songs beside me, which are certainly the *worst* of my productions, as will make about one hundred pages close printed, and about two hundred, printed as the *Minstrelsy* is. Now, although I will not proceed without your consent and advice, yet I would have you to understand that I expect it, and have the scheme much at heart at present. The first thing that suggested it, was their extraordinary repute in Ettrick and its neighbourhood, and being everlastingly plagued with writing copies, and promising scores which I never meant to perform. As my last pamphlet was never known, save to a few friends, I wish your advice what pieces of it are worth preserving. The "Pastoral" I am resolved to insert, as I am "Sandy Tod." As to my manuscripts, they are endless; and as I doubt you will disapprove of publishing them wholesale, and letting the good help off the bad, I think you must trust to my discretion in the selection of a few. I wish likewise to know if you think a graven image on the first leaf is any recommendation; and if we might front the songs with a letter to you, giving an impartial account of my manner of life and education, and, which if you pleased to transcribe, putting He for I. Again, there is no publishing a book without a patron, and I have one or two in my eye, and of which I will, with my wonted assurance to you, give you the most free choice. The first is Walter Scott, Esq., Advocate, Sheriff-depute of Ettrick Forest, which, if permitted, I will address you in a dedication singular enough. The next is Lady Dalkeith, which, if you approved of, you must become the Editor yourself; and I shall give you my word for it, that neither word nor sentiment in it shall offend the most delicate ear. You will not be in the least jealous, if, alongst with my services to you, I present my kindest compliments to the sweet little lady whom you call Charlotte. As for Camp and Walter (I beg pardon for this pre-eminence), they will not mind them if I should exhaust my eloquence in compliments. Believe me, Dear Walter, your most devoted servant,

JAMES HOGG[1].

Scott, as might be expected, did not consent to the simple scheme of "putting He for I," but he accepted the dedication, wrote a prefatory letter to the Memoir, and persuaded Constable to take the book. Even after that there was considerable delay in its publication, due perhaps to the unsettled state of Hogg's affairs, the Harris scheme and his subsequent residence in England, but at last in 1807 *The Mountain Bard* was published with the Memoir of which parts have been quoted already. The Shepherd's account of the origin of his book deserves to be given.

In 1802, *The Minstrelsy of the Scottish Border* came into my hands; and though I was even astonished to find such exact copies of many old songs, which I had heard sung by people who never could read a song, but had them handed down by tradition; and likewise at the conformity of the notes, to the traditions and superstitions which are, even to this day, far from being eradicated from the minds of the people among our mountains,—yet, I confess, that I was not satisfied with many of the imitations of the ancients. I immediately chose a number of traditional facts, and set about imitating the different manners of the ancients myself. The chief of these are, *The Death of Douglas, Lord of Liddesdale*, *The Heir of Thirlestane*, *Sir David Graham*, *The Pedlar*, and *John Scott of Harden*, by the Scotts of Gilmanscleuch.

The last title must be a slip for *The Murder of John Scott*—the ballad which is now called *Gilmanscleuch*. In the third edition, instead of this sentence there is:

These ballads you have seen: and as they are the first things which you have approved, I have some thoughts of intruding myself once more on the public.

[1] Lockhart, II, pp. 169–72.

a rather obscure statement which hardly fits Hogg's circumstances in 1821. It may be a survival from the first draft of the Memoir, written perhaps in 1803 or 1804; *Douglas*, *Sir David Graham* and *The Pedlar* all appeared in the *Scots Magazine* in 1804–5.

The contents of *The Mountain Bard* vary considerably in different editions[1], and there is even some difference in the texts of the poems; there are two distinct versions, for instance, of *Sir David Graham*[2]. As might be expected, there are traces of the *Minstrelsy* in several of the ballads, but most of all in this. According to Hogg's prefatory note, it was founded on *The Twa Corbies*:

> It appears as if the bard had found his powers of description inadequate to a detail of the circumstances attending the fatal catastrophe, without suffering the interest already roused to subside, and had artfully consigned it over to the fancy of every reader to paint in what way he chose; or else that he lamented the untimely fate of a knight, whose base treatment he durst not otherwise make known than in that short parabolical dialogue. That the original is not improved in the following ballad will but too manifestly appear upon perusal.

The last sentence is merely Hogg doing his best to be modest; he gives a good many details with evident satisfaction, though in his first version he balks when he actually comes to the fatal catastrophe. The ghost of Sir David appears to his lady, who here seems to have had some hand in his murder:

> His grim, grim eyelids didna move;
> His thin, thin cheek was deadly pale;
> His mouth was black, and sair he strove
> T' impart to her some dreadful tale.

---

[1] *Vide* Bibliography, pp. 186–7.

[2] Or Graeme; Hogg himself changed the spelling of the name.

For thrice his withered hand he waved,
  And laid it on his bleeding breast.
Hast thou a tender heart received?
  How thou wilt tremble at the rest!

Fain wad I tell what there befel,
  But it's unmeet for mortal ear:
The dismal deeds on yonder fell
  Wad shock a human heart to hear.

And that is all. Hogg never quite cured himself of the habit of saying, "I wants to make your flesh creep" and then not doing it. The revised and longer version is more like *The Three Ravens* than *The Twa Corbies*: the lady is faithful and goes mad for grief:

There's a lady has lived in Hoswood tower,
  'Tis seven years past on St Lambert's day,
And aye when comes the vesper hour
  These words an' no more can she say:

"They slew my love on the wild Swaird green,
  As he was on his way to me;
An' the ravens picked his bonnie blue een,
  An' the tongue that was formed for courtesye.

"My brothers they slew my comely knight,
  An' his grave is red blood to the brim:
I thought to have slept out the lang, lang night,
  But they've wakened me, and wakened not him!"

That is very much better than the ghost.

Most of the poems in *The Mountain Bard* are good, especially those which are most distinctly not imitations of the ancients, *Farewell to Ettrick* and *The Author's Address to his auld dog Hector*; indeed Hogg never did anything better in its way than the *Address*:

Come, my auld, towzy, trusty friend,
  What gars ye look sae dung wi' wae?
D'ye think my favour's at an end,
  Because thy head is turnin' gray?

Although thy strength begins to fail,
  Its best was spent in serving me;
An' can I grudge thy wee bit meal,
  Some comfort in thy age to gie?

For mony a day, frae sun to sun,
  We've toiled fu' hard wi' ane anither;
An' mony a thousand mile thou'st run,
  To keep my thraward flocks thegither.

To nae thrawn boy nor naughty wife,
  Shall thy auld banes become a drudge;
At cats an' callans a' thy life,
  Thou ever bor'st a mortal grudge;

An' whiles thy surly look declared,
  Thou lo'ed the women warst of a';
Because my love wi' thee they shared,
  A matter out o' right or law.

When sittin' wi' my bonnie Meg,
  Mair happy than a prince could be,
Thou placed thee by her other leg,
  An' watched her wi' a jealous ee.

An' then at ony start or flare,
  Thou wad'st hae worried furiouslye;
While I was forced to curse an' swear,
  Afore thou wad'st forbidden be.

Yet wad she clasp thy towzy paw;
  Thy gruesome grips were never skaithly
An' thou than her hast been mair true,
  An' truer than the friend that gae thee.

* * * *

I ne'er could thole thy cravin' face,
  Nor when ye pattit on my knee;
Though in a far an' unco place,
  I've whiles been forced to beg for thee.

Even now I'm in my master's power,
  Where my regard may scarce be shown;
But ere I'm forced to gie thee o'er,
  When thou art auld an' senseless grown,

I'll get a cottage o' my ain,
  Some wee bit cannie, lonely biel',
Where thy auld heart shall rest fu' fain,
  An' share wi' me my humble meal.

Thy post shall be to guard the door
  Wi' gousty bark, whate'er betides;
Of cats an' hens to clear the floor,
  An' bite the flaes that vex thy sides.

When my last bannock's on the hearth,
  Of that thou sanna want thy share;
While I hae house or hauld on earth,
  My Hector shall hae shelter there.

And should grim death thy noddle save,
  Till he has made an end o' me;
Ye'll lye a wee while on the grave
  O' ane wha aye was kind to thee.

There's nane alive will miss me mair;
  An' though in words thou can'st not wail,
On a' the claes thy master ware,
  I ken thou'lt smell an' wag thy tail.

The worst things in the volume are *Robin and Nanny*, which is weak, and *Sandy Tod*, which is very weak, though Hogg had a tenderness for it. According to the 1807 Memoir, it was inspired by the behaviour of a lad at Straiton who "went out at night, and attacked the moon with great rudeness and vociferation." But according to the 1803 letter to Scott, "The 'Pastoral' I am resolved to insert, as I am 'Sandy Tod'"; possibly in four years Hogg had forgotten this "amour." The *Tweeddale Raide*, which did not appear in the first edition, was written not by James Hogg, but by his nephew Robert Hogg.

The Pedlar is a good ghost story with some very good eerie stanzas at the beginning, beside which the end is dull, and yet the end is a remarkable instance of the judgment of Heaven: a bone of the murdered man bleeds when the murderer touches it long afterwards. The bone is not in the first version, which appears in the *Scots Magazine*, and the story is the better for its absence. Hogg had an unlucky trick of destroying with a few words the eerieness he had made; that is not quite done here, but there is an atrocious example of this kind of bathos in *The Wife of Crowle*; when the ghost

> has offered his hand with expression so bland

to his mother—an action too condescending to be filial—there is really nothing else to be done with him.

The history has got mixed in *Mess John*, but apart from that excusable fault it is a good story of black magic. Scott seems to have been fond of it, for he quotes it in the notes to *Marmion* and tells the story in one of the notes to *Old Mortality*. It also contains another of Hogg's gems of expression:

> His face was like the rising moon,
> Imblushed with evening's purple dye.

Willie Wilkin contains even blacker magic than *Mess John*. *Gilmanscleuch* was another of Scott's favourites, and *The Fray of Elibank* does not spoil its story—it glorifies a real or supposed ancestor of the Shepherd's.

But the most enjoyable things in *The Mountain Bard* are the footnotes, which contain some of Hogg's best stories. Sometimes the end of a ballad is there in prose—"After the subject of a ballad is fairly introduced, great particularity is disgusting; therefore, the lass of Craigieburn, after this line, is no more mentioned. But the story adds, that she died of a broken heart, and of the heats which she got in being forced to run so fast." Of a different kind are the story of the great and worthy Mr Boston's dealing with the ghost of the pedlar, and the still better story of the Rev. Henry Davieson's laying of Buckholm's ghost; the ill-luck of the millers of Thirlestane; the note on Hogg's ancestors, however much of it he invented; the water-cow in the notes to *Mess John*, and the other note which foreshadows *The Brownie of Bodsbeck*; the Devil's fight with Hab Dob and Davie Din; and the various superstitions and bits of magic of which some are given in the notes to *The Pedlar* and others scattered in different places. There Hogg was on his own ground, and it is only to be wished that he had cultivated it more.

The Mountain Bard brought Hogg a fair sum of money, and he made a little more out of an essay which received a prize from the Highland Society—*The Shepherd's Guide: being a practical treatise on the diseases of sheep, their causes, and the best means of preventing them; with observations on the most suitable farm-stocking for the various climates of this country.* It seems to be a careful piece of work, and indeed he knew his trade, if he would only have been more faithful to it. He was always in danger, as Scott once remarked, of neglecting his hirsel for his poem-making.

Yet the Shepherd's ambition, never to be fulfilled, was to be a successful stock-farmer. He had for some years past been endeavouring to better his position, but so far his efforts had come to nothing. His attempt to settle in Harris, which fell through in 1804, was followed, after a short stay in Cumberland, by his engagement as shepherd at Mitchel Slack, where he remained till 1807. In 1806 he began to undertake the valuation of land, an occasional business which he did not finally abandon until 1811, and in 1807, finding himself with a small capital made out of literature, he joined partnership with a friend, Adam Brydon of Aberlosk—the "Edie o' Aberlosk" of some of his sketches—and took the farm of Locherben in Yarrow. Almost at once they were in difficulties, and though a letter of Scott's casts most of the blame on Brydon, there is evidence that he was not wholly responsible for their failure. Hogg's friend John Morrison makes it clear in his *Random Reminiscences* that the social instincts of the Shepherd had a good deal to answer for.

Morrison was a surveyor who came into contact with many celebrities of his time and was on intimate terms with Hogg, who addressed more than one set of verses to him. Soon after the taking of Locherben Morrison happened to be surveying in Dumfriesshire and went to see how Hogg was getting on and to give him some money on behalf of Scott, who was already uneasy about him. Hogg was not at home, and after making the best of conversation with his housekeeper, a very pretty girl, Morrison departed unsatisfied. Some time later he tried again, and was not reassured by what he saw:

> (When I paid a second visit to Locherben) my pretty housekeeper was then gone. It was the time of sheep-shearing, which was just finished. Masters and men were sitting round a small cask of whisky, drinking it raw out of a tea-cup. They were all rather merry. I sat with them for some time and was regaled with some excellent mutton-ham, cakes and butter, whisky and water....
>
> The establishment at Locherben soon after was broken up—how could it stand?—and Mr Hogg, with a small reversion, took on lease a farm on the Water of Scar, in the parish of Penpont, about seven miles west from Locherben. Corfardine was its name. I happened to be at Eccles with Mr Maitland a few days, and one forenoon paid him a visit, distant about three miles. The ground was covered with snow; and, on entering the farm, I found all the sheep on the wrong side of the hill. Hogg was absent, and had been so for some days, feasting, drinking, dancing and fiddling, etc., with a neighbouring farmer. His housekeeper was the most ugly, dirty goblin I had ever beheld; a fearful contrast to his former damsel.

Hogg appeared presently and announced that he had been looking for sheep, but does not seem to have been vexed by Morrison's broad hint that that was a lie. They discussed the situation amicably, and Morrison strongly advised giving up the farm and going to Edinburgh. It was not, however, until after several other schemes had fallen through, and the failure was too obvious for Hogg to persuade himself that he could yet recover his losses, that in 1810 he resigned for the time being all his ambitions as a farmer and embarked on the almost equally hopeless task of making his fortune by literature in Edinburgh.

4. *EARLY DAYS IN EDINBURGH*

Hogg's first months in Edinburgh might have proved disastrous but for the goodness of two friends, John Grieve and his partner, Mr Scott; by business they were hatters, and as for their characters, what Lockhart writes of Grieve may safely be applied to Scott also—"a man of cultivated mind and generous disposition, and a most kind and zealous friend of the Shepherd." Both did all they could to help him, and for six months he was actually living with them. Gradually his circle of acquaintances widened, and chief among his new friends was James Gray, formerly master in the Grammar School at Dumfries, where he had known Burns, and at this time one of the classical masters in the High School. Gray's first wife had been Mary Phillips, and though she had now been dead some years and he had married again, the ties of friendship were strong between him and the Phillips family. His sister-in-law Margaret was a frequent visitor in his house, and Hogg, meeting her there, soon fell in love with a seriousness which he had never shown before and displayed a constancy and steadiness of purpose of which we might otherwise have considered him incapable. Margaret Phillips was his moral superior: a woman of dignity, resolution and loyalty, with so unfailing a recognition of goodness that the mere fact of her love for the Shepherd raises our opinion of him. He does not seem to have been oppressed by any sense of unworthiness, but he was conscious of the practical difficulties in their way. She came of good, even gentle, stock in Annandale, and her relations were hardly willing for some time to receive him as an equal; besides, his financial position was deplorable. From Hogg's point of view, the history of the next ten years of his life is the history of his attempts, not merely to make a living, but to prosper sufficiently to render marriage possible.

As early as the summer of 1810 he published *The Forest Minstrel*, a collection of poems by various hands, his own contribution being the largest and Laidlaw's *Lucy's Flitting* the best. Thomas Mouncey Cunningham, Allan's brother, with whom Hogg exchanged poetical epistles in the *Scots Magazine* in 1805–6, sent several poems, and one of them, *Ayont the Mow*, has found its way into Thomson as the Shepherd's.

I have not seen the first edition, and *The Forest Minstrel* is not included in the collections of 1822 and 1838–40. The earliest edition I have been able to examine is the little volume of 1840 which contains *The Mountain Bard* as well; there is nothing in this which is not Hogg's, but it does not agree, either in the poems it contains, in their order, or sometimes even in their text, with Thomson's version. It certainly does not follow the first edition, for it includes *The Minstrel Boy*, which was not written before 1813, *When Maggy Gangs Away*, which was written after Hogg's marriage, and *When the Kye comes Hame*, which was probably not written long before 1822. On the other hand, it does not include *Gracie Miller*, *Bauldy Frazer* and *Caledonia*, which were certainly in the 1810 edition, or *Bonny Dundee*, *Mary at her Lover's Grave*, and *Hap and rowe the feetie*, which were probably there; they had all been previously published and are in Thomson's *Minstrel*. Thomson must be nearer the original edition, though his text does not always agree with the text of the quotations in the review which appeared in the *Scots Magazine* in August 1810. This review quotes *The Bonny Lass of Deloraine*, *Caledonia*, *On Ettrick Clear*, *My Peggy and I*, and *The Haymakers*, the reviewer observing of the last, "It may not be amiss to produce part of it as an awful warning"—though the verses had already appeared in the magazine. In October 1810 *Prince Owen and the Seer* and *Gracie Miller* are given in full in the poetry columns with a reference to the *Minstrel*; in the 1831 *Songs* Hogg adds *The Flower* and *A Widow's Wail* to the list, and the notes to the *Jacobite Relics* prove that *Bauldy Frazer* and *The Emigrant* were there. Not many awful warnings are in *The Forest Minstrel* as we have it, but it does not contain any of the Shepherd's best songs; it was simply an expedient for making money, and not even a successful expedient.

The next experiment was a weekly paper, and on September 1, 1810, appeared the first number of *The Spy: a Periodical Paper of Literary Amusement and Instruction*. The editor was Hogg, who was also the author of by far the larger part of the contents. He was not, one might suppose, the person best qualified to be editor of a paper of literary instruction, and Scott among others tried to dissuade him from the enterprise, but Hogg's confidence was unshakable; he had tried his hand at literary criticism in the *Scots Magazine* in 1806 and had much more to say, and, he declared, if his works were not sae yelegant as those of the eighteenth century essayists, they were mair original. Hogg was always proud of his originality and afraid of losing it, to prevent which catastrophe, according to R. P. Gillies, he read very little. That plan does not always succeed, and it was not altogether successful with the Shepherd; Scott told Byron in 1813 that when he first knew Hogg the Shepherd was both indignant and horrified when parallel passages to his own poems were pointed out in authors whom he had never read. The originality which displayed itself in *The Spy*, however, was not much to the taste of its readers, and the third and fourth numbers, which contained the first draft of *Basil Lee—The Berwickshire Farmer*, also called *On Instability in one's Calling*—deprived Hogg of half his subscribers. Long afterwards, Mrs S. C. Hall complained that Hogg sent for her *Juvenile Forget-me-not* either ghost stories or stories of seduction; indeed, he wrote very few stories for adults which had not one or other of these themes, and although there is a good deal of variety in ghosts, tales of seduction grow monotonous. *The Berwickshire Farmer* is one of his earliest, dullest, and, in spite of his indignant disclaimers, coarsest. He "despised the fastidiousness and affectation of the people," who retorted by giving up his paper. It ran for nearly a year and then he had to make an end.

Copies of *The Spy* are so rare now that the *Cambridge History of English Literature* even asserts that none are known, but there is a copy in the British Museum. Some of the essays and some of the literary criticisms may be by other hands, though most bear marks of the Shepherd, but with the possible exception of these and certain exception of a few others[1], a very small

[1] In No. XXXVI there is a letter by James Thomson, and in the same number a translation from Petronius Arbiter which is more likely to be by Gray, or James Park, who wrote the imitation of Catullus in No. V, than by Hogg himself; in No. XLVII there are some verses by Burns "never before printed"—*Ah! woe is me, my mother dear*; Leyden's *Lines on Assaye* are in No. IX; *The Sailor Boy*, by B. W., in No. XXVI; *Address to the Setting Moon*, by W. G., in No. XXVIII; *To the patriots of Spain*, by Philo-Britannus, in No. XLVI; and *To Miss Helen K—*, by J. G., in No. XLVIII. Professor T. Gillespie, the Rev. William Gillespie,

quantity in a year's files of a magazine, Hogg seems to have written everything. It is, when all allowances have been made, a sufficiently remarkable achievement.

The best of the stories were afterwards reprinted in the *Winter Evening Tales*, and the others were not worth reprinting. Hogg probably, though not certainly, wrote the unsigned poems, which are in his weaker manners, but some of the poetry which he acknowledged is excellent. *Lord Huntly* is there, a *Glenfinlas* kind of story; and *Lock the door, Lariston*, one of the best of war-songs:

"Lock the door, Lariston, lion of Liddesdale;
Lock the door, Lariston, Lowther comes on;
The Armstrongs are flying,
The widows are crying,
The Castletown's burning, and Oliver's gone!

"Lock the door, Lariston—high on the weather-gleam
See how the Saxon plumes bob on the sky—
Yeoman and carbineer,
Billman and halberdier,
Fierce is the foray, and far is the cry!

"Bewcastle brandishes high his broad scimitar;
Ridley is riding his fleet-footed gray;
Hidley and Howard there,
Wandale and Windermere;
Lock the door, Lariston; hold them at bay.

"Why dost thou smile, noble Elliot of Lariston?
Why does the joy-candle gleam in thine eye?
Thou bold border ranger,
Beware of thy danger;
Thy foes are relentless, determined, and nigh."

J. Black of the *Morning Chronicle*, and Robert Sym, the uncle of John Wilson and afterwards the "Timothy Tickler" of the *Noctes Ambrosianae*, are known to have given some slight assistance, but it is impossible to identify their contributions with certainty.

Jock Elliot raised up his steel bonnet and lookit,
His hand grasped the sword with a nervous embrace;
"Ah, welcome, brave foemen,
On earth there are no men
More gallant to meet in the foray or chase!

"Little know you of the hearts I have hidden here;
Little know you of our moss-troopers' might—
Linhope and Sorbie true,
Sundhope and Milburn too,
Gentle in manner, but lions in fight!

"I have Mangerton, Ogilvie, Raeburn and Netherbie,
Old Sim of Whitram, and all his array;
Come all Northumberland,
Teesdale and Cumberland,
Here at the Breaken tower end shall the fray!"

See how they wane—the proud files of the Windermere!
Howard! ah, woe to thy hopes of the day!
Hear the wide welkin rend,
While the Scots' shouts ascend—
"Elliot of Lariston, Elliot for aye!"

Hogg afterwards added two more verses, descriptive of the battle, before the last, but they are not necessary and they are rather too poetical.

Just as good in another way is *The Auld Man's Fareweel to his Wee House:*

I like ye weel, my wee auld house,
Though laigh the wa's an' flat the riggin';
Though round thy lum the sourick grows,
An' rain-draps gaw my cozy biggin'.

Lang hast thou happit mine an' me,
My head's grown gray aneath thy kipple;
An' aye thy ingle cheek was free
Baith to the blind man an' the cripple;

An' to the puir forsaken wight
Wi' bairnie at her bosom cryin';
My cot was open day an' night,
Nor wanted bed for sick to lie in.

. . . . . .

Troth, I maun greet wi' thee to part,
  Though to a better house I'm flittin';
Sic joys will never glad my heart
  As I've had by thy hallan sittin'.

. . . . . .

I canna help but haud thee dear,
  My auld, storm-battered hamely shielin';
Thy sooty lum an' kipples clear
  I better lo'e than gaudy ceilin'.

Thy roof will fa', thy rafters start,
  How damp an' cauld thy hearth will be!
Ah, sae will soon ilk honest heart,
  That erst was blithe an' bauld in thee.

I thought to cower aneath thy wa',
  Till death had closed my weary e'en;
Then left thee for the narrow ha',
  Wi' lowly roof o' swaird sae green.

Fareweel, my house an' burnie clear,
  My bourtree bush an' bowzy tree;
The wee while I maun sojourn here,
  I'll never find a hame like thee!

The songs in *The Spy* are at the worst easier than Hogg's early verses, though he himself condemned them as melodious but "often deficient in real stamina." That is true of some: the elegant feebleness of the *Hymn to the Evening Star* is as amazing as its Catholic imagery; but it is not true of all. *Morning* is not feeble, and *What gars the parting day-beam blush?* is good even here in its first form. Hogg afterwards recast it as a *Courting Song*. Of the other poems the most important are two which were afterwards inserted in *The Queen's Wake*, *King Edward's Dream* and *The Fate of Macgregor*; and Hogg's first attempt to produce an "Antient Fragment," supposed to be found among someone's papers and like his others of that kind in its extraordinary spelling and Hogg-like language. If it were properly spelt it would be neither very good nor very bad; in its actual state it is merely irritating.

On the failure of *The Spy* Hogg took the advice of Grieve and returned to poetry. In 1811 he prepared *The Queen's Wake* for the press and offered it first to Constable, whose terms however he considered too low. Hogg was at the time earning a little money as secretary to a debating club called the Forum, and according to his account a certain young publisher named Goldie, whose acquaintance he had made at the meetings of this club, begged to be allowed the honour of publishing his book. Against this version of events Goldie afterwards declared that he had never been a member of the Forum or attended its meetings, and that Hogg "waited on (him), because, as he said, Mr Constable had refused to publish for him. This declaration of his was accompanied with observations on Mr Constable's behaviour to him, too coarse and vulgar to be repeated." Mr Goldie was a gentleman of refined taste, though he was annoyed when Hogg said so.

At least Goldie published the book, in 1813, and presently issued the unsold copies with a new title-page; this re-issue counts as the second edition. Goldie also published a completely new edition, known as the third, and *The Hunting of Badlewe*, one of Hogg's unactable and almost unreadable poetical dramas, and went bankrupt when about half the third edition of *The Queen's Wake* was sold. Fortunately for the Shepherd, Blackwood was one of the trustees and sold the remainder of the edition for him on commission, and in the end Hogg was rather a gainer by the bankruptcy. This remainder of the third edition is known as the fourth; a fifth was published by subscription in the spring of 1819, and a sixth in the late summer of the same year.

Goldie seems to have been merely unfortunate and to have treated Hogg very fairly, but when Hogg published his revised Memoir in 1821 he asserted that he had not been treated fairly over the third edition. An unprejudiced person reading even Hogg's account would not take that view, since he himself says he went behind Goldie's back to Constable to ask him to publish this edition, as there were already rumours of Goldie's failure. Goldie retorted vigorously in *A Letter to a Friend in London*—rather too vigorously, indeed. Hogg had reported a harmless though probably imaginary conversation between himself and a Mr William Dunlop on the publication of *The Queen's Wake*; at the worst it is only one of the Shepherd's devices for indulging his vanity by putting his own opinion of himself into the mouth of another person, but Goldie refers to it as "a story which wears such an appearance of low and vulgar blackguardism, that it is hard to believe it possible to have happened—but between persons of the most abandoned habits." It is merely couched in broad Scots, but Goldie displays virtuous indignation and a pleasantly extensive vocabulary in his references to it:

> If anything like this interview ever happened, no man who had any regard to decency or decorum himself, or valued these qualities in others, would, on any account, have defiled his pages with a detestable and revolting slang, equally offensive to pure religion and sound morals, and calculated even to degrade the nymphs of Billingsgate, or the pickpockets of St Giles's. But I understand Mr Dunlop is above the influence of such abuse: he is an ostensible member of our national church, and lately filled the office of one of the chief magistrates of the metropolis of his country with equal credit to himself and advantage to the public.

It is to be hoped that Mr William Dunlop was grateful to his defender.

The Queen's Wake is one of those works with some reputation which hardly anyone reads, and yet most of it is worth reading at least once. The setting is good—the arrival of Queen Mary in Scotland, and the interludes between the three nights of the Wake—and the descriptions of the bards who strove for the golden harp are sometimes memorable: Rizzio, who sang first and pleased the Queen best; Gardyn, who sang of Young Kennedy and deserved the fate of that bard of Galloway who was hissed; the bard of Fife, vigorous enough in mind for all his feeble gait; the bard of Ettrick, Hogg himself; the bard of Ern, who sang of Kilmeny and did not get what he deserved; the nameless bard whose

fair face and forehead high
Glowed with intrusive[1] modesty—

so that it is surprising to learn that he stands not for the Shepherd but for Grieve; the borderer who over-strained himself in singing; the sixteenth bard—Allan Cunningham—who went on too long; and the bard who sang of M'Kinnon in Gaelic, to the bewilderment of the Court. Gardyn won the prize, but "the poor bard of Ettrick" showed his disappointment so plainly that the Queen in pity gave him another. It is here that the Shepherd first accuses Scott of trying to prevent him from making any more poetry—an almost incredible charge in that form, though Scott may have told him that he could not hope to make his living by poetry and had better attend more closely to his business[2].

[1] So Hogg: some editions emend to *intrinsic* or *instinctive*, but *intrusive* is likely to be the true reading. Cf. pp. 136–7 here.

[2] Compare Scott's letter to Lady Dalkeith, August 24th, 1811—"The poor fellow has just talent sufficient to spoil him for his own trade, without having enough to support him by literature." (Lockhart, III, pp. 363–4.)

Of the separate poems, two could hardly be better—*The Witch of Fife* and *Kilmeny*. Some could hardly be worse, and worst of all, worse even than *Malcolm of Lorn*, which Hogg himself condemned as feeble, is *Young Kennedy*, whose singer at first was level with the bard of Ettrick and finally won the prize. *Young Kennedy* is an amazing poem. Macdougal, whose daughter Kennedy loved, died suddenly:

> Though grateful the hope to the death-bed that flies,
> That lovers and friends o'er our ashes will weep;
> The soul, when released from her lingering ties,
> In secret may see if their sorrows are deep.
> Who wept for the worthy Macdougal?—Not one!
> His darling Matilda, who, two months agone,
> Would have mourned for her father in sorrow extreme,
> Indulged in a painful delectable dream.

She married Young Kennedy, but on the bridal night the revengeful ghost of her father drove the bridegroom out to his destruction, and Matilda survived only long enough, after an interval of madness, to tell the tale.

It is a relief to come to *The Witch of Fife*, that glorious comic ballad of witchcraft[1]. It was not consistently comic at first, but ended lamentably with the death of the witch's auld guidman. Scott begged him off, and the Shepherd added the last thirteen riotous stanzas:

> The reike flew up in the auld man's face,
> And choukit him bitterlye;
> And the lowe cam up with ane angry blese,
> And it syngit his auld breek-knee.

---

[1] The story, like so many of Hogg's best plots, is traditional. Cf. the tale of the Piskies in the Cellar in Hunt's *Popular Romances of the West of England*, 1st Series, p. 76; and Scott's introduction to *The Young Tamlane* in the *Minstrelsy*.

He lukit to the land fra whence he cam,
  For lukis he culde get nae mae;
And he thochte of his deire littil bairnis at hame,
  And O the auld man was wae!

But they turnit their facis to the sun
  With gloffe and wonderous glair,
For they saw ane thing beth lairge and dun,
  Comin swaipin' down the ayr.

That burd it cam fra the landis o' Fyfe,
  And it cam rycht tymeouslye,
For quha was it but the auld manis wyfe,
  Just comit his dethe to see?

Scho put ane reide cap on hie heide,
  And the auld guidman lookit fain,
Then whisperit ane word intil his lug,
  And tovit to the air again.

The auld guidman he gae ane bob,
  I' the mids o' the burnyng lowe;
And the sheklis that band him to the ring,
  They fell fra his armis like towe.

He drew his breath, and he said the word,
  And he said it with muckil glee,
Then set his fit on the burnyng pile,
  And away to the ayr flew he.

Till aince he clerit the swirlyng reike,
  He lukit beth ferit and sad;
But whan he wan to the lycht blue ayr,
  He lauchit as he'd been mad.

His armis war spred, and his heid was hiche
  And his feite stack out behynde;
And the laibies of the auld manis cote
  War wauffing in the wynde.

And aye he neicherit, and aye he flew,
  For he thochte the ploy se raire;
It was like the voice of the gainder blue,
  Quhan he flees throu the ayr.

He lukit back to the Carlisle men
  As he borit the norlan sky;
He noddit his heide, and gae ane girn,
  But he nevir said guid-bye.

They vanisht far i' the liftis blue wale,
  Ne mair the English saw,
But the auld manis lauch cam on the gale,
  With a lang and a loud gaffa.

Earl Walter and *Mary Scott* are long ballads of the kind that Hogg wrote for *The Mountain Bard*, the second even longer in the later editions than in the first; and most of the other songs are either of this kind or of the *Young Kennedy* kind, with good odd lines and passages but with a fatal inclination to bathos. The metre may be partly to blame: it is difficult to tell a tragic tale in the lolloping line of *Young Kennedy*, and it is nearly always the tragic tales that Hogg chooses to tell in this way. The verse of *Kilmeny* is free, but for this once, and never in the same degree again, Hogg did what he was trying to do. It is, as it deserves to be, the most famous of his poems, too familiar for quotation to be necessary. The Shepherd sought often after that unearthly beauty, but he never found it again for more than a few lines. There is a touch of it in the mermaid and her song in *The Abbot M'Kinnon*, but it is only a touch.

After the two great poems of *The Queen's Wake*, this song of the seventeenth bard is the best, but it is only fair to a prelate who, however questionable his morals were, was probably exceedingly orthodox, to protest against the story. A lying spirit may have taken the name of St Columba, but the abbot would never have believed him.

The Queen's Wake was at least successful enough to encourage Hogg, and in the next few years appeared his other long poems. The first was *Mador of the Moor*, which was a holiday task, and began as "a poem descriptive of the river Tay." The descriptive passages are the best, but the story is very poor. Hogg had the ambition, for which it would be unfair to condemn him, of rivalling Scott and Byron, especially Scott, whom he followed in his long poems and stories—though he asserted loudly that he was no imitator—and never, except in one or two ballads, with any good result. There is a hint of Scott in the story of *Mador*, which is a distorted *Lady of the Lake*, and of Byron in the verse, the Spenserian stanza, which Hogg learnt from him. Hogg was proud of his use of the stanza, and had a theory of it which helps to explain the jerkiness of *Mador*:

> I thought it so formed, that every verse ought to be a structure of itself, resembling an arch, of which the two meeting rhymes in the middle should represent the keystone, and on these all the strength and flow of the verse should rest.

The natural consequence of this theory is that his Alexandrines are nearly always awkwardly attached to a stanza which could do very well without them. In Ila Moore's song to her child they serve as a refrain.

Mador was written in 1814 but not published until after *The Pilgrims of the Sun*. Hogg had planned a volume to be called *Midsummer Night Dreams*, but he could not at the time get the poems which were to form it published together. In the 1822 collected edition there is a section with this heading, including *The Pilgrims of the Sun*, *Connel of Dee*, *Superstition*, *The Gyre Caryl*, *The Haunted Glen*, *The Mermaid*, *Verses to the Comet of* 1811, *The Powris of Moseke*, *The Field of Waterloo*, and *Verses to Lady Anne Scott*. The first three poems belonged to the original scheme, the last two seem to have little to do with it.

The Pilgrims of the Sun was published separately in 1815, in Scotland by Blackwood, in England by Murray, who had serious doubts about it and in the end was only persuaded to take it by Byron. Hogg could not understand such hesitation, and wrote to Murray in January 1815:

> I cannot help smiling at your London critics. They must read it over again. I had the best advice in the three kingdoms on the poem—men whose opinions, even given in a dream, I would not exchange for all the critics in England, before I ever proposed it for publication. I will risk my fame on it to all eternity[1].

But the Shepherd would be forgotten by this time if his fame were to rest on *The Pilgrims of the Sun.* It is an endeavour to expand *Kilmeny*, and *Kilmeny* will not bear expansion and elaboration of this sort. The poem begins with a description of Mary Lee of Carelha' and her virtues, and then tells how she falls into a deathlike trance and is carried away from her body to the sun, whence she is shown by an angelic guide the kingdoms of the universe and their inhabitants. Hogg has theories, perhaps noteworthy in him, on the purification of the soul in successive worlds before it is fit for eternal happiness. Mary returns to her body and presently marries a stranger poet, Hugo of Norroway, who resembles her guide, and Hogg concludes with a gentle suggestion that he is their descendant.

Hogg's last ambitious poem was *Queen Hynde*, published at the end of 1824. He considered it infinitely superior to *The Queen's Wake*, and was as ready to stake his credit on it as on *The Pilgrims of the Sun*, with as little reason. There is a beautiful young queen, and a mischievous maiden, and a gallant prince in disguise who is not as interesting as he ought to be, and terrific combats, and a happy ending which comes gratefully to a reader exhausted by the effort to read it all. Hogg observed regretfully that "it was unfortunate that the plot should have been

[1] Smiles, *A Publisher and his Friends*, vol. I, pp. 345–6.

laid in an age so early that we have no interest in it"—an explanation which may have satisfied him. But the truth is that *Queen Hynde* is half as long again as *The Queen's Wake* and not half so amusing. The Shepherd tried to be humorous and tried to throw in moral reflections, and the humour is rather more tedious than the reflections. There are, as there are in his feeblest poems, gleams of beauty, but it is hardly worth while to hunt for them; and more than any other of Hogg's poems, *Queen Hynde* is a weak following of Scott.

Unfortunately Hogg's rhymed romances were not as profitable to their author as Scott's had been, and but for other friendly help the poor Shepherd might have fared badly enough. Scott, trying here and there on his behalf, had naturally spoken for him to the Buccleuchs, and Hogg had seconded the appeal by dedicating *The Forest Minstrel* to the Duchess—receiving a hundred guineas in return—and by subsequently, in March 1814, writing to her one of the oddest letters which even Hogg ever wrote:

MAY IT PLEASE YOUR GRACE,—I have often grieved you by my applications for this and that: I am sensible of this, for I have had many instances of your wishes to be of service to me, could you have known what to do for that purpose. But there are some eccentric characters in the world, of whom no person can judge or know what will prove beneficial, or what may prove their bane. I have again and again received of your grace's private bounty, and though it made me love and respect you the more, I was nevertheless grieved at it. It was never your grace's money that I wanted, but the honour of your countenance; indeed, my heart could never yield to the hope of being patronized by any house save that of Buccleuch, whom I deemed bound to cherish every plant that indicated anything out of the common way on the braes of Ettrick and Yarrow.

I know you will be thinking that this long prelude is to end with a request: No, madam! I have taken the resolution of never making another request. I will however tell you a story, which is, I believe, founded on a fact:—

There is a small farm at the head of a water called —— possessed by a mean fellow named ——. A third of it has been taken off and laid into another farm—the remainder is as yet unappropriated. Now, there is a certain poor bard, who has two old parents, each of them upwards of eighty-four years of age; and that bard has no house nor home to shelter those poor parents in, or cheer the evening of their lives. A single line from a certain very great and very beautiful lady, to a certain Mr Riddle, would insure that small pendicle to the bard at once. But she will grant no such thing! I appeal to your grace if she is not a very bad lady that!—I am your grace's ever obliged and grateful

JAMES HOGG,
The Ettrick Shepherd.

The Duchess felt hardly justified in turning out someone else to make room for Hogg, but she mentioned his case to her husband, and her death five months later, which might have shattered his expectations, had the effect of making the Duke look on his fortunes as a sacred legacy. The farm of Altrive Lake in Yarrow was then vacant, and it was offered to Hogg at a rent which was to be nominal but never reached the stage of being named. As soon as he could get a good enough house built, Hogg could marry and return to the countryside where he was at home and at his best. But there were still delays which occupied several years, and in them he not only entered into the second most important literary relation of his life but also produced some of his most amusing work.

5. *LATER LIFE IN EDINBURGH*: THE POETIC MIRROR *AND* BLACKWOOD'S MAGAZINE

HOGG had by this time a large circle of literary acquaintances. One introduction had led to another, and besides being on terms of intimacy with many of the lesser men, he knew Wordsworth and Southey, he knew Byron at least through correspondence and possibly personally, and he was a member of what is sometimes called the Blackwood Group: that group of clever, mostly young, men who were responsible for the brilliance and the personalities of the early years of *Blackwood's Magazine*. The most important members of that group, besides Hogg himself, were John Wilson, to his contemporaries "the author of *The Isle of Palms*," though that is little read now, later Professor of Moral Philosophy and as unlike the conventional idea of a professor as could be, but even to his own time best known, and not yet forgotten, as the Christopher North of the *Noctes Ambrosianae*; Lockhart, in those days a mercilessly clever young man with a deadly power of sarcasm and a mischievous delight in hoaxing his friends and the public; and, a few years later, Maginn, whom Thackeray drew in his decay as Captain Shandon, but whose memory is on the whole more truthfully as well as more kindly preserved in the wistfully humorous lament of the older Lockhart over "bright broken Maginn." They were like a set of undergraduates with plenty of wits and no respect for higher powers, and the

Shepherd moved among them with breathless and awed enjoyment of their wickedness, whether it was directed against himself—Lockhart never told him the truth but once, he declared, and then it was by accident—or whether he was allowed to join in it at the expense of other people.

While Hogg was waiting to settle at Altrive Lake, it occurred to him that he might as well make a little profit out of his literary friends. In that letter to Murray in which the doubting publisher was assured that *The Pilgrims of the Sun* was an excellent poem, Hogg also enquired anxiously after possible new editions of *The Queen's Wake*—he expected one to be necessary every six months—and continued, "Will our 'Repository' not go on? I have at least a volume of very superior poetry."

The adjective might lead one to suppose that the poetry was his own, but the *Repository*, otherwise *The Thistle and The Rose*, otherwise and finally *The Poetic Mirror*, was intended to be a collection like *The Forest Minstrel*, with more distinguished contributors but published in the same way for the Shepherd's benefit. There never was a man whose friends were more eager to help him and, to use Scott's expression, call the attention of the public to him now and then. The measures which they took were perhaps not always well chosen for his dignity, but the intention was most often kindly.

On this occasion Scott was asked to send a poem, but refused and brought the Shepherd's wrath upon him; it seems to have been then that Hogg wrote to him beginning "Damned Sir" and ending "Yours with disgust"—a conclusion which he used also in writing to Blackwood in moments of annoyance. Scott took no notice of the letter or its writer, but learning a few months later that Hogg was ill[1], he behaved as he might have been expected to behave, enquiring anxiously after him and making himself responsible for the expenses of the illness. Hogg found out what had happened and wrote a queer, muddled, pathetic apology which was answered by an invitation to breakfast, and all ended happily. Wordsworth sent a poem, Byron half promised help but was slow in giving it. To Murray, who had suggested that marriage might have caused the delay and that a letter to Lady Byron might bear double fruit, Hogg replied approving the suggestion but expressing a manly independence which is really edifying: "There is nothing I am so afraid of as teazing or pestering my superiors for favours. Lord B. knows well enough that without his support at first, the thing will not go on, and as I am sure he is a kind soul, I think I will for the present trust to himself." Hogg had written to Byron on his marriage: "I wished she might prove both a good *mill* and a *bank* to him; but I much doubted they would not be such as he was calculating on. I think he felt that I was using too much freedom with him." Byron answered with "rather a satirical, bitter letter." He did not in the end send anything for the *Mirror*.

Finally the *Mirror* was abandoned in its original shape, Wordsworth's poem was returned to him, and the Shepherd invented verses that might have been written by the authors to whom he had applied, composed a suitable preface, and presented to the world *The Poetic Mirror, or The Living Bards of Britain*, at first without his own name. His scheme of an

[1] The illness, I am afraid, was Hogg's own fault, the result of a succession of nights of hard drinking with the Right and Wrong Club.

anthology had been known for some time, and Croker, reviewing the *Mirror* in the *Quarterly*, supposed that a *Peter Bell* trick had been played on Hogg—a joke which Hogg would have enjoyed but does not seem to have known. It is possible—it was certainly believed at the time—that he had a little assistance. *The Morning Star* was supposed to be by Wilson himself, whom it imitated, and Maginn, in a moment of just anger with the Shepherd, went rather beyond justice and declared that all the best things had been written by Wilson. The *Epistle to Mr R— S—* was not Hogg's and according to him was not intended as an imitation of Scott, which however it is.

It seems natural to compare *The Poetic Mirror* with *Rejected Addresses*, but the comparison is not quite fair. The *Mirror* is not entirely parody and was not intended to be parody so much as imitation sometimes perfectly sincere. It is not a distorting mirror so much as one with occasional flaws. Deliberate parody comes out in a few lines of *Wat o' the Cleuch*[1], in *Isabelle*, in the three extracts from *The Recluse*, in the Southey parodies—of which *Peter of Barnet* is bad and only the *Curse* itself amusing—and in a few lines of *The Morning Star*. *The Gude Greye Katt* is not so good a self-parody that it would not pass for serious in any

[1] Hogg did not waste jokes; one here is repeated in the later *Russiadde*. In *Wat o' the Cleuch* it is

> Ere the weapon's swing was sped,
> Sometimes it severed kinsman's head;

in the *Russiadde*

> Nor once perceived that as he drew
> Each stroke, as many Scots he slew.

Someone seems to have been trying to make Hogg admire Virgil. The *Russiadde* is half a self-parody with occasional asides which may be paraphrased, "Who says I can't write heroic poetry as well as Virgil?"

other company, and it is even possible that it was intended for the original serious *Repository*; and *The Guerilla*, *The Cherub* and the last two pieces are perfectly serious. But *Isabelle* is good parody, however sacrilegious it may be, and only there and in *The Recluse* did Hogg let himself go[1].

It is a strange and lovely night,
A grayish pale, but not white!
Is it rain, or is it dew,
That falls so thick I see its hue?
In rays it follows, one, two, three,
Down the air so merrily,
Said Isabelle; so let it be!

Why does the lady Isabelle
Sit in the damp and dewy dell,
Counting the racks of drizzly rain,
And how often the rail cries over again?
For she's harping, harping in the brake,
Craik, craik—Craik, craik—
Ten times nine, and thrice eleven;
That last call was a hundred and seven.
Craik, craik—the hour is near—
Let it come, I have no fear!
Yet it is a dreadful work, I wis,
Such doings in a night like this!

Sounds the river harsh and loud?
The stream sounds harsh, but not loud.
There is a cloud that seems to hover
By western hill the churchyard over;
What is it like?—'Tis like a whale;
'Tis like a shark with half the tail,

---

[1] Mr Ernest Hartley Coleridge suggests in his edition of *Christabel* (p. 105) that Hogg may also have written *Christobell. A Gothic Tale* (v. *European Magazine*, LXVII, pp. 345–6), signed V. But the other poems by V. in the magazine during 1815–16 make it fairly certain that he was not Hogg. *The Warden of Carlisle* especially (May, 1815, pp. 442–3) is most unlike Hogg's Border ballads.

Not half, but third and more;
Now 'tis a wolf, and now a boar;
Its face is raised—it cometh here;
Let it come—there is no fear.
There's two for heaven, and ten for hell,
Let it come—'tis well—'tis well!
Said the lady Isabelle.

What ails that little cut-tailed whelp,
That it continues to yelp, yelp?
Yelp, yelp, and it turns its eye
Up to the tree and half to the sky;
Half to the sky and full to the cloud,
And still it whines and barks aloud.
Why I should dread I cannot tell;
There is a spirit; I know it well!
I see it in yon falling beam—
Is it a vision or a dream?
It is no dream, full well I know,
I have a woeful deed to do!
Hush, hush, thou little murmurer;
I tell thee, hush—the dead are near!

. . . .

Hogg never wearied of parodying Wordsworth. Besides dealing with him in *The Poetic Mirror* in a manner which shall be shown, he published in 1829 in the *Edinburgh Literary Journal* two numbers of *A New Poetic Mirror*—an *Ode to a Highland Bee* by Mr W. W. and a song by Mr T. M.; and in 1830 appeared *Andrew the Packman. After the manner of Wordsworth.* There is more of parody in *Andrew the Packman* than in the *Ode*, and the Moore song is again simply an imitation. Whether Hogg had left himself any right to parody or imitate Moore may be questioned[1], but Wordsworth was fair game and Hogg commonly does him justice. It is not easy to beat the impishness of the extracts from *The Recluse*, where more than Wordsworthian flatness is mixed with lines

[1] On that point, see pp. 151–4.

which might deceive the elect to admiration if they were quoted apart from their context. Wordsworth had once hurt Hogg's feelings, as Hogg explains in his *Autobiography*:

> It was the triumphal arch scene....It chanced one night, when I was there (i.e. Rydal Mount) that there was a resplendent arch across the zenith, from the one horizon to the other, of something like the aurora borealis, but much brighter....Well, when word came into the room of the splendid meteor, we all went out to view it; and, on the beautiful platform at Mount Ryedale, were all walking, in twos and threes, arm-in-arm, talking of the phenomenon, and admiring it. Now, be it remembered, that Wordsworth, Professor Wilson, Lloyd, De Quincey, and myself, were present, besides several other literary gentlemen, whose names I am not certain that I remember aright. Miss Wordsworth's arm was in mine, and she was expressing some fears that the splendid stranger might prove ominous, when I, by ill luck, blundered out the following remark, thinking that I was saying a good thing:—"Hout, me'm! it is neither mair nor less than joost a treeumphal airch, raised in honour of the meeting of the poets." "That's not amiss—eh? eh?—that's very good," said the Professor, laughing. But Wordsworth, who had De Quincey's arm, gave a grunt, and turned on his heel, and leading the little opium chewer aside, he addressed him in these disdainful and venomous words:—"Poets? poets? What does the fellow mean? Where are they?" Who could forgive this? For my part I never can, and never will!...The "*Where are they?*" was too bad! I have always some hopes that De Quincey was *leeing*, for I did not myself hear Wordsworth utter the words.

The Shepherd took a fair revenge. The first extract from *The Recluse*, *The Stranger*, is not the worst:

> A boy came from the mountains, tripping light
> With basket on his arm—and it appeared
> That there was butter there, for the white cloth,
> That over it was spread, not unobserved,
> In tiny ridges gently rose and fell,
> Like graves of children covered o'er with snow
> And by one clumsy fold the traveller spied
> One roll of yellow treasure, all as pure
> As primrose bud reflected in the lake.

"Boy," said the stranger, "wilt thou hold my steed
Till I walk round the corner of that mere?
When I return I will repay thee well."
The boy consented—touched his slouching hat
Of broad unequal brim with ready hand,
And set his basket down upon the sward.

The traveller went away—but ere he went
He stroked his tall brown steed, and looked at him
With kind, but yet not unregretful eye.
The boy stood patient—glad was he to earn
The little pittance; well the stripling knew
Of window in the village, where stood ranged
The brown and tempting cakes well sprinkled o'er
With the sham raisin and deceitful plum;
And, by corporeal functions swayed, his mind
Forestalled the luxury with supreme delight.

Long, long he patient stood; the day was hot,
The butter ran in streamlets, and the flies
Came round in thousands—o'er the horse's head
A moving, darkening canopy they hung,
Like the first foldings of the thunder-cloud
That, gathering, hangs on Bowfell's hoary peak.

The stranger came not back; the little boy
Cast many a wistful look—his mind was mazed,
Like as a brook that travels through the glade,
By complicated tanglement involved,
Not knowing where to run; and haply he
Had sunk inert, but that in patience, or
Perhaps incited by a curious mind,
He cast his eyes to east, and west, and north;
But nothing save the rocks, and trees, and walls,
(Of grey stones built, and covered on the top
Sheepfold-wise, with a cope of splintered flags,
That half-diverging stood upon their edge
And half-reclining lay) came in the range
Of his discernment. Some full bitter tears
At length came flowing down the poor boy's cheek.

The stranger did not return, and the horse presently broke free and ran away.

No more the poor boy cried—he lifted up
His basket from the earth into the air,
That unviewed element that circumfolds
The earth within its bosom; there he felt
With his left hand how it affected was
By the long day and burning sun of heaven.
It was all firm and flat—no ridges rose
Like graves of children—basket, butter, cloth,
Were all one piece coherent. To his home
The boy returned right sad and sore aghast.
No one believed his tale; they deemed it was
A truant idler's story, in excuse
Of charge neglected. Days and months passed on,
And all remained the same; the maidens sung
Along the hayfield; at the even-tide
The dance and merriment prevailed; the sky
Was pure as heretofore: the mid-day winds
Arose and ruffled all the peaceful lake;
The clouds of heaven passed over—nature all
Appeared the same as if that stranger wight
Had never been—save that it was observed
That Daniel Crosthwaite, who, beside the tarn,
From good Sir William rented a few fields,
Appeared at church with a much better hat
Than he was wont, for it was made of down
That by the broad Ontario's shores had grown
On the sleek beaver; on his window too
A book one day was seen, and none could tell
How it came there—it was a work in the
French tongue, a novel of Voltaire: these things
Were noted, whispered, and thought of no more.

And so it goes on to the discovery of the stranger's skeleton by Wordsworth and his companions, and Wordsworth's moralisings on it in the style in which Wordsworth would moralise, until he is interrupted by a sight

fraught with wonder and astonishment.
It was a tadpole—somewhere by itself
The creature had been left, and there had come
Most timeously, by Providence sent forth,
To close this solemn and momentous tale.

There is not much malice in this, or in *The Flying Tailor*. Hugh Thwaites was frail when he was born:

But mark the wondrous change: ere he was put
By his mother into breeches, Nature strung
The muscular part of his economy
To an unusual strength; and he could leap,
All unimpeded by his petticoats,
Over the stool on which his mother sat
When carding wool, or cleansing vegetables,
Or meek performing other household tasks.
Cunning he watched his opportunity,
And oft, as house affairs did call her thence,
Over leapt Hugh, a perfect whirligig,
More than six inches o'er the astonished stool!
What boots it to narrate, how at leap-frog
Over the breeched and unbreeched villagers
He shone conspicuous? Leap-frog do I say?
Vainly so named. What though in attitude
The Flying Tailor aped the croaking race,
When issuing from the weed-entangled pool,
Tadpoles no more, they seek the new-mown fields
A jocund people, bouncing to and fro
Amid the odorous clover—while amazed
The grasshopper sits idle on the stalk,
With folded pinions, and forgets to sing?
Frog-like, no doubt, in attitude he was;
But sure his bounds across the village green
Seemed to my soul—(my soul for ever bright
With purest beams of sacred poesy)—
Like bounds of red-deer on the Highland hill,
When, close environed by the tinchel's chain,
He lifts his branchy forehead to the sky,
Then o'er the many-headed multitude
Springs belling half in terror, half in rage,
And fleeter than the sunbeam or the wind,
Speeds to his cloud-lair on the mountain-top.

No more of this: suffice it to narrate,
In his tenth year he was apprenticed
Unto a master tailor, by a strong
And regular indenture of seven years,
Commencing from the date the parchment bore,

And ending on a certain day, that made
The term complete of seven solar years.
Oft have I heard him say, that at this time
Of life he was most wretched; for, constrained
To sit all day cross-legged upon a board,
The natural circulation of the blood
Thereby was oft impeded, and he felt
So numbed at times, that when he strove to rise
Up from his work, he could not, but fell back
Among the shreds and patches that bestrewed
With various colours, brightening gorgeously,
The board all round him—patch of warlike red
With which he patched the regimental suits
Of a recruiting military troop,
At that time stationed in a market-town
At no great distance—eke of solemn black
Shreds of no little magnitude, with which
The parson's Sunday coat was then repairing,
That in the new-roofed church he might appear
With fitting dignity, and gravely fill
The sacred seat of pulpit eloquence,
Cheering with doctrinal point and words of faith
The poor man's heart, and from the shallow wit
Of atheist drying up each argument;
Or sharpening his own weapons, only to turn
Their point against himself, and overthrow
His idols with the very enginery
Reared 'gainst the structure of our English church.

. . . .

But other doom was his. That very night
A troop of tumblers came into the village,
Tumbler, equestrian, mountebank—on wire,
On rope, on horse, with cup and balls—inten
To please the gaping multitude, and win
The coin from labour's pocket—small perhaps
Each separate piece of money, but when joined
Making a good round sum, destined ere long
All to be melted (so these lawless folk
Name spending coin in loose debauchery)—
Melted into ale—or haply stouter cheer,
Gin diuretic, or the liquid flame
Of baneful brandy, by the smuggler brought
From the French coast in shallop many-oared,

Skulking by night round headland and through bay,
Afraid of the king's cutter, or the barge
Of cruising frigate, armed with chosen men,
And with her sweeps across the foamy waves
Moving most beautiful with measured strokes.

It chanced that as he threw a somerset
Over three horses (each of larger size
Than our small mountain-breed), one of the troop
Put out his shoulder, and was otherwise
Considerably bruised, especially
About the loins and back. So he became
Useless unto that wandering company,
And likely to be felt a sore expense
To men just on the eve of bankruptcy;
So the master of the troop determined
To leave him in the workhouse, and proclaimed
That if there was a man among the crowd
Willing to fill his place and able to,
Now was the time to show himself. Hugh Thwaites
Heard the proposal as he stood apart
Striving with his own soul—and with a bound
He leapt into the circle and agreed
To supply the place of him who had been hurt.
A shout of admiration and surprise
Then tore heaven's concave, and completely filled
The little field, where near a hundred people
Were standing in a circle round and fair.
Oft have I striven by meditative power,
And reason working 'mid the various forms
Of various occupations and professions,
To explain the cause of one phenomenon
That, since the birth of science, hath remained
A bare enunciation, unexplained
By any theory, or mental light
Streamed on it by the imaginative will,
Or spirit musing in the cloudy shrine,
The penetralia of the immortal soul.
I now allude to that most curious fact,
That 'mid a given number, say threescore,
Of tailors, more men of agility
Will issue out, than from an equal show

From any other occupation—say
Smiths, barbers, bakers, butchers, or the like.
. . . . .
First, then, I would lay down this principle,
That all excessive action by the law
Of nature tends unto repose. This granted,
All action not excessive must partake
The nature of excessive action—so
That in all human beings who keep moving,
Unconscious cultivation of repose
Is going on in silence. Be it so.
Apply to men of sedentary lives
This leading principle, and we behold
That, active in their inactivity,
And unreposing in their long repose,
They are in fact the sole depositaries
Of all the energies by others wasted,
And come at last to teem with impulses
Of muscular motion, not to be withstood,
And either giving vent unto themselves
In numerous feats of wild agility,
Or terminating in despair and death.
. . . . .

Hugh Thwaites's apprenticeship was not wasted, for during it he developed a philosophy of clothes:

A pair
Of breeches, to his philosophic eye,
Were not what unto other folks they seem,
Mere simple breeches; but in them he saw
The symbol of the soul—mysterious, high
Hieroglyphics! such as Egypt's priest
Adored upon the holy Pyramid,
Vainly imagined tomb of monarchs old,
But raised by wise philosophy, that sought
By darkness to illumine, and to spread
Knowledge by dim concealment—process high
Of man's imaginative, deathless soul.
. . . . .

James Rigg shows something rather worse than bad taste in its jesting over the accident which caused the hero's blindness, but parts of it are very good, as for example the painstaking effort to describe the effect of James Rigg's voice:

> Something in his voice,
> While thus he spake of simplest articles
> Of household use, yet sunk upon my soul,
> Like distant thunder from the mountain-gloom
> Wakening the sleeping echoes; so sublime
> Was that old man, so plainly eloquent
> His untaught tongue, though something of a lisp
> (Natural defect), and a slight stutter too,
> (Haply occasioned by some faint attack,
> Harmless, if not renewed, of apoplex),
> Rendered his utterance most peculiar;
> So that a stranger, had he heard that voice
> Once only, and then travelled into lands
> Beyond the ocean, had on his return,
> Meet where they might, have known that curious voice
> Of lisp and stutter, yet I ween withal
> Graceful, and breathed from an original mind.
> . . . . . .

Wordsworth seems to have been unconscious of ever having given offence to the Shepherd, and not to have been offended himself by *The Poetic Mirror*; probably he never read it. They remained on friendly terms, and even the Shepherd's vanity would have acknowledged the *Extempore Effusion on the Death of James Hogg* as sufficient amends for a worse crime than that of which he tried to believe Wordsworth guiltless.

As a matter of fact, though Hogg seems never to have realised it, he himself had once hurt Wordsworth's feelings. The two were taking a walk one day near Rydal, and Wordsworth had been showing Hogg lakes, not the large kind but mountain tarns. Presently Hogg began to be tired, and Wordsworth said in an encouraging tone, "I'll just show you another lake, and then we'll go homewards." To which Hogg ruthlessly replied, "I dinna want to see ony mair *dubs*. Let's step in to the public and hev a wee drap o' whusky, and then we'll hame!"

The pleasantest thing about that incident is that it brought out an unexpected humorous recognition in Wordsworth, who used to tell the story with delight, explaining that after the first shock he could not feel offended at the insult to his country: "the *dubs* was so characteristic of the man." It was at least as characteristic as "Poets! Where are they?" and Wordsworth does not come badly out of his intercourse with the Shepherd.

The bankruptcy of Goldie, which caused Hogg's introduction to Blackwood, affected the whole of the rest of his career. He had since 1800 contributed largely to magazines, and from the date of the establishment of *Blackwood's Magazine* almost all his stories and poems appeared first in magazines and annuals, the greater number in *Blackwood's*, but many in *Fraser's*, the *Scots Magazine* and the *Edinburgh Literary Journal*, with scattered pieces in *The Anniversary*, *The Juvenile Forget-me-not*, *The Metropolitan*, and probably more which I have not seen. Many of them were never reprinted, and some of these unreprinted pieces are at least as good as some which Thomson included. It is true that Thomson made very little research, if he made any, into Hogg's scattered writings, but compiled his edition with certain omissions from the *Tales and Sketches* of 1836–7 and the *Poems* of 1838–40; but there are some things which he ought to have noticed at least in his preface. As far as the verses are concerned, Thomson has the best and Hogg would have done well to leave in *Blackwood's* some of those which he recovered for *A Queer Book*, but not all the tales in *Blackwood's* and elsewhere deserve utter oblivion. There is, for example, in *Fraser's*, the story *On the Separate Existence of the Soul*, in which a seraph is thus described in memorable words:

> The radiant being had neither wings nor female habiliments, but appeared much rather like a prince newly arisen from his bed, and arrayed in a tinsel nightgown and slippers.

A few more amusing bad things like this might have been preferred to such dull bad things as *Trials of Temper*, which no one would have missed if it had been left in *Blackwood's*.

Hogg's relations with *Blackwood's* were very variable: with *Fraser's*, friendly, except just after the publication of *The Domestic Manners and Private Life of Sir Walter Scott*. The *Scots Magazine* was kind to him, and most of the smaller periodicals treated him with respect. The story of his dealings with *Blackwood's* and its dealings with him has often been told by himself and others, but there are a few facts which may still be remarked.

The Shepherd's connection with the magazine began with the first number, though he was not, as he claimed to be, its founder[1]. He contributed verse and prose to the first three numbers, and he had a hand in the *Chaldee MS* in the rejuvenated magazine. Blackwood had founded it in more or less declared rivalry to Constable's *Edinburgh Magazine*, and he put in charge of it joint editors who did not carry out his intentions for it and finally deserted him and went over to Constable. It was an annoying affair, but

[1] R. P. Gillies made the same claim on his behalf, stating in his *Memoirs* (Vol. II, pp. 231–2), that he himself wrote a review of Hogg's *Dramatic Tales* for the first number. But this review is mentioned in the February number for 1818 as arriving too late for inclusion, and the magazine first appeared in April 1817.

Hogg had the idea of turning the tables on the editors and Constable by telling the story in the manner of the prophetical books of the Bible. His draft was worked over and expanded by Lockhart and Wilson, and the result was the *Chaldee MS*, which caused such scandal that it was left out of later copies of that issue of *Blackwood's*. Hogg is sometimes accused, not quite fairly, of claiming the whole plan and working out of the *Chaldee MS*; the plan he did claim, but beyond that he named as his only the first two chapters, part of the third and part of the last—leaving, it must be confessed, very little to his collaborators. He spoke from memory, but appealed for confirmation to the proof-slips, which are now in the British Museum and do not altogether bear out his statements. Chapter I is fully corrected by him. Chapter II, the catalogue of the beasts who came to "Ebony's" assistance, needs correction but has received none. Chapter III is corrected as far as v. 38, which is almost at the end of the catalogue of Constable's beasts, and there are no more corrections, though again they are needed, until Chapter IV, v. 32, after the list of Constable's human helpers. From this point to the end the corrections are by Hogg, who replaced the original v. 34 by three new verses.

It would seem from this that Hogg's daughter, Mrs Garden, was right in disallowing "the more profane"—and witty—parts as her father's. How much also of the parts which he corrected had been made up "in full divan," Hogg contributing a good deal but not all, it is impossible to say. "They interlarded it with a good deal of devilry of their own, which I had never thought of," he wrote himself.

On the other hand, Hogg took some pains to show that he could have written the whole of the *Chaldee MS* if he had chosen. In his note to No. LIX—*Johnny Cope*—in the second volume of the *Jacobite Relics* he gives two chapters of the same sort of thing:

> The following curious Chaldee Manuscript, intituled "The Chronicles of Charles the Young Man," was published about this time.

This was in 1821; next year he was pressing on Blackwood *John Paterson's Mare*,

> as No. 1 of an allegorical history of our miscellaneous literature. I cannot conceive, even with its previous faults, why your editors rejected it, for I am sure that a more harmless good-natured allegory was never written. It is, besides, quite unintelligible without a key, which should never be given. I think it will be next to the Chaldee in popularity, as it is fully as injurious[1].

Hogg was frequently self-contradictory in his statements, but I do not think he ever went further than in this letter.

John Paterson's Mare was never published, nor, apparently, were the allegories mentioned in another letter of the Shepherd's:

> I am writing for another magazine, with all my birr, and intend having most excellent sport with it, as the editors will not understand what one sentence of my celebrated allegories mean till they bring the whole terror of Edinburgh aristocracy upon them[2].

It is possible that these allegories, *John Paterson's Mare* particularly, were not written in the Chaldee manner, but still Hogg was not tired of that form of joking. In *The Three Perils of Man* the Friar tells a story in the Chaldee style, and there is a short passage of the same kind in *The Three Perils of Woman.* It is not difficult to write in the fashion of the Authorised Version, and Hogg's later attempts are sufficiently "Chaldean" in their language, but they have hardly a trace of wit.

[1] Mrs Oliphant, *William Blackwood and his Sons*, vol. 1, p. 348.
[2] *L.c.* 1, p. 337.

Hogg makes one serious accusation against the authorities of *Blackwood's*, especially Wilson—that of printing his name in full to poems, letters and essays which he himself never saw. This refers only to the early days of the magazine, before 1821; the accusation is made in the 1821 Memoir and kept by an oversight in later editions; he had already complained unsuccessfully in October 1820. After 1821 he was not touched except in reviews of his books and in the *Noctes Ambrosianae*, and in neither is he credited with writings not his own. Later his complaint was that he was treated with too little respect in the *Noctes*, and that rejected manuscripts were not returned to him; the earlier complaint does not reappear, except in reprints of the Memoir, and seems on examination to be overdrawn.

Before 1821 there are in the magazine three sets of verses and one letter ascribed to Hogg which he almost certainly did not write. The "essays" of his accusation is a rhetorical addition: there are none[1]. Of the spurious contributions, none seems to have

[1] The following are not included by Thomson in his edition, and were never reprinted by the Shepherd:

Poems:	Sonnet to the Publisher ...	II, 610 (reverse).
	Song to a Salmon, and other "Tent" verses	v, 610, 640.
	Sonnet	VI, 464.

Of these the "Tent" verses are certainly not genuine, and I do not think the sonnets are. There seems however to have been a friendly joke against the Shepherd about his or other men's sonnets, for in vol. v, p. 205, R. P. Gillies has a sonnet *On seeing a Spark fall from the Ettrick Shepherd's Pipe*, which concludes:

Learn to write sonnets, Hogg, and thou shalt merit
Applause with deathless Petrarch evermore.

Hogg's or another's, the sonnets are very bad.

angered him at the time; it was his friends who were annoyed. The verses supposed to be composed by him during the prolonged imaginary picnic in the "Tent" he took as a joke; he had himself offered help, though his letter was lost, and he considered what was published "excellent sport, and very good-natured sport besides." His only grievance was that his "pieces" were refused, and he could not understand the anger of his friends[1]. In the spring of 1820 he did indeed declare

no one has any right to publish aught in my name without consulting me,

referring either to the Letter or to the Sonnet in the January number (Vol. VI, pp. 390–3 and 464); but he was having business disagreements with Blackwood at the time and probably wrote more roughly than he felt. He was calm by October, when his friends were again up in arms, perhaps because of the account in the June number of his wedding, to which he

Letters: Enclosing a fragment of *The Mad Banker of Amsterdam* and referring to a letter just received from

"the Odontist"	VI, 390–3.
Containing *Cow Wat*	VII, 630–1.
To his (Edinburgh) Reviewer ...	VIII, 67–76.

The *Cow Wat* letter would have been obviously genuine even if Mrs Oliphant had not found the *Cow Wat* manuscript. The letter to the Reviewer is also genuine, at least in part, though it has obviously been edited; it is the one in which Hogg acknowledged the authorship of *Donald M'Gillavry* (v. p. 39). The first is probably by Lockhart, but Hogg was in the "Odontist" joke. The Odontist suffered in the same way as Hogg, but more severely. He was a dentist of Glasgow, Dr Scott, on whom Lockhart fathered his own *Lament for Captain Paton* and other verses, to the great indignation of the supposed author.

[1] *Vide* his letter to Blackwood, *William Blackwood and his Sons*, I, 325–6.

himself refers as "a joke, an even-down quiz without much ill-meaning." The truth would seem to be that when Hogg was first troubled by the disrespectful behaviour of his colleagues, he relieved himself by making a general accusation of another kind of ill-treatment, which had been shown to him but not to such an extent as his readers might suppose from his own words.

Real cause for anger was given to him in 1821 by the review of the revised Memoir which preceded the third edition of *The Mountain Bard*. This review begins with a complaint against Hogg's presumption in publishing autobiographies at all, and especially in such numbers; then deals unkindly with various writings and statements of the Shepherd; and finally comes to his chief offence, the claim to the authorship of the *Chaldee MS*, of whose origin the reviewer professes to give the true account. The beginning of the article is merely loutish, but the end atones:

> The *Chaldee Manuscript*! Why, no more did he write the Chaldee Manuscript than the five books of Moses....You yourself, Kit, were learned respecting that article; and myself, Blackwood, and a reverend gentleman of this city, alone know the perpetrator. The unfortunate man is now dead, but delicacy to his friends makes me withhold his name from the public. It was the same person who murdered Begbie! Like Mr Bowles and Ali Pacha, he was a mild man, of unassuming manners—a scholar and a gentleman. It is quite a vulgar error to suppose him a ruffian. He was sensibility itself, and would not hurt a fly. But it was a disease with him "to excite popular emotion." Though he had an amiable wife, and a vast family, he never was happy, unless he saw the world gaping like a stuck pig. With respect to his murdering Begbie, as it is called, he knew the poor man well, and had frequently given him both small sums of money, and articles of wearing apparel. But all at once it entered his brain, that, by putting him to death in a sharp, and clever, and mysterious manner, and seeming also to rob him of an immense number of banknotes, the city of Edinburgh would be thrown into

a ferment of consternation, and there would be no end of the "public emotion," to use his own constant phrase on occasions of this nature. The scheme succeeded to a miracle. He stabbed Begbie to the heart, robbed the dead body in a moment, and escaped. But he never used a single stiver of the money, and was always kind to the widow of the poor man, who was rather a gainer by her husband's death. I have reason to believe that he ultimately regretted the act; but there can be no doubt that his enjoyment was great for many years, hearing the murder canvassed in his own presence, and the many absurd theories broached on the subject, which he could have overthrown by a single word.

Mr —— wrote the *Chaldee Manuscript* precisely on the same principle on which he murdered Begbie; and he used frequently to be tickled at hearing the author termed an assassin. "Very true, very true," he used to say on such occasions, shrugging his shoulders with delight, "he is an assassin, sir; he murdered Begbie";—and this sober truth would pass, at the time, for a mere *jeu d'esprit*,—for my friend was a humourist, and was in the habit of saying good things. The Chaldee was the last work, of the kind of which I have been speaking, that he lived to finish. He confessed it and the murder, the day before he died, to the gentleman specified, and was sufficiently penitent, yet, with that inconsistency not unusual with dying men, almost his last words were, (indistinctly mumbled to himself), "It ought not to have been left out of the other editions."

After this plain statement Hogg must look extremely foolish. We shall next have him claiming the murder, likewise, I suppose; but he is totally incapable of either.

At the end of this amazing article there is a note by "Christopher North," explaining that it is only an example of the puff collusive and even insinuating that the unfortunate Shepherd may have written it himself. Hogg seems to have been fairly easily pacified, though he thought at one moment of taking legal proceedings against the writer[1] and the magazine, but from this he was dissuaded, fortunately for him-

[1] Supposed to be Wilson, but the Begbie part is not like Wilson. It was probably touched up by Lockhart or De Quincey.

self, by Scott[1]. After that he was free from annoyance except in the *Noctes Ambrosianae*: a large exception, but one that was very much his own fault. When a man is eager to contribute to a series in which he is mocked as often as he is held up to admiration, it is a little unreasonable of him to complain of being made ridiculous. In 1831 Lockhart was doing his best to get a pension for Hogg, who was as usual in financial difficulties, and took occasion to remark, in an article in the *Quarterly*, that Hogg was not the boozing buffoon which some people, judging from his dramatic character, supposed him to be, but a respectable citizen. Wilson retorted in *Blackwood's* that anyone who thought or called Hogg a boozing buffoon was himself a braying jackass, but there can be no doubt that the *Noctes* portrait of Hogg did him some harm; it may not be entirely accurate to say that he is ever represented simply as a boozing buffoon, but he certainly disposes of a pretty large quantity of toddy, and he is frequently in ridiculous situations. On the other hand, the Ettrick Shepherd of those delightful dialogues is more consistently poetical and witty in his conversation than the Shepherd of real life. His account of his adventures with that remarkable animal the Bonassus, or his dreams, or his experiences in a previous existence as the Terrible Tawney of Timbuctoo, even his literary and moral judgments, have the accent of Hogg with a smaller proportion of valueless matter than Hogg's own prose writings. "What's a Noctes without a Shepherd?" as he truly remarks in one of them. As a matter of fact, in spite of occasional outbursts of remonstrance he was proud of his share in them, and even while his songs were

[1] Scott's letter on the subject is in Mrs Garden's *Memorials*, 3rd edition, pp. 135–8.

appearing there tried to play the same game in the *Edinburgh Literary Journal* in 1828–9 with two numbers of *Noctes Bengerianae*[1] which are sufficient to show how little right he had to claim much of the prose of the original *Noctes*. And again, after quarrelling with Blackwood in 1833, he tried to begin a series in *Fraser's*, writing to Maginn ("Oliver York"):

> I have been the hero of the *Noctes* all along, and there is no man has so good a right to carry it on as I have. I told North lately, in a letter, that I began *Blackwood's Magazine*, and by — I would end it: therefore, none of your London whims; but let my articles retain their original title. But, if you like, you may make it A NEW SERIES.

Maginn, being the friend of both sides, excused himself from publishing any *Noctes Ambrosianae*, but printed part of the dialogue, which described the Shepherd's London adventures in the preceding year, and all the songs[2].

[1] The name was taken from Mount Benger, the farm which Hogg most unwisely took soon after his marriage in addition to Altrive.

[2] The second, *King Willie*, had already appeared in *Blackwood's*—Hogg often published the same poem in several magazines—and the third, *Hey, then up we go*, had appeared in the *Jacobite Relics* and is here again disowned by Hogg.

There is some evidence, given by Rogers in his *Modern Scottish Minstrel* (vol. IV—in some copies this has the title-page of II—pp. 115, 166, 271), that Hogg has also been wrongly credited with the fourth, *M'Kimmon*, and the seventh, *Rise! rise! Lowland and Highland Men*, and with one of the songs in the *Noctes Bengerianae, O saw you this sweet bonnie lassie*. The last Hogg disclaims: his Nancy says "a J and an H stand for" the writer's name, but "it is not a song o' our master's"; he may also have disclaimed the others, but Maginn's compression of his *Noctes Ambrosianae* has left that obscure. According to Rogers, Hogg took copies of the songs when they were sent to him for approval, and after that either returned or lost the originals; and then the copies were found among his papers and taken for his own work. Rogers ascribes *M'Kimmon*—in his version *M'Crimman*—to George

Hogg quarrelled with Blackwood and the Blackwood group more than once, but all the quarrels, with one exception, were made up and forgotten; the Shepherd did not usually bear malice for long, and there was a certain absurdity about him which made it hard for anyone to take his transgressions with great seriousness. Publishers especially, in spite of their habit of going bankrupt at the most inconvenient moments for him, did not deal badly with him. Murray used to send parcels of books which he thought would improve the Shepherd's mind—one was *Emma*, of which it would be pleasant to have Hogg's opinion; Constable was gracious; and Blackwood went so far in his friendship as to help Hogg to Longman's acquaintance when Hogg thought he was not being well enough paid by Blackwood himself. But the poor Shepherd was always in financial trouble, and only ceaseless activity enabled him to avoid complete ruin.

Allen, *Rise! rise!* to John Imlah, and *O saw you* to James Home. Rogers's note does not seem to have attracted much attention, for *Rise! rise!* is given as Hogg's with no remark in Hadden's *Story of James Hogg*, *M'Kimmon* in the selections by Mrs Garden and Dr Wallace, and both in the *Cambridge History of English Literature*. All that can be said is that they are extraordinarily like Hogg at his best, and if they are not his they ought to be.

6. *ALTRIVE LAKE AND MOUNT BENGER*

HOGG moved to Altrive in 1817, and by 1820 his prospects were sufficiently good to justify him in marrying. There are pleasant glimpses of the last preparations for the wedding and of the manners of the time in Hogg's letters: his idea, which roused his bride's gentle mockery, of a suitable wedding dress—white muslin, with a white satin Highland bonnet with white plumes and veil, which, as he explains, is both highly becoming and convenient, for "married country ladies wear such bonnets at table, instead of caps, when visiting"; the presentation of a hat to the minister—Hogg in fact seems to have presented hats to two ministers, the one whom he had wished to perform the ceremony and the one who actually did so; and the fortunately obsolete custom of taking "a female friend" on the honeymoon. After all delays the Shepherd and his Margaret were married in April 1820 and, as far as they were personally concerned, lived happy ever after.

From other points of view, however, their misfortunes began almost at once. The first was comic—an attack of measles which amused as much as it distressed the elderly bridegroom—but others were more serious. Hogg's father-in-law, a fairly wealthy man, had promised a dowry with his daughter, and on the strength of this expectation Hogg leased the large and extravagant farm of Mount Benger, which had already ruined two men in six years, for a term of nine years. In a very short time Mrs Hogg's parents, owing to heavy financial losses, were in the position of needing help instead of giving it, and Hogg found himself obliged to support them. To do him justice, he accepted the duty cheerfully. Then there was presently a family—a son and four daughters survived him—and with admirable public spirit he arranged that the children of the neighbourhood should share their schooling. He lodged and boarded the schoolmaster and repaired a half-ruined hut to serve as the school-house, the Yarrow school being some distance away, actually ten miles from the upper end of Yarrow parish. The kirk itself was five miles from Mount Benger, and it must have been a goodly sight to see the Hogg family driving thither in "the caravan," a light cart covered by a movable tin dome, painted green, and with green baize curtains at each end—nearly as remarkable a conveyance as the "Runaway Bedstead" of the Baring Goulds.

To the ordinary expenses of farming and house-keeping must be added those which were the penalties of celebrity—swarms of visitors who arrived with or without warning. In that lonely place, fourteen miles from the nearest market town, they could not be sent away unrefreshed, and they sometimes presumed on the Shepherd's hospitality. One day there were fourteen unexpected guests to dinner, and hungry and weary strangers would arrive at odd hours with the certainty of receiving comfort, food and warmth and, very possibly, a bed. As well as giving them such physical entertainment, the Shepherd was obliged to show them some personal courtesy, sometimes to take them about and display the sights of the countryside or to accompany them fishing or shooting, and Mount Benger suffered.

A welcome and unexacting but only occasional visitor was Scott, whom little Jamie Hogg always remembered as "the man wi' the guid knife," a fascinating weapon which contained a saw. One day when Scott had been dining at Mount Benger he took up little Margaret Hogg and kissed her and then, laying his hand on her head, said, "God Almighty bless you, my dear child!" The mother burst into tears, explaining afterwards, "O, I thought if he had but just done the same to them all, I do not know what in the world I would not have given!" He was, she felt, one of the stable things in the world, and their mutual respect is brought out in Hogg's story of their last meeting:

> The last time Margaret saw him was at his own house in Maitland Street, a very short time before he finally left it. We were passing from Charlotte Square to make a call in Laurieston, when I said, "See, yon is Sir Walter's house, at yon red lamp." "O, let me go in and see him once more!" said she. "No, no, Margaret," said I, "you know how little time we have, and it would be too bad to intrude on his hours of quiet and study at this time of the day." "O, but I must go in," said she, "and get a shake of his kind honest hand once more. I cannot go by." So . . . in we went, and were received with all the affection of old friends, but his whole discourse was addressed to my wife, while I was left to shift for myself among books and newspapers. He talked to her of our family, and of our prospects of being able to give them a good education, which he recommended at every risk, and at every sacrifice. He talked to her of his own family one by one, and of Mr Lockhart's family, giving her a melancholy account of little Hugh John Lockhart—

—until Hogg, feeling that he deserved as much attention as his wife, broke into the grave conversation with a ludicrous remark on Sir Walter's braw gown.

Usually when Hogg went to Edinburgh, as he did on business once or twice a year, he went alone, leaving his wife with perfect confidence to rule the household. He would stay at Watson's Selkirk and Peebles Inn, visiting friends and attending to business, and on the last night before his return to Yarrow he would give a party. Robert Chambers was present at one at least of these feasts and has left a lively description of it[1]:

In the course of the forenoon, he would make a round of calls, and mention, in the most incidental possible way, that two or three of his acquaintances were to meet that night in the Candlemaker Row at nine, and that the addition of this particular friend whom he was addressing, together with any of *his* friends he chose to bring along with him, would by no means be objected to. It may readily be imagined that, if he gave this hint to some ten or twelve individuals, the total number of his visitors would not probably be few. In reality, it used to bring something like a Highland host upon him. Each of the men he had spoken to came, like a chief, with a long train of friends, most of them unknown to the hero of the evening, but all of them eager to spend a night with the Ettrick Shepherd. He himself stood up at the corner of one of Watson's largest bedrooms to receive the company as it poured in. Each man, as he brought in his train, would endeavour to introduce each to him separately, but would be cut short by the lion with his bluff good-humoured declaration: "Ou ay, we'll be a' weel acquent by and by."

The first two clans would perhaps find chairs, the next would get the bed to sit upon; all after that had to stand. This room being speedily filled, those who came subsequently would be shown into another bedroom. When it was filled too, another would be thrown open, and still the cry was: "They come!" At length, about ten o'clock, when nearly the whole house seemed "panged" with people, as he would have himself expressed it, supper would be announced....All the warning Mr Watson had got from Mr Hogg about this affair was a hint, in passing out that morning, that *twae-three* lads had been speaking of supping there that night. Watson, however, knew of old what was meant by *twae-three*, and had laid out his largest room with a double range of tables, sufficient to accommodate some sixty or seventy people....

At length all is arranged; and then, what a strangely miscellaneous company is found to have been gathered together! Meal-

[1] *The Candlemaker Row Festival*, originally printed in *Chambers's Journal*, but more conveniently to be read in W. Chambers's *Memoir of Robert Chambers*, pp. 247–54.

dealers are there from the Grass-market, genteel and slender young men from the Parliament House, printers from the Cowgate, and booksellers from the New Town. Between a couple of young advocates sits a decent grocer from Bristo Street; and amidst a host of shop-lads from the Luckenbooths, is perched a stiffish young probationer, who scarcely knows whether he should be here or not, and has much dread that the company will sit late. Jolly, honest-like bakers, in pepper-and-salt coats, give great uneasiness to squads of black coats in juxtaposition with them; and several dainty-looking youths, in white neckcloths and black silk eye-glass ribbons, are evidently much discomposed by a rough tyke of a horse-dealer who has got in amongst them, and keeps calling out all kinds of coarse jokes to a crony about thirteen men off on the same side of the table. Many of Mr Hogg's Selkirkshire store-farming friends are there, with their well-oxygenated complexions and Dandie-Dinmont-like bulk of figure; and in addition to all comers, Mr Watson himself, and nearly the whole of the people residing in his house at the time. If a representative assembly had been made up from all classes of the community, it could not have been more miscellaneous than this company, assembled by a man to whom, in the simplicity of his heart, all company seemed alike acceptable.

Then follows the account of the supper itself, which though it might be noisy and prolonged to four or five o'clock in the morning, was innocent mirth and had no bad consequences.

There may be some question, however, whether the greatest occasion of Hogg's life, when he shone in his glory at a Burns and Hogg dinner in London, did not have bad consequences. Perhaps Carlyle and Lockhart were right in thinking that his head was a little turned by his honours. Or perhaps that was a harsh judgment. At least there can be no doubt that Hogg was thoroughly lionised and thoroughly enjoyed himself when he went to London in 1832.

He had always wished to go, and a dozen years earlier Scott had tried to take him along to the coronation of George IV. It was just after the bankruptcy of Hogg's father-in-law had upset all his calculations with regard to the leasing, stocking and farming of Mount Benger, and Scott thought that if he went to London and produced a coronation ode, a little dexterous use of influence might get a place or pension which would help him out of his difficulties. Whether the friendly piece of jobbery would have succeeded cannot be decided, for Hogg, his responsibilities as a newly-established farmer heavy upon him, did not feel justified in missing St Boswell's Fair, and "with the tear in his eye," as he expressed it, refused the invitation. His devotion to duty was not rewarded with success at Mount Benger, and at the end of his nine-year lease he found himself poorer than when he started. He returned to live at Altrive Lake and then, with the hope of raising money, went to London to arrange with Cochrane the bookseller the publication of a collected edition of his works. As so often happened to those with whom Hogg was connected, bankruptcy fell upon Cochrane shortly afterwards and the Shepherd was none the better for the scheme, but he had at least had his glorious hour.

Blackwood's and especially the *Noctes Ambrosianae* had made his name familiar to most people, and his days were filled with engagements throughout the three months of his stay. He was, as he wrote to his wife, "positively worried with kindness," and in an earlier letter he describes the kind of thing that happened to him.

When invited, I accept on condition that there is not to be a party. "Oh no! there shall be no party, just a few friends, merely a family party." Well, I go at seven o'clock, no fashionable dinners before that. By the time we get a few glasses of wine drunk, the rapping at the door begins and continues without intermission for an hour and a half. Then we go upstairs and find both drawing-rooms crammed as full as ever you saw sheep in a fold. And then I am brought in and shown, like any other wild beast, all the ladies curtseying and flattering and begging for one shake of my hand. Such flummery I never saw in this world, and every night I am taken in this way.

In spite of his protestations, one suspects that the Shepherd did not really dislike all this fêting. The climax came on January 25th, when a public dinner was held to celebrate the birthday of Burns, and Hogg was the guest of honour. For once in his life he received, as he himself confessed, his fill of flattery, "even to fulsomeness and running over....I was the hero of the evening, and every gentleman and nobleman ended with some encomiums of me, Lockhart in particular abounded with them. It was a glorious speech, but is said to be badly reported in the papers this morning." The galleries were filled with ladies, and the Shepherd felt honest compassion for them at their being admitted "merely to *smell* a good dinner, without being permitted either to eat or drink." He might have extended his pity to half the guests, for S. C. Hall tells us that twice as many assembled as had been expected, and each steward was forced to stand guard over those whom he had succeeded in supplying with food, while the hungry raged in vain and two pipers paced round the room and drowned their clamour. But for the Shepherd it was a very superior occasion.

After all this it must have been good for him to receive from his wife a letter of such gentle shrewdness as one of Sir James Barrie's heroines might have written: "Leave before you are threadbare. I do not exactly mean your coat, but leave the Londoners something to guess at. By the by, the coat is no joke either, for you are apt to wear it too long....I should rather wear a worse gown than you should appear in a shabby coat. It is pitiful to think of your going about with great holes in your stockings." And at the end of March he returned to her care and to his endeavours to get his affairs into order, for the glory of the visit to London had brought little or no material profit. He was over sixty, and the most of his work was done, with small gain to himself.

7. *THE TALES OF THE SHEPHERD*

THE stories which Hogg himself had selected as his best[1] were published in six volumes in 1837, just after his death, and Thomson adopted this selection with four omissions which are not very easy to explain. *The Surpassing Adventures of Allen Gordon* makes large demands on its readers' faith, but it is no worse as a story than *Basil Lee*, and it has one very attractive character, a tame Polar bear. *Cousin Mattie*, *The Bush aboon Traquhair*—a pastoral drama—and possibly *The Prodigal Son* may have been omitted for moral reasons, and the second at least is a poor thing. Hogg considered himself a moral teacher, as much in his novels as when he mounted the pulpit in *The Spy* or the *Lay Sermons*, but his idea of edification was not the same as Thomson's. Thomson was within his rights in rejecting bodily what displeased him; his does not pretend to be a complete edition; but it is hard to forgive him his mutilation of *The Brownie of Bodsbeck*, from which he omitted Davie Tait's prayer, though he allowed the prayers given in *The Shepherd's Calendar*. His editing of the other tales is less drastic than Hogg's own, which had reduced *The Three Perils of Man* to the comparatively modest *Siege of Roxburgh* and omitted entirely the portentous *Three Perils of Woman* and dull *Altrive Tales*. There is still dullness and clumsy jesting enough in the tales, but the worst things have gone.

[1] According to the publisher, Scott helped in the revision of some, but the titles of these are not given. Hogg had asked Lockhart to edit them for him, but Lockhart wisely refused to take the responsibility.

A parallel might be drawn between Hogg's tales and his poems. There are the pastoral sketches, such as the last chapters of *The Shepherd's Calendar*, which are as natural and humorous as the best of the songs; the stories of murders and the faery world might be paired with the ballads, the ambitious historical romances with the longer poems; and just as he produced one masterpiece in verse, *Kilmeny*, so he did in prose, *The Confessions of a Justified Sinner*. There are of course leakages from one compartment to another, and *The Confessions* contains something of nearly all.

Broadly speaking, Hogg is at his best in prose, as in poetry, when he is not trying to follow Scott too closely. It was the success of the Waverley novels and the consequent fashion of historical romances that drew from him *The Brownie of Bodsbeck*, for which we should be thankful; but Scott's novels are also responsible for the works of Hogg which are the most awful of his awful warnings. Now and then the best Hogg breaks in with a song or a touch of grotesque humour or a scrap of living tradition, but he ought never to have attempted historical romances about anyone earlier than the Covenanters. For them he had tradition to help him, but for earlier times he had no knowledge behind him, and if he ever read up his subject he did not understand what he read.

The Brownie of Bodsbeck was the first of these romances and by far the best[1], because it has to do with the kinds of life that Hogg knew and the traditions which were most familiar to him. Its relation to *Old Mortality*

[1] *The Confessions of a Justified Sinner*, though it is dated a century before Hogg, hardly comes into the same category. The story could not have been developed so well if it had been placed in any other time, but the history is subordinate to the other elements.

is not easy to make out. Hogg himself stated that it was written first and had to be changed so as not to seem a plagiary. The Brownie has so little character in the present version that he might as well be called Balfour of Burleigh as Brown of Caldwell, but he may have had more originally; Nanny is a little like some of Scott's old women, but yet not near enough to be considered a copy; on the other hand, even making all allowance for the traditional view of Claverhouse, it seems at least possible that Hogg deliberately darkened his lines in his revision, out of a desire to correct what he thought false in Scott's portrait. The best thing in the story, Davie Tait's prayer, is certainly not at all indebted to Scott, but comes out of Hogg's own experience. There are other prayers in Chapter VII which he repeats in the *Prayers* of *The Shepherd's Calendar* and assigns to their true author, Adam Scott in Upper Dalgleish; they are good, but Davie Tait's is glorious.

> There is scarcely a boy in the country who cannot recite scraps of Davie Tait's prayer; but were I to set all that is preserved of it down here, it might be construed as a mockery of that holy ordinance, than which nothing is so far from my heart or intention.

Thomson takes advantage of this to leave the prayer out, but Hogg goes on and gives "the sublime part of it."

> But the last time we gathered oursels before thee, we left out a wing o' the hirsel by mistake, an' thou hast paid us hame i' our ain coin. Thou wart sae gude than as come to the sheddin thysel, an' clap our heads, an' whisper i' our lugs, "dinna be disheartened, my puir bits o' waefu' things, for though ye be the shotts o' my hale fauld, I'll take care o' ye, an' herd ye, an' gie ye a' that ye hae askit o' me the night." It was kind, an' thou hast done it; but we forgot a principal part, an' maun tell thee now, that we have had another visitor sin' ye war here, an' ane

wha's back we wad rather see than his face. Thou kens better thysel than we can tell thee what place he has made his escape frae; but we sair dread it is frae the boddomless pit, or he wadna hae ta'en possession but leave. Ye ken, that gang tried to keep vilent leasehaud o' your ain fields, an' your ain ha', till ye gae them a killiecoup. If he be ane o' them, O come thysel to our help, an' bring in thy hand a bolt o' divine vengeance, het i' the furnace o' thy wrath as reed as a nailstring, an' bizz him an' scouder him till ye dinna leave him the likeness of a paper izel, until he be glad to creep into the worm-holes o' the earth, never to see sun or sterns mair. But, if it be some puir dumfoundered soul that has been bumbased and stoundit at the view o' the lang Hopes an' the Downfa's o' Eternity, comed daundering away frae about the laiggen girds o' Heaven to the waefu' gang that he left behind, like a lost sheep that strays frae the rich pastures o' the south, an' comes bleating back a' the gate to its cauld native hills, to the very gair where it was lambed and first followed its minny, ane canna help haeing a fellow-feeling wi' the puir soul after a', but yet he'll find himsel here like a cow in an unco loan. Therefore, O furnish him this night wi' the wings o' the wild gainner or the eagle, that he may swoof away back to a better hame than this, for we want nane o' his company. An' do thou give to the puir stray thing a weel-hained heff and a beildy lair, that he may nae mair come straggling amang a stock that's sae unlike himsel, that they're frightit at the very look o' him.

Thou hast promised in thy Word to be our shepherd, our guider an' director; an' thy word's as gude as some men's aith, an' we'll haud thee at it. Therefore take thy plaid about thee, thy staff in thy hand, an' thy dog at thy fit, an' gather us a' in frae the cauld windy knowes o' self-conceit—the plashy bogs an' mires o' sensuality, an' the damp flows o' worldly-mindedness, and wyse us a' into the true bught o' life, made o' the flakes o' forgiveness and the door o' loving-kindness; an' never do thou suffer us to be heftit e'ening or morning, but gie lashin' meals o' the milk of praise, the ream o' thankfulness, an' the butter o' good-works. An' do thou, in thy good time an' way, smear us ower the hale bouk wi' the tar o' adversity, weel mixed up wi' the meinging of repentance, that we may be kiver'd ower wi' gude bouzy shake-rough fleeces o' faith, a' run out on the hips, an' as brown as a tod. An' do thou, moreover, fauld us owernight, an' every night, in within the true sheep-fauld o' thy covenant, weel buggen wi' the stanes o' salvation, an' caped wi' the divots o' grace. An' then wi' sic a shepherd, an' sic a sheep-fauld, what hae we to be feared for? Na, na! we'll fear naething but sin!—We'll never mair scare at the poolly-woolly o' the whaup, nor swirl at the gelloch o' the ern; for if the arm of our Shepherd be about us for good, a' the imps, an' a' the powers o' darkness, canna wrang a hair o' our tails.

How near this style of eloquence was to reality may be seen by referring to the genuine prayers in *The Shepherd's Calendar:*

One of the most notable men for this sort of family eloquence was Adam Scott, in Upper Dalgleish. I had an uncle who herded with him, from whom I heard many quotations from Scott's prayers, a few of which are as follows:—

"We particularly thank thee for thy great goodness to Meg, and that ever it came into your head to take any thought of sic an useless baw-waw as her." (This was a little girl that had been somewhat miraculously saved from drowning.)

"For thy mercy's sake—for the sake of thy poor sinfu' servants that are now addressing thee in their ain shilly-shally way, and for the sake o' mair than we dare weel name to thee, hae mercy on Rob. Ye ken yoursel he is a wild mischievous callant, and thinks nae mair o' committing sin than a dog does o' licking a dish; but put thy hook in his nose, and thy bridle in his gab, and gar him come back to thee wi' a jerk that he'll no forget the langest day he has to leeve."

"Dinna forget poor Jamie, wha's far away frae amang us the night. Keep thy arm o' power about him, and oh, I wish ye wad endow him wi' a like spunk and smeddum to act for himsel. For if ye dinna, he'll be but a bauchle in this world, and a backsitter in the neist."

"We're a' like hawks, we're a' like snails, we're a' like slogie riddles; like hawks to do evil, like snails to do good, and like slogie riddles, that let through a' the good, and keep the bad."

"Bring down the tyrant and his lang neb, for he has done muckle ill the year, and gie him a cup o' thy wrath, and gin he winna tak that, gie him kelty." (*Kelty* signifies double, or two cups. This was an occasional petition for one season only, and my uncle never could comprehend what it meant.)

The last two prayers are used in the seventh chapter of *The Brownie of Bodsbeck*. There is also a flavour of

Davie Tait in these two of "an old relation of my own," probably the Laidlaw uncle who sang ballads in his profaner moods:

"And mairower and aboon, do thou bless us a' wi' thy best warldly blessings—wi' bread for the belly and theeking for the back, a lang stride and a clear ee-sight. Keep us from a' proud prossing and upsetting—from foul flaips, and stray steps, and from all unnecessary trouble."

"And when our besetting sins come bragging and blowstering upon us, like Gully o' Gath, O enable us to fling aff the airmer and hairnishin o' the law, whilk we haena proved, and whup up the simple sling o' the gospel, and nail thes mooth stanes o' redeeming grace into their foreheads."

Another of Hogg's relations was that James Laidlaw whose prayer for Cow Wat the Shepherd gave in a letter printed in *Blackwood's* (vol. VI, pp. 630–1); unfortunately it has never been reprinted except by Mrs Oliphant, who did not know that it had been published at all and, by misreading "Hell" as "will," found it difficult to make sense of it. This is the story:

I remember, and always will, a night that I had with him about seventeen years ago. He and one Walter Bryden, better known by the appellation of Cow Wat, Thomas Hogg, the celebrated flying Ettrick tailor, and myself, were all drinking in a little change house one evening. After the whisky had fairly begun to operate, Laidlaw and Cow Wat went to loggerheads about Hell, about which their tenets of belief totally differed. The dispute was carried on with such acrimony on both sides, that Wat had several times heaved his great cudgel, and threatened to knock his opponent down. Laidlaw, perceiving that the tailor and I were convulsed with laughter, joined us for some time with all his heart; but all at once he began to look grave, and the tear stood in his eye. "Aye, ye may laugh!" said he; "great gomerals! It's weel kend that ye're just twae that laugh at everything that's good. Ye hae mair need to pray for the poor auld heretick than laugh at him, when ye see that he's on the braid way that leads to destruction. I'm really sorry for the poor auld scoundrel after a', and troth I think we sude join an' pray for him. For my part I sal lend my mite." With that he laid off his old slouched hat, and kneeled down on the floor, leaning forward on a chair, where he prayed a long prayer for Cow Wat, as he familiarly termed him, when representing his forlorn case to his Maker. I do not know what I would give now to have a copy of that prayer, for I never heard anything like it. It was so cutting, that before the end Wat rose up, foaming with rage, heaved his stick, and cried, "I tell ye, gie ower, Jamie Laidlaw, I winna be prayed for in that gate."

If there were different places and degrees of punishment, he said, as the auld hoary reprobate maintained—that was to say, three or four hells—then he prayed that poor Cow Wat might be preferred to the easiest ane. "We couldna expect nae better a place," he said, "for sic a man, and indeed we would be ashamed to ask it. But on the ither hand," continued he, "if it be true that the object of our petition cheated James Cunningham an' Sandy o' Bowerhope out o' from two to three hunder pounds o' lamb-siller, why, we can hardly ask sic a situation for him; an' if it be farther true that he left his ain wife, Nanny Stothart, and took up wi' another (whom he named, name and surname), really we have hardly the face to ask any mitigation for him at a'."

The tailor and I, and another one, I have forgot who it was, but I think it was probably Adie o' Aberlosk, were obliged to hold Wat by main force upon his chair till the prayer was finished.

Some of the songs in *The Brownie of Bodsbeck* may also be partly traditional; Nanny's in Chapter v, especially the shorter versions of the first edition, are much more like the real thing than Hogg's usually are.

The Woolgatherer, which was published with the *Brownie*, has no history in it but plenty of good stories. *The Hunt of Eildon* has very little history; it is confused magic, mostly voluntary or involuntary skin-changing, and there seems to be no particular reason why it should either begin or end where it does. A story not unlike it, but much more pointed, is *The Witches of Traquhair* in *The Shepherd's Calendar*.

The Brownie of Bodsbeck appeared in 1818, the *Winter Evening Tales* in 1820. These tales are nearly all in prose, but only one of the prose tales is strictly an historical romance, and that is the inept *Bridal of Polmood,* which has already been noticed for the sake of the old song embedded in it. In the *Winter Evening Tales* it has an introductory chapter explaining that the story was told by an old gentleman in a stage-coach, but this was afterwards omitted. The scene is laid in the court of Scotland in the early sixteenth century, and as Hogg knew nothing either of courts or of the sixteenth century the result of his combined ignorance and boldness is a story madder than most. Blackwood refused it, to the great indignation of Hogg, who asserted in his *Autobiography* that it had been acknowledged by all who read it as the most finished and best tale that he ever produced. Most of its readers will be rather of Blackwood's opinion. There is not much hope for a romancer who kills one of his characters and then, deciding that he needs him, brings him to life again with the calm explanation that

> King James, who was well versed in everything relating to the human frame, was the best surgeon, and the most skilful physician then in the realm, succeeded at last in restoring him to life.

Two years later Hogg published his most ambitious romance, in three volumes—*The Three Perils of Man; or War, Women, and Witchcraft.* He afterwards pretended to think poorly of it:

> I dashed on, and mixed up with what might have been made one of the best historical tales our country ever produced, such a mass of diablerie as retarded the main story, and rendered the whole perfectly ludicrous.

This main story, stripped of the diablerie, is *The Siege of Roxburgh,* which is not as good as Hogg thought it might have been—there are too many improbabilities of character and situation for that—but is yet better than might be expected by a reader coming to it from *The Three Perils of Man*. The third Peril, Witchcraft, has vanished entirely; that is, Chapters x, xi and xii of Vol. i, the whole of Vol. ii, and the first five chapters of Vol. iii have been taken away, and so has everything that depends on them in the later part of the story. Michael Scott has disappeared with his wizardry, and the Warden gets full credit for the device which took the castle; all the company that went to Aikwood has disappeared, except Charlie Scott, whose dignity, though never very great, has gained much by the omissions which concern him; and as a natural consequence the stories told at Aikwood have also disappeared. Hogg might have found an excuse for bringing them in somewhere else, but he does not seem to have thought it worth while. They delay the action, and though Charlie's history of his first stour is spirited—the Laidlaws show to as much advantage in it as in the siege itself—Gibbie's is not the only one which ought to have brought punishment on the teller.

Hogg found room, however, for some of the rejected passages in different places. *The Hymn to the Devil* and the *Poet's Tale*—which is here printed as prose but is really bad blank verse—were published again in magazines[1], and Gibbie's Tale is in the *Altrive Tales*. It may be questioned whether they are worth rescuing, but Hogg did well to save one other thing,

[1] The *Hymn to the Devil* is in the *Noctes*, No. 19 (*Blackwood's*, vol. xvii, pp. 367–9); *The Three Virgins* in *Fraser's*, vol. xi, pp. 666–79, where it is called *The Three Sisters*, omitting the introduction, the *Hymn to the Redeemer* and six verses of the *Hymn to Odin*. The *Hymn to the Redeemer* was reprinted with slight alterations in *The Amulet*, 1835, pp. 118–20.

the Poet's Song. According to him it slipped in casually—he speaks almost as if it made itself:

> When *The Three Perils of Man* came first to my hand, and I saw this song put into the mouth of a drunken poet, and mangled in the singing, I had no recollection of it whatever. I had written it off-hand along with the prose and quite forgot it.

He revised it after discovering it and reprinted it more than once in slightly differing versions; it is in No. 8 of the *Noctes* (*Blackwood's*, vol. XIII, p. 598) and in the *Songs*, and Thomson printed two versions in his edition. Even in its earlier form it shines out of *The Three Perils of Man*, and Hogg improved it in his revision. It is one of the best of his songs, *When the Kye comes hame*, and one of the most popular. Hogg had reason to be proud of it, and in spite of his expressed contempt for *The Three Perils of Man* one suspects that he had some tenderness for the whole book; at least he thought it worth while to complain that Scott stole the main plot for *Castle Dangerous* and Allan Cunningham the rest for *Sir Michael Scott*.

The Three Perils of Woman; or Love, Leasing, and Jealousy is not an exact parallel to *The Three Perils of Man*. It is not a continuous story, and the first tale, the more wildly improbable, is not historical. The second, which includes the second and third Perils, is Jacobite.

A curious testimony to the rage for "Scotch novels" of any kind is given by *Les trois écueils des femmes*, a French translation made anonymously in 1825. The translator has shortened the original considerably, cutting out, for example, all the Scots in the first story. It was probably incomprehensible. "Leasing" seems to have been misread as "Learning"; it is translated "La science"[1]. There are a good many mistranslations, of which this that follows is the best for which the translator alone is responsible. Hogg wrote (*Perils*, II, 171–2):

> She made the pipers of all the regiments to join, and push on after the fliers, playing, with all their might, "Away, Whigs, away!"

The translator renders it thus (*Écueils*, III, 50–1):

> Elle réunit tous les musiciens des régimens, qui chantaient de toutes leurs forces: "Éloignez-vous! wighs, éloignez-vous!"

That translator deserves to be remembered with Du Maurier's Laure, who translated Tennyson to her Isidore:

> "Cassez-vous, cassez-vous, cassez-vous,
> O mer, sur vos froids gris cailloux!"

This Jacobite story is dull, but not so absurd as *The Bridal of Polmood*. Hogg knew his ground fairly well. Better again are some of the *Tales of the Wars of Montrose*, especially those which least attempt to be historical. The *Edinburgh Baillie* is not good, and *Sir Simon Brodie* is feeble, but *Wat Pringle* is a lively story and may, as Colonel Fitzwilliam Elliot points out in *The Trustworthiness of the Border Ballads*, contain some real tradition. *Mary Montgomery* is the best of the three remaining stories; *Colonel Peter Aston* would be better if Hogg were less concerned to bring in his history, and *Julia M'Kenzie* gains by having no history in it.

The best of the partly historical shorter tales is *The Cameronian Preacher's Tale*. Again the history does not get in the way—it would even be hard to say within a century what the date of the story is—and there is a concentration and restraint in the telling

[1] But the book was advertised in *Blackwood's*, vol. XIII, p. 481, as *The Three Perils of Woman: Love, Learning, and Jealousy*; and in No. 7 of the *Noctes* Hogg remarks, "I fixed on Love, Learning and Laziness."

which Hogg rarely showed. The reason may be that it is a story of the supernatural: when a ghost or anything of its like comes in, Hogg knows what he is about and wastes no words, but when he has nothing behind him but his own invention, he tries to get out of difficulties by long and uninteresting descriptions or conversations, or heavy jesting. He needs something of the marvellous before he can make a story probable.

There is no want of horrible probability in *The Confessions of a Justified Sinner*, afterwards renamed *The Confessions of a Fanatic* because the earlier title shocked the pious. Hogg himself seems to have been startled when he read it over; it was first published anonymously with a frontispiece "facsimile" of part of Robert Colwan's MS, and Hogg explains in his *Autobiography* that he durst not put his name to it because "it was a story replete with horrors." It is certainly not a book to be read before going to bed in the dark. Professor Saintsbury considers it too good for Hogg and suggests that Lockhart may have revised it, but there is no convincing reason for depriving the Shepherd of the full credit for his work. He could write well, when he took the trouble, and for once he did consistently. The *Confessions* are written in his usual style and are hardly more closely woven and concentrated than passages in his other stories. There are even some blunders in the use of words, which Lockhart would not have been likely to pass in revision. There is, for example, the extraordinary use of "unguent" in the prefatory Editor's Narrative:

> Hers were not the tenets of the great reformers, but theirs mightily overstrained and deformed. Theirs was an unguent hard to be swallowed; but hers was that unguent embittered and over-heated until nature could no longer bear it.

Another word, not wrong in itself but not common in literary use, is "alongst," which occurs in the description of the finding of the manuscript:

> The title page is written, and is as follows:
>
> THE PRIVATE MEMOIRS
> AND CONFESSIONS
> OF A JUSTIFIED SINNER:
> WRITTEN BY HIMSELF.
> FIDELI CERTA MERCES.
>
> And, alongst the head, it is the same as given in the present edition of the work.

The Shepherd's descendants owned, at least as late as 1898, a MS of the *Confessions* in his own handwriting; I am not sure that this can be considered a final proof of his authorship, but it carries some weight[1].

The germ of the book is the letter, *A Scots Mummy*, which appeared in *Blackwood's* in 1823 (vol. XIV, pp. 188–90), and is quoted almost in full at the end of the *Confessions*. It is impossible to make out whether Hogg had the whole story in his mind then or whether it developed afterwards by degrees. Some of the ideas seem to have haunted him and demanded to be treated again: *The Brownie of the Black Haggs*, a good story, and *The Strange Letter of a Lunatic*, a weaker one, both take them up. The Brownie has several of the characteristics of "my illustrious friend," and his story even catches some of the horror of the *Confessions*.

The original *Confessions* contain a few passages afterwards omitted—by Hogg himself, not his editor—of which the longest are John Barnet's remarks on Robert Colwan's paternity, Penpunt's reflections on Cameronian principles, and Lucky Shaw's story of

[1] *Vide* Ettrick Shepherd Memorial Volume, 1898.

the narrow escape of the people of Auchtermuchty. They are good in themselves, especially the last:

It was but the year afore the last, that the people o' the town o' Auchtermuchty grew so rigidly righteous, that the meanest hind among them became a shining light in ither towns an' parishes. There was nought to be heard, neither night nor day, but preaching, praying, argumentation, an' catechising in a' the famous town o' Auchtermuchty. The young men wooed their sweethearts out o' the Song o' Solomon, an' the girls returned answers in strings o' verses out o' the Psalms. At the lint-swinglings, they said questions round; and read chapters, and sang hymns at bridals; auld and young prayed in their dreams, an' prophesied in their sleep, till the deils in the farrest nooks o' hell were alarmed, and moved to commotion. Gin it hadna been an auld carl, Robin Ruthven, Auchtermuchty wad at that time hae been ruined and lost for ever. But Robin was a cunning man, an' had rather mae wits than his ain, for he had been in the hands o' the fairies when he was young, an' a' kinds of spirits were visible to his een, an' their language as familiar to him as his ain mother tongue. Robin was sitting on the side o' the West Lowmond, ae still gloomy night in September, when he saw a bridal o' corbie craws coming east the lift, just on the edge o' the gloaming. The moment that Robin saw them, he kenned, by their movements that they were craws o' some ither warld than this; so he signed himself, and crap into the middle o' his bourock. The corbie craws came a' an' sat down round about him, an' they poukit their black sooty wings, an' spread them out to the breeze to cool; and Robin heard ae corbie speaking, an' another answering him; and the tane said to the tither: "Where will the ravens find a prey the night?"—"On the lean crazy souls o' Auchtermuchty," quo the tither.—"I fear they will be o'er weel wrappit up in the warm flannens o' faith, an' clouted wi' the dirty duds o' repentance[1], for us to mak a meal o'," quo the first.—"Whaten vile sounds are these that I hear coming bumming up the hill?" "O these are the hymns and praises o' the auld wives and creeshy louns o' Auchtermuchty, wha are gaun crooning their way to heaven; an' gin it warna for the shame o' being beat, we might let our great enemy tak them. For sic a prize as he will hae! Heaven, forsooth! What shall we think o' heaven, if it is to be

[1] It is perhaps a little remarkable that "craws o' some ither warld than this" should speak in the style of Davie Tait.

filled wi' vermin like thae, amang whom there is mair poverty and pollution than I can name."[1] "No matter for that," said the first, "we cannot have our power set at defiance; though we should put them in the thief's hole, we must catch them, and catch them with their own bait, too. Come all to church to-morrow and I'll let you hear how I'll gull the saints of Auchtermuchty. In the mean time, there is a feast on the Sidlaw hills to-night, below the hill of Macbeth,—Mount, Diabolus, and fly." Then, with loud croaking and crowing, the bridal of corbies again scaled the dusky air, and left Robin Ruthven in the middle of his cairn.

The next day the congregation met in the kirk of Auchtermuchty, but the minister made not his appearance. The elders ran out and in, making inquiries; but they could learn nothing, save that the minister was missing. They ordered the clerk to sing a part of the 119th Psalm, until they saw if the minister would cast up. The clerk did as he was ordered, and by the time he reached the 77th verse, a strange divine entered the church, by the *western door*, and advanced solemnly up to the pulpit.

Thence he preached a sermon proving all the people of Auchtermuchty to be in the highroad to hell unless they changed their opinions and modes of worship:

The good people of Auchtermuchty were in perfect raptures with the preacher, who had thus sent them to hell by the slump, tag, rag, and bobtail! Nothing in the world delights a truly religious people so much as consigning them to eternal damnation. They wondered after the preacher—they crowded together, and spoke of his sermon with admiration, and still as they conversed, the wonder and the admiration increased; so that honest Robin Ruthven's words would not be listened to. It was in vain that he told them he heard a raven speaking, and another raven answering him: the people laughed him to scorn, and kicked him out of their assemblies, as one who spoke evil of dignities; and they called him a warlock, an' a daft body, to think to mak language out o' the crouping o' craws.

The sublime preacher could not be heard of, although all the

[1] "If these gang to heaven, we'll a' be sae shockit,
Your garret o' blue will but thinly be stockit."
Balmaquhapple.

country was sought for him, even to the minutest corner of St Johnston and Dundee; but as he had announced another sermon on the same text, on a certain day, all the inhabitants of that populous country, far and near, flocked to Auchtermuchty. Cupar, Newburgh, and Strathmiglo, turned out men, women, and children. Perth and Dundee gave their thousands; and from the East Nook of Fife to the foot of the Grampian Hills, there was nothing but running and riding that morning to Auchtermuchty. The kirk would not hold the thousandth part of them. A splendid tent was erected on the brae north of the town, and round that the countless congregation assembled. . . .

The great preacher appeared once more, and went through his two discourses with increased energy and approbation. All who heard him were amazed, and many of them went into fits, writhing and foaming in a state of the most horrid agitation. Robin Ruthven sat on the outskirts of the great assembly, listening with the rest, and perceived what they, in the height of their enthusiasm, perceived not,—the ruinous tendency of the tenets so sublimely inculcated. Robin kenned the voice of his friend the corby-craw again, and was sure he could not be wrang: sae when public worship was finished, a' the elders an' a' the gentry flocked about the great preacher, as he stood on the green brae in the sight of the hale congregation, an' a' were alike anxious to pay him some mark o' respect. Robin Ruthven came in amang the thrang . . . . and, with the greatest readiness and simplicity, just took haud o' the side an' wide gown, an' in the sight of a' present, held it aside as high as the preacher's knee, and behold, there was a pair o' cloven feet! The auld thief was fairly catched in the very height o' his proud conquest, an' put down by an auld carl. He could feign nae mair, but gnashing on Robin wi' his teeth, he darted into the air like a fiery dragon, an' keust a reid rainbow ower the taps o' the Lowmonds.

A' the auld wives an' weavers o' Auchtermuchty fell down flat wi' affright, an' betook them to their prayers aince again, for they saw the dreadfu' danger they had escapit, an' frae that day to this it is a hard matter to gar an Auchtermuchty man listen to a sermon at a', an' a harder ane still to gar him applaud ane, for he thinks aye that he sees the cloven foot peeping out frae aneath ilka sentence.

Hogg would seem to have come to look on this and the other passages as digressions and taken them out accordingly, but though the book as a whole may be better for their absence, he must have regretted them. There is hardly a superfluous paragraph in *The Confessions of a Fanatic*. The *Fanatic* used to be easier to find than the *Justified Sinner*, because of its inclusion by Thomson. In 1895 however the original text was published by Shiels under the title of *The Suicide's Grave*—the title which Hogg gave it when he acknowledged it in 1828—and a new edition has recently been issued under the original title.

The story begins leisurely, but the pace quickens after the appearance of "my illustrious friend." Here is part of Robert Colwan's version of events which are described from another standpoint in the Editor's Narrative:

> My illustrious friend still continuing to sound in my ears the imperious duty to which I was called, of making away with my sinful relations, and quoting many parallel actions out of the Scriptures, and the writings of the holy Fathers, of the pleasure the Lord took in such as executed His vengeance on the wicked, I was obliged to acquiesce in his measures, though with certain limitations. . . .
>
> My heart now panted with eagerness to look my brother in the face: on which my companion, who was never out of the way, conducted me to a small square in the suburbs of the city, where there were a number of young noblemen and gentlemen playing at a vain, idle, and sinful game, at which there was much of the language of the accursed going on; and among these blasphemers he instantly pointed out my brother to me. I was fired with indignation at seeing him in such company, and so employed; and I placed myself close beside him to watch all his motions, listen to his words, and draw inferences from what I saw and heard. In what a sink of sin was he wallowing! I resolved to take him to task, and if he refused to be admonished, to inflict on him some condign punishment; and knowing that my illustrious friend and director was looking on, I resolved to show some spirit. Accordingly, I waited until I heard him profane his Maker's name three times, and then, my spiritual indignation being roused above all restraint, I went up and kicked him. Yes, I went boldly up and struck him with my foot, and meant to

have given him a more severe blow than it was my fortune to inflict. It had, however, the effect of rousing up his corrupt nature to quarrelling and strife, instead of taking the chastisement of the Lord in humility and meekness. He ran furiously against me in the choler that is always inspired by the wicked one; but I overthrew him, by reason of impeding the natural and rapid progress of his unholy feet, running to destruction. I also fell slightly; but his fall proving a severe one, he arose in wrath, and struck me with the mall which he held in his hand, until my blood flowed copiously; and from that moment I vowed his destruction in my heart. But I chanced to have no weapon at that time, nor any means of inflicting due punishment on the caitiff, which would not have been returned double on my head, by him and his graceless associates. I mixed among them at the suggestion of my friend, and following them to their den of voluptuousness and sin, I strove to be admitted among them, in hopes of finding some means of accomplishing my great purpose, while I found myself moved by the spirit within me so to do. But I was not only debarred, but, by the machinations of my wicked brother and his associates, cast into prison....

My reverend father took this matter greatly to heart, and bestirred himself in the good cause till the transgressors were ashamed to show their faces. My illustrious companion was not idle: I wondered that he came not to me in prison, nor at my release; but he was better employed, in stirring up the just to the execution of God's decrees: and he succeeded so well, that my brother and all his associates had nearly fallen victims to their wrath: but many were wounded, bruised, and imprisoned, and much commotion prevailed in the city. For my part, I was greatly strengthened in my resolution by the anathemas of my reverend father, who, privately (that is, in the family capacity), in his prayers, gave up my father and brother, according to the flesh, to Satan, making it plain to all my senses of perception, that they were beings given up of God, to be devoured by fiends or men, at their will and pleasure, and that *whosoever* should slay them, would do God good service....

Immediately after this I was seized with a strange distemper, which neither my friends nor physicians could comprehend, and it confined me to my chamber for many days; but I knew myself that I was bewitched, and suspected my father's reputed concubine of the deed. I told my fears to my reverend protector, who hesitated concerning them, but I knew by his words and looks that he was conscious I was right. I generally conceived myself to be two people. When I lay in bed, I deemed there were two of us in it; when I sat up, I always beheld another person, and always in the same position from the place where I sat or stood, which was about three paces off me towards my left side. . . . The most perverse part of it was, that I rarely conceived *myself* to be any of the two persons. I thought for the most part that my companion was one of them, and my brother the other; and I found, that to be obliged to speak and answer in the character of another man, was a most awkward business at the long run.

Who can doubt, from this statement, that I was bewitched, and that my relatives were at the ground of it . . . .?

I say I was confined a month. I beg he that readeth to take note of this, that he may estimate how much the word, or even the oath, of a wicked man is to depend on. For a month I saw no one but such as came into my room, and for all that, it will be seen, that there were plenty of the same set to attest upon oath that I saw my brother every day during that period; that I persecuted him with my presence day and night; while all the time I never saw his face, save in a delusive dream. I cannot comprehend what manoeuvres my illustrious friend was playing off with them about this time; for he, having the art of personating whom he chose, had peradventure deceived them, else so many of them had never all attested the same thing. I never saw any man so steady in his friendships and attentions as he; but as he made a rule of never calling at private houses, for fear of some discovery being made of his person, so I never saw him while my malady lasted; but as soon as I grew better, I knew I had nothing ado but to attend at some of our places of meeting, to see him again.

So the story goes on, with the more and more embarrassing and horrible attentions of "my illustrious friend," until at last Robert Colwan hangs himself in a hay-rope made of green risp:

This was accounted a great wonder, and every one said, if the devil had not assisted him it was impossible the thing could have been done; for in general, these ropes are so brittle, being made of green hay, that they will scarcely bear to be bound over the rick. And the more to horrify the good people of this neighbourhood, the driver said, when he first came in view, *he could almost give his oath* that he saw two people busily engaged at the hay-rick, going round it and round it, and he thought they were dressing it[1].

The *Justified Sinner* is the best of all Hogg's stories, but to judge by the number of its editions *The Long Pack* is the most popular; a good murder story, but no better than others and probably only liked for local reasons; Mrs Gaskell has a garbled version of it, without any reference to Hogg, in *Cranford*. It was first published separately and reprinted in the *Winter Evening Tales*, which also contains several other stories of murders, ghosts and the like, most of the *Spy* stories, and three stories in verse. Of the longer tales *The Renowned Adventures of Basil Lee* is easily the worst: it was intended, as its first title in *The Spy* implies, to show the evil results of instability in one's calling, but no casual reader would guess that or anything else to be the moral. *The Love Adventures of Mr George Cochrane* is, on Hogg's own admission, partly autobiographical, but it is to be hoped that the Shepherd did not cut such a poor figure in love as his hero. The *Country Dreams and Apparitions* are, as might be expected, better reading; the first, *John Gray o' Middleholm*, which was never reprinted, is a story of buried treasure, in which Hogg uses what seems to be a variant of the old tale of the gossiping wife who spread the report that crows had flown out of her husband's mouth.

In the *Winter Evening Tales* two articles, *Storms* and *A Country Wedding*, are put together under the heading of *The Shepherd's Calendar*, but they are not included by Thomson in the later *Shepherd's Calendar*, though he has them both in his edition. Only five or six stories in the so-called *Shepherd's Calendar* have anything to do with shepherds or sheep; the rest are

[1] In all these extracts there is a good deal of grammar which is not Lockhart's. The fluctuation between homely Scots and stilted English again is characteristic of Hogg.

traditional stories and tales of Hogg's own invention, published in *Blackwood's*, sometimes with the general heading and sometimes without it[1], between 1818 and 1829 and collected into a volume in 1829. Hogg seems to have had some idea of classifying them, but he did not carry out his intention with any regularity. Thus Chapters I and II—I give for convenience Thomson's numbers, which do not agree exactly even with the rearranged *Shepherd's Calendar* of 1829—are in *Blackwood's* headed "Class Second. Deaths, Judgments, and Providences." Chapter XII, which follows them, is "Class Five, The Lasses." Chapters IV and V are "Dreams and Apparitions"; Chapter IX "Dreams and Apparitions. Part II"; Chapter XI "Dreams and Apparitions"; Chapter VII "Dreams and Apparitions. Part IV"; Chapter X, following, leaps suddenly to "Class IX. Fairies, Brownies, and Witches"; and Chapter XVI, with a slight variation, is "Class IX. Fairies, Deils, and Witches."

The manner of their classification after all matters very little. There is a good deal of fine confused feeding in them, especially in the tales of the supernatural and those chapters, hardly tales, which deal with the shepherd's life and odd country characters. Hogg's own relations and neighbours were of rich and surprising originality, and it is to be wished that he had preserved more stories of them at the expense of his excursions into historical romance. Besides those with a remarkable gift for prayer, there were people like Will o' Phaup, Hogg's maternal grandfather:

He was the last man of this wild region, who heard, saw, and conversed with the fairies; and that not once or twice, but at

[1] Without it are *Further Anecdotes of the Shepherd's Dog*, *The Marvellous Doctor*, *A Strange Secret* (= only the first half of Chapter XIII in Thomson), and *The Brownie of the Black Haggs*.

sundry times and seasons. . . . Will was coming from the hill one dark misty evening in winter, and, for a good while, imagined he heard a great gabbling of children's voices, not far from him, which still grew more and more audible; it being before sunset, he had no spark of fear, but set about investigating whence the sounds and laughter proceeded. He at length discovered that they issued from a deep cleuch not far distant, and thinking it was a band of gipsies, or some marauders, he laid down his bonnet and plaid, and creeping softly over the heath, reached the brink of the precipice, peeped over, and to his utter astonishment, beheld the fairies sitting in seven circles, on a green spot in the bottom of the dell, where no green spot ever was before. They were apparently eating and drinking; but all their motions were so quick and momentary, he could not well see what they were doing. Two or three at the queen's back appeared to be baking bread. The party consisted wholly of ladies, and their number was quite countless—dressed in green pollonians, and grass-green bonnets on their heads. He perceived at once, by their looks, their giggling, and their peals of laughter, that he was discovered. Still fear took no hold of his heart, for it was daylight, and the blessed sun was in heaven, although obscured by clouds; till at length he heard them pronounce his own name twice; Will then began to think it might not be quite so safe to wait till they pronounced it a third time, and at that moment of hesitation it first came into his mind that it was All Hallow Eve! There was no further occasion to warn Will to rise and run; for he well knew the fairies were privileged, on that day and night, to do what seemed good in their own eyes. "His hair," he said, "stood all up like the birses on a sow's back, and every bit o' his body, outside and in, prinkled as it had been brunt wi' nettles." He ran home as fast as his feet could carry him, and greatly were his children astonished (for he was then a widower) to see their father come running like a madman, without either his bonnet or plaid. He assembled them to prayers, and shut the door, but did not tell them what he had seen for several years.

It was Will too who followed a party of fairies, supposing them to be some of his neighbours, "up a wild glen called Enterlony," until "a voice out of the crowd called to him in a shrill laughing tone, 'Ha, ha, ha! Will o' Phaup, look to your ain hearthstane the night.'"

When Will had become a right old man, and was sitting on a little green hillock at the end of his house one evening, resting himself, there came three little boys up to him, all exactly like one another, when the following short dialogue ensued between Will and them:—

"Goode'en t'ye, Will Laidlaw."

"Goode'en t'ye, creatures. Whare ir ye gaun this gate?"

"Can ye gie us up-putting for the night?"

"I think three siccan bits o' shreds o' hurchins winna be ill to put up. Where came ye frae?"

"Frae a place that ye dinna ken. But we are come on a commission to you."

"Come away in, then, and tak sic cheer as we hae."

Will rose and led the way into the house, and the little boys followed; and as he went, he said carelessly, without looking back, "What's your commission to me, bairns?" He thought they might be the sons of some gentleman, who was a guest of his master's.

"We are sent to demand a silver key that you have in your possession."

Will was astounded; and standing still to consider of some old transaction, he said, without lifting his eyes from the ground—"A silver key? In God's name, where came ye frae?"

There was no answer, on which Will wheeled round, and round, and round; but the tiny beings were all gone, and Will never saw them more. At the name of God, they vanished in the twinkling of an eye.

Will had once a Rip van Winkle vision, but without any unhappy consequences to himself. The Shepherd expresses no opinion as to the kind of creature seen then, but in *The Woolgatherer* the herd-boy Barnaby has an explanation of the various kinds of beings which may be met. *The Woolgatherer* is a good story; it appeared first, in a shorter form, as *The Country Laird* in *The Spy*, and the longer form is made long by the change in the character of Barnaby, who becomes much more voluble than he originally was and tells some of Hogg's best traditional stories.

The deil an' his agents, they fash nane but the gude fock, the Cameronians, an' the prayin' ministers, an' sic like. Then the bogles, they are a better kind o' spirits; they meddle wi' nane but the guilty, the murderer, an' the mansworn, an' the cheater o' the widow an' fatherless; they do for *them*. Then the fairies, they're very harmless, they're keener o' fun an' frolic than aught else; but if fock neglect kirk ordinances, they see after *them*. Then the brownie, he's a kind o' half-spirit half-man; he'll drudge an' do a' the wark about the town for his meat, but then he'll no work but when he likes for a' the king's dominions. That's precisely what we a' believe here awa', auld an' young.

The best and most horrible of the lad's stories is that of the wicked laird, of which Scott gives part in his note to *Lady Anne* in the *Border Minstrelsy*

It was the Laird o' Ettrickhaw; he that biggit his house amang the widow's corn, and never had a day to do weel in it. It isna yet a full age sin' the foundation-stane was laid, an' for a' the grandeur that was about it, there's nae man at this day can tell where the foundation has been, if he didna ken before.

With the help of "hurkle-backit Charley Johnston" the laird used to dispose of his illegitimate children and their mothers. Then he was haunted and took to drinking:

He durst never mair sleep by himsel while he lived: but that wasna lang, for he took to drinking, and drank, and swore, and blasphemed, and said dreadfu' things that folk didna understand. At length, he drank sae muckle ae night out o' desperation, that the blue lowe came burning out at his mouth, and he died on his ain hearth-stane, at a time o' life when he should scarcely have been at his prime.

But it wasna sae wi' Charley! He wore out a lang and hardened life; and at the last, when death came, he coudna die. For a day and two nights they watched him, thinking every moment would be the last, but always a few minutes after the breath had left his lips, the feeble cries of infants arose from behind the bed, and wakened him up again. The family were horrified; but his sons and daughters were men and women, and for their ain sakes they durstna let ane come to hear his confessions. At last, on the third day at two in the morning, he died clean away. They watched an hour in great dread, and then streekit him, and put the dead-claes on him, but they hadna weel done before there were cries, as if a woman had been drowning, came from behind the bed, and the voice cried, "O, Charley, spare my life! Spare my life! For your own soul's sake and mine, spare my life!" On which the corpse again sat up in the bed, pawled wi' its hands, and stared round wi' its dead face. The family could stand it nae langer, but fled the house, and rade and ran for ministers, but before any of them got there, Charley was gane. They sought a' the house and in behind the bed, and could find naething; but that same day he was found about a mile frae his ain house, up in the howe o' the Baileylee-linn, a' torn limb frae limb, an' the dead-claes beside him. There war twa corbies seen flying o'er the muir that day, carrying something atween them, an' fock suspectit it was Charley's soul, for it was heard makin' a loud maen as they flew o'er Alemoor. At the same time it was reportit, that there was to be seen every morning at two o'clock, a naked woman torfelling on the Alemoor loch, wi' her hands tied behind her back, and a heavy stane at her neck.

The last sentence is an example of Hogg's inclination to go on too long and supply unnecessary details, but for all that the story is very good. Nearly all his later stories are of dreams and apparitions, and the reading of many of them awakens a certain unwillingness to look at the door.

How much of this effect is due to the stories themselves and how much to the telling of them it is difficult to say. At his best Hogg has a command of language which contrasts strongly with the thinness of many uneducated writers who, using an unfamiliar dialect, are afraid of misusing it. Hogg never suffered from that fear, and when he makes mistakes his blunders have an attractive heartiness and completeness. In the narrative parts of his prose stories, except when he is telling them dramatically, he seems at the first glance to use English, with a marked love of "langnebbit" words. Hence the "unguent hard to be swallowed" of *The Confessions of a Justified Sinner*; and hence too this in *Disagreeables*:

> I wish all blustering chaps were dead,
> That's the true bathos to have done with them.

He did not know the meaning of unguent or bathos, but they were good words. This affection for good words, regardless of their accepted meaning, had sometimes disastrous consequences.. It is possible to see what he was trying to say in these lines from *Queen Hynde*, but the words do not mean what Hogg intended them to mean, and he can hardly be allowed the privilege of Humpty Dumpty:

> Ah, how unlike art thou to those
> (Warm friends profess'd, yet covert foes)
> Who witness'd, grinning with despite,
> A peasant's soul assume its right;
> Rise from the dust, and mounting o'er
> Their classic toils and boasted lore,
> Take its aerial seat on high
> Above their buckram fulgency.
> In vain each venom'd shaft they tried,
> The impartial world was on his side;
> Their sport was marr'd—lost was the game—
> The halloo hush'd and eke the name!
> Then lower stoop'd they for a fee
> To poor and personal mockery;
> The gait, the garb, the rustic speech,
> All that could homely worth appeach,
> Unweariedly, time after time,
> In loathed and everlasting chime
> They vended forth. Who would believe
> There were such men? and who not grieve
> That they should stoop, by ruthless game,
> To stamp their own eternal shame?
> While he, the butt of all their mocks,
> Sits throned amid his native rocks
> Above their reach, and grieves alone
> For their unmanly malison.

One feels that this was perhaps not the best way in which to retort upon the Shepherd's critics.

But even when apparently writing English, Hogg heard Scots in his mind. His rhymes in his later poems, where he is usually fairly accurate, often will not fit in English, but will in Scots. Here is an example from *Elen of Reigh:*

> What am I raving of just now?
> Forsooth I scarce can say to you—
> A moonlight river beaming by,
> Or holy depth of virgin's eye!
> Unconscious bard! what perilous dreaming!
> Is nought on earth to thee beseeming?
> Will nothing serve but beauteous women?—
> No, nothing else. But 'tis strange to me,
> If you never heard aught of Elen of Reigh.

Here and there he attempts to reproduce the Highland or the north of England speech, with only fair success. But when he takes to his Scots without disguise, he shows a humorous appreciation and right use of words, which may be illustrated by a passage in *The Brownie of Bodsbeck.* John Hoy the Shepherd is being examined by Claverhouse about the soldiers who have been found murdered in the linn:

"How did it appear to you that they had been slain? Were they cut with swords, or pierced with bullets?"

"I canna say, but they war sair hashed."

"How do you mean when you say they were hashed?"

"Champit like; a' broozled and jurmummled, as it were."

"Do you mean that they were cut, or cloven, or minced?"

"Na, na,—no that ava. But they had gotten some sair doofs. They had been terribly paikit and daddit wi' something."

"I do not in the least conceive what you mean."

"That's extr'ord'nar, man—can ye no understand folk's mother-tongue? I'll mak it plain to ye. Ye see, whan a thing comes on ye that gate, that's a dadd—sit still now. Then a paik, that's a swap or a skelp like—when a thing comes on ye that way, that's a paik. But a doof's warst ava—it's—"

"Prithee hold; I now understand it all perfectly well."

There are few very unusual words and forms in the Scots of Hogg; the most unusual are *oord*—became—and its past participle *wort*:

> I was just standin' looking about me amang the lang hags that lead out frae the head o' the North Grain, and considering what could be wort of a' the sheep. (*Brownie of Bodsbeck*, Ch. III.)
>
> "Ye'll mind your eldest brother weel eneugh. Did ye ever ken what oord o' him?"
>
> "No; I am sorry to say I never did."
>
> "And do you mind your sister-in-law, Miss Fanny, the bonniest o' them a'? Oogh? Or did ye ever ken what came o' her?" (*Baron St Gio.*)

But as a rule he is not hard reading even for a Southron, who guesses at most of the expressive words and is lazily content to let the rest go, just as he does in reading Scott. And at his very best, in *The Confessions of a Justified Sinner* or in such passages of *The Brownie of Bodsbeck* as John Hoy's account of the apparition on the night of the soldiers' murder, Hogg can without apprehension challenge comparison with Scott. He has not Scott's range and variety or anything like his knowledge of humanity, but he shares with Scott the faculty of rising to strange heights in dealing with the supernatural.

8. *LATER POEMS AND SONGS*

NEARLY all Hogg's verses from about 1820 onwards appeared first in *Blackwood's* or *Fraser's*. They are represented fairly well by the *Songs* of 1831 and by the collection which he published in 1832—*A Queer Book*, which is a medley of ballads, serious and half-serious, descriptive and sentimental poems, and two or three political allegories; but there are still many which he never reprinted. *Fraser's* was neglected in the *Poems* of 1838 and consequently by Thomson, who however includes most of the *Blackwood* poems.

Most of the later ballads are very long, and some of them are marred by Hogg's attempts at archaic spelling. Those which were never reprinted after the *Queer Book*, and those which are still in the files of *Fraser's* or *Blackwood's*, are distinguished by their extra length and wildness, and in all there is nothing which Hogg had not done before, either in *The Mountain Bard* or in *The Queen's Wake*. *The Laird of Lun*, *Crawford John* and some others are perhaps partly traditional. *The Wife of Ezdel-More* takes up the idea, already used in one of Hogg's stories—*The Hunt of Eildon*—of lovers turned into birds, and does not improve it. *The Witch of the Grey Thorn* has a good gruesome plot, but it rivals *Young Kennedy* in language:

> The Monarch was roused, and pronounced in his wrath
> A sentence unseemly, the Archbishop's death.

Why unseemly is hard to say, for the Archbishop had been plotting the Monarch's death. There are several ballads or other narratives of the faery world and a land of innocence, but none of the careful descriptions has the charm of *Kilmeny*, and some fall into bathos. And there are several flights through the air and expeditions to hell or heaven, but none has the careless joy of *The Witch of Fife*.

The graver poems, however, include some of the best things which Hogg ever wrote. His verses *On the Lifting of the Banner of Buccleuch* are finer than Scott's on the same subject, the *Lines to Sir Walter Scott* are charming in their ease, and the *Verses to Lady Anne Scott*, of which he was so proud that he reprinted them more than once or twice, are deserving of his pride. Even better is *St Mary of the Lowes*:

O lone St Mary of the waves,
  In ruin lies thine ancient aisle,
While o'er thy green and lowly graves
  The moorcocks bay, and plovers wail:
  But mountain spirits on the gale
Oft o'er thee sound the requiem dread;
  And warrior shades, and spectres pale,
Still linger by the quiet dead.

Yes, many a chief of ancient days
  Sleeps in thy cold and hallowed soil:
Hearts that would thread the forest maze,
  Alike for spousal or for spoil;
  That wist not, ween'd not, to recoil
Before the might of mortal foe,
  But thirsted for the Border broil,
The shout, the clang, the over-throw.

Here lie those who, o'er flood and field,
  Were hunted as the osprey's brood;
Who braved the power of man, and seal'd
  Their testimonies with their blood:
  But long as waves that wilder'd flood,
Their sacred memory shall be dear,
  And all the virtuous and the good
O'er their low graves shall drop the tear.

. . . .

Here lie old Border bowmen good;
  Ranger and stalker sleep together,
Who for the red-deer's stately brood
  Watch'd, in despite of wind and weather,
  Beneath the hoary hills of heather;
Even Scotts and Kerrs, and Pringles, blended
  In peaceful slumbers, rest together,
Whose fathers there to death contended.

Here lie the peaceful, simple race,
  The first old tenants of the wild,
Who stored the mountains of the chase
  With flocks and herds—whose manners mild
  Changed the baronial castles, piled
In every glen, into the cot,
  And the rude mountaineer beguiled,
Indignant, to his peaceful lot.

. . . .

There is a more homely pathos in *The Monitors*:

The lift looks cauldrife i' the west,
  The wan leaf wavers fra the tree,
The wind touts on the mountain's breast
  A dirge o' waesome note to me.
  It tells me that the days o' glee,
When summer's thrilling sweets entwined,
  An' love was blinkin' in the e'e,
Are a' gane by an' far behind;

That winter wi' his joyless air,
  An' grizzly hue, is hasting nigh,
An' that auld age, an' carkin' care,
  In my last stage afore me lie.
  Yon chill and cheerless winter sky,
Troth, but 'tis eerisome to see,
  For ah! it points me to descry
The downfa's o' futurity[1].

---

[1] Compare "the lang Hopes an' the Downfa's o' Eternity" in Davie Tait's prayer in *The Brownie of Bodsbeck*, v. pp. 114–6. Hogg has not improved the expression in his verse.

I daurna look into the east,
  For there my morning shone sae sweet;
An' when I turn me to the west,
  The gloaming's like to gar me greet.
  The deadly hues o' snaw and sleet
Tell of a dreary onward path;
  Yon new moon on her cradle sheet
Looks like the Hainault scythe of death.

. . . .

"But, bard—ye dinna mind your life
  Is waning down to winter snell—
That round your hearth young sprouts are rife,
  An' mae to care for than yoursell."
  Yes, that I do—that hearth could tell
How aft the tear-drap blinds my e'e;
  What can I do, by spur or spell,
An' by my faith it done shall be.

And think—through poortith's eiry breach
  Should want approach wi' threatening brand,
I'll leave them canty sangs will reach
  From John o' Groats to Solway strand.
  Then what are houses, goud, or land,
To sic an heirship left in fee?
  An' I think mair o' auld Scotland,
Than to be fear'd for mine or me.

. . . .

There are faults of expression here and there, but more noticeable is a dignity not very common in the Shepherd's writings.

The political poems are an odd and with few exceptions uninteresting collection, ranging from loyal songs on the King's birthday to "screeds on politics" and complicated allegories like the prophetical part of *Kilmeny* but weaker. Hogg was a good Tory by instinct, not, one suspects, very much by reason. One of the last of the allegories, *An Auld Wife's Dream*, which appeared in *Fraser's* in 1833, is also one of the best, at least in its lively opening:

> November wind had toutit loud,
>   An' tirled the wan leaves frae the trees;
> The cauld hues o' the winter cloud
>   Were ghaistly fearsome-like to see:
>   Where auld John Graeme, o' Goudie-lee,
> Gat up ae morn frae 'mang the claes,
>   An' buff'd the blankets wi' his knee,
> To fley away the greedy flaes.

It was actually written in November of the preceding year, and Hogg's note, warning people to be ready for the worst, shows well enough the fears which filled some minds after the passing of the Reform Bill. His apprehensions may seem a little excessive, but they were sincere; he even asserted in conversation and again in the *Domestic Manners* that the Whig ascendancy in the Cabinet killed Sir Walter. A few of the political verses are spirited, but most of them, especially the allegories and dreams in which Hogg delighted, need and do not deserve a good deal of annotation to make them intelligible.

It is interesting to notice how varied Hogg's metres are even in his earliest verses. He played with blank verse and heroic couplets, these being the instruments of a correct poet, but ballad-measures, even if slightly prosaic in his first ballads, came to him almost naturally, and he used the regular octosyllabic couplet, in *Geordie Fa's Dirge* and elsewhere, with an ease which points to some previous practice. Ballad measures and the short couplet remained his favourite verses for narrative, but he experimented in other forms, and *The Pilgrims of the Sun* is a sort of sampler intended to display his skill in various kinds of verse. It begins in the fashion of his ballads:

Of all the lasses in fair Scotland,
  That lightly bound o'er muir and lee,
There's nane like the maids of Yarrowdale,
  Wi' their green coats kilted to the knee.

The second part is in blank verse, which Hogg considered more suitable for sacred matters; he seems to imply that it was the measure of Hebrew poetry, but he may be only thinking confusedly of *Paradise Lost*:

Harp of Jerusalem!—how shall my hand
Awake thy hallelujahs?—How begin
The song that tells of light ineffable,
And of the dwellers there; the fountain pure
And source of all, where bright archangels dwell,
And where, in unapproached pavilion, framed
Of twelve deep veils, and every veil composed
Of thousand thousand lustres, sits enthroned
The God of Nature?—O thou harp of Salem,
Where shall my strain begin?

The third part is in the heroic couplet:

Imperial England, of the ocean born,
Who from the isles beyond the dawn of morn,
To where waste oceans wash Peruvia's shore,
Hast from all nations drawn thy boasted lore!
Helm of the world, whom seas and isles obey,
Though high thy honours, and though far thy sway,
Thy harp I crave, unfearful of thy frown;
Well may'st thou lend what erst was not thine own.

That is, the heroic couplet is not a Scots but originally a foreign and then an English metre, and when we return to Scotland we must use something else:

Here I must seize my ancient harp again,
And chaunt a simple tale, a most uncourtly strain.

He does it in the fourth part by using first a couplet of four trisyllabic feet, and then the free short couplet of mixed dissyllabic and trisyllabic feet; it is the verse of *Kilmeny*, but not so well managed as in *Kilmeny*:

> The night-wind is still, and the moon in the wane,
> The river-lark sings on the verge of the plain;
> So lonely his plaint by the motionless reed
> It sounds like an omen or tale of the dead.
>
> . . . .
>
> Her lady mother, distracted, and wild
> For the loss of her loved, her only child,
> With all her maidens tracked the dew—
> Well Mary's secret bower she knew.
> Oft had she traced, with fond regard,
> Her darling to that grove, and heard
> Her orisons the green bough under,
> And turned aside with fear and wonder.

Speaking generally, Hogg could manage a regular trisyllabic metre better in a song than in a narrative poem, probably because in a song he had usually some tune in his head to support him. *Balmaquhapple* sings itself without notes; *The Witch of the Grey Thorn* may be in the metre of *Bonny Dundee*, but it will not go to that or any other tune.

For long sustained narrative Hogg mostly used the regular octosyllabic couplet, employing the Scott variant with shorter recurring lines of three feet only once, in the first twenty lines of *Queen Hynde*. He may have been afraid of seeming to imitate Scott, and some of these lines are certainly very like Scott:

> Nations arose and nations fell,
> But still his sacred citadel
> Of Grampian cliff and trackless dell
>   The Caledonian held:
> Grim as the wolf that guards his young,
> Above the dark defile he hung,
> With targe and claymore forward flung;
> The stoutest heart, the proudest tongue,
>   Of foeman there was quell'd.

The plumed chief, the plaided clan,
Mock'd at the might of mortal man;
Even those the world who overran
  Were from that bourn expell'd.

In songs Hogg was sometimes bound by the tune, but when he made his songs first and tunes afterwards he preferred simple stanzas of four or eight lines, sometimes with a refrain. He avoided, almost as if deliberately, the peculiarly "Scottish" forms: the Hallowe'en stanza he used only once, in *The Mistakes of a Night*, and Burns's other favourite stanza also only once, in the *Verses for the Eye of Mr David Tweedie of that Ilk:*

Ye auld catwuddied, canker'd carle,
What set you on to growl an' snarl,
An' try to raise your puny quarrel
  Wi' folks afore ye,
Wha wadna gie an auld tar barrel
  For half-a-score o' ye?[1]

The Battle of Busaco is written on the pattern of *Hohenlinden*, perhaps "as a per contra"[2] to that poem, but Hogg may merely have been trying the stanza to see how he liked it; *The Dawn of July 1810* is in the same stanza, and both poems appeared first in *The Spy* with only a few weeks between them. The *Skylark* stanza appears two or three times, but is nowhere successful except in *The Skylark.* It does not really fit a serious poem, *To the Genius of Shakespeare*, the point of which is that so many great minds have appeared

[1] Never reprinted; they appeared in *The Edinburgh Literary Journal*, vol. III, pp. 276–7. Mr David Tweedie had sent, through Hogg, a review of poets to the *Journal*, concerning which Hogg remarked in a letter to Blackwood, "Tweedie has not been half so severe upon (D. M. Moir) as me." (Mrs Oliphant, I, p. 356.) But it is possible that Mr David Tweedie was one of Hogg's disguises.

[2] *Vide* pp. 151–4.

in Scotland of late that there is the only possible place for another Shakespeare to be born:

Then here, by the sounding sea,
Forest, and greenwood tree,
Here to solicit thee cease shall we never:
Yes, thou effulgence bright,
Here must thy flame relight,
Or vanish from Nature for ever and ever!

But in some of his best poems there is a stanza exactly suited for grave reflection, rhyming *ababbcbc* in lines of four feet. Once or twice he tried variants of it; in *The Lady's Dream* with the fourth and eighth lines usually of three feet, and in *On Carmel's Brow* with all the even lines of three feet; but he was happiest when he kept to the form with four feet in each line. It was early a familiar measure in Scots and in English; it occurs in several stanzas of some versions of *Take thy old cloak about thee*:

King Stephen was a worthy peer;
His breeches cost him but a crown;
He held them sixpence all too dear,
Therefore he called the tailor loun.
He was a king and wore the crown,
And thou's but of a low degree;
It's pride that puts this country down:
Man, take thy old cloak about thee!

Hogg may have got it from that, or from Burns, or from poems which he read in Ramsay's *Evergreen* or *The Minstrelsy of the Scottish Border*. The old song on the Battle of Harlaw has it:

Frae Dunideir as I cam throuch,
Doun by the Hill of Banochie,
Allangst the Lands of Garioch,
Grit Pitie was to heir and se
The Noys and dulesum Hermonie
That evir that dreiry Day did daw,
Cryand the Corynoch on hie,
Alas! alas! for the Harlaw.

So have *The Raid of the Reidswire* and a good proportion of the poems in the *Evergreen*. In England the stanza was used in Hogg's own time by Crabbe in those strange kindred poems, *Sir Eustace Grey* and *The World of Dreams:*

They placed me where those streamers play,
  Those nimble beams of brilliant light;
It would the stoutest heart dismay
  To see, to feel, that dreadful sight:
  So swift, so pure, so cold, so bright,
They pierced my frame with icy wound;
  And all that half-year's polar night,
Those dancing streamers wrapp'd me round.

But the stanza was old in England too; Lawrence Minot used it in *The Taking of Calais* and the main part of the song on King Edward's landing and march through France, and so did the author of *The Plowman's Tale*. In this last poem the *c* rhyme is ingeniously carried on from stanza to stanza until rhymes fail; and some of the Scots poets treated the last line of the stanza as a refrain or half-refrain, with something of the same result, Burns, for example, in *Mary Morison*. Hogg does not seem to have been attracted by such subtleties, but used the simple form with dignity in *St Mary of the Lowes* and *The Monitors*, as the quotations from these will have shown, and in some of his songs.

Whether justly or unjustly it is hard to say, but it is the songs of the Shepherd which have done most to keep his name alive. Some were made to old tunes, some had tunes composed for them by himself, some were written and left to take their chance of finding a tune, but there are few which do not demand to be sung. He published them in his own volumes of poetry, in magazines, and in various "Garlands" with music by himself and others, and in 1831 he collected them nearly all into one volume with notes on the tunes and any stories of the publication or composition of the verses which he thought likely to interest the public.

Some of Hogg's self-criticisms are worth noticing, and there is a good deal of himself in his other remarks. Thus *A Witch's Chant*

> is a most unearthly song, copied from an unearthly tragedy of my own (i.e. *All-Hallow Eve*)....The poetry of the play has astounded me. The following is but a flea-bite to some of it.

The Flowers of Scotland

> was written to the popular air of "The Blue Bells of Scotland," at the request of a most beautiful young lady, who sung it particularly well. But several years afterwards I heard her still singing the old ridiculous words, which really like the song of the whilly-whaup, "is ane shame till heirre." I never thought her so bonny afterwards; but neither she was.

Of *I'll no wake wi' Annie*:

> I composed this pastoral ballad, as well as the air to which it is sung, whilst sailing one lovely day on St Mary's Loch; a pastime in which, above all others, I delighted, and of which I am now most shamefully deprived. Lord Napier never did so cruel a thing, not even on the high seas, as the interdicting of me from sailing on that beloved lake, which if I have not rendered classical, has not been my blame. But the credit will be his own, —that is some comfort.

A rather different complexion is put on the interdiction by Dr Russell in his *Reminiscences of Yarrow* (p. 87); Hogg had erected a boathouse without leave and then requested that Lord Napier should "debar all others, and grant the proprietorship solely to him." The boathouse was removed, the request refused, and Hogg took his revenge. The affair does not show him in a very favourable light, but there is another story to be made out which illustrates Lockhart's remark on another occasion[1]: "To say nothing about modesty, his notions of literary honesty were always exceedingly loose; but at the same time, we must take into account his peculiar notions, or rather no notions, as to the proper limits of a joke."

Whether Hogg's curious honesty or his equally curious notion of a joke was responsible here it is difficult to say, but what he did was to take some of the best known of the *Irish Melodies* and turn them to his own use. The results of his handling can hardly be called parodies—most of them are too serious for that—and they are not exactly imitations. He called his *Minstrel Boy* a "per contra" to Moore's—an odd phrase which yet in a measure describes these songs. Hogg's Minstrel Boy goes to the glen; the wave is made for the slave instead of the sea's being made for the free; the maiden who is entreated to rove through Morna's grove rejects the prayer with rudeness; the hour when daylight springs is as dear to Hogg as the hour when daylight dies to Moore; and so on. The Shepherd does not seem to have been conscious at first that he had done anything unusual in this adaptation without acknowledgment of another man's poems, but Moore's publishers protested and the sheets containing the verses were cancelled when Hogg tried, about 1822, to publish them. Longmans were at that time the London publishers of both poets, and there seems to have been a private arrangement to suppress the verses. Either Moore never knew that anything of the sort had ever happened or he knew and bore no malice. There is none, at least, in the references to Hogg in his *Diary*. Blackwood and

[1] *Life of Scott*, II, 172. He is referring to Hogg's suggestion that Scott should copy out Hogg's autobiography, "putting he for I" (v. p. 52).

Cadell published the 1831 Songs, and this may explain how it was that Hogg was able to print the verses there. It is instructive to trace his emotions through his notes in this volume of 1831: first blustering defiance, then unquiet, and a kind of ungracious apology which is unpleasantly like the references to Lockhart in *The Domestic Manners of Sir Walter Scott.*

The series begins with *The Minstrel Boy*, which

> was written as a *per contra* to Mr Moore's song to the same air. But either he or his publishers, or both, set up their birses, and caused it and a great many more to be cancelled,—the most ridiculous of all things, in my opinion, I ever knew. It was manifestly because they saw mine were the best. Let them take that! as Gideon Laidlaw said when the man died who had cheated him.

The Maid of the Sea

> is one of the many songs which Moore caused me to cancel, for nothing that I know of, but because they ran counter to his. It is quite natural and reasonable that an author should claim a copyright of a sentiment; but it never struck me that it could be so exclusively his, as that another had not a right to contradict it. This, however, seems to be the case in the London law; for true it is that my songs were cancelled, and the public may now judge on what grounds, by comparing them with Mr Moore's. I have neither forgot nor forgiven it; and I have a great mind to force him to cancel Lalla Rookh for stealing it wholly from the Queen's Wake, which is so apparent in the plan, that every London judge will give it in my favour, although he ventured only on the character of one accomplished bard, and I on seventeen. He had better have let my few trivial songs alone.

Go Home to your Rest is

> another of the proscribed M'Gregors; but here he is again, and sung to the well-known old air of "The Dandy O."

The next which Hogg gives, though he shows some hesitation, is *There's Gowd in the Breast*, which was not "proscribed"; it shares only the tune with *Let Erin Remember.*

O'er the Ocean Bounding

is another of the proscription list; but here, let them turn the blue bonnet wha can. Our forefathers had *cried down* songs, which all men and women were strictly prohibited from singing, such as "O'er Boggie," and "The wee Cock Chicken," etc., because Auld Nick was a proficient at playing them on the pipes. The London people have done the same with a number of mine; but I hereby cry them up again, and request every good singer in Britain and Ireland, and the East Indies, to sing the following song with full birr to the sweet air, "Maid of the Valley."

If e'er I am Thine

was written to an Irish air, called "The Winding Sheet," and harmonized by Smith; but was, I believe, one of the suppressed ones.

How dear to me the Hour

is likewise on the proscription list—a proscribed rebel against the sovereign authority of Mr Little the Great; but if I have trod too near the heels of his dignity, I am sure it was through no ill intention.

These are all, but it is not difficult to see why the publishers interfered. Moore sings:

Come o'er the sea,
Maiden! with me,
Mine through sunshine, storm, and snows—

and Hogg:

Come from the sea,
Maiden, to me,
Maiden of mystery, love and pain.

Moore begins his second verse:

Is not the Sea
Made for the Free,
Land for courts and chains alone?

To which Hogg replies with admirable sense:

Is not the wave
Made for the slave,
Tyrant's chains and stern control?

The most surprising thing is that Hogg should have taken so much trouble when he could make better songs without getting into another man's debt, and it is even more surprising when one considers that he very seldom took up the old songs which anyone might fairly refashion. In the light of all the other proof of his anxiety not to compromise his originality, the Moore incident looks like an unsuccessful joke.

Hogg's criticism is not always certain. He saw, for instance, that *The Skylark* was good, but exalted it at the expense of *Bonnie Prince Charlie*—"one of my worst," he says incorrectly. It is in fact a good example of what he calls his "desperate Jacobite effusions," of which not all are very desperate, but most are very lively. Best of them all is *Donald M'Gillavry*, which, as we have seen[1], Hogg put into the *Jacobite Relics* unsigned for fun, thereby bringing forth from his Edinburgh Reviewer praise which must have been wished back again. The praise was deserved and the trick was one of Hogg's most successful jokes, better in some ways than the *Chaldee* affair.

Donald's gane up the hill hard an' hungry,
Donald's come down the hill wild an' angry;
Donald will clear the gouk's nest cleverly;
Here's to the king, an' Donald M'Gillavry!
Come like a weigh-bauk, Donald M'Gillavry,
Come like a weigh-bauk, Donald M'Gillavry;
Balance them fair, an' balance them cleverly,
Off wi' the counterfeit, Donald M'Gillavry!

Donald's come o'er the hill trailin' his tether, man;
As he war wud, or stanged wi' an ether, man;
When he gaes back, there's some will look merrily;
Here's to King James an' Donald M'Gillavry!
Come like a weaver, Donald M'Gillavry,
Come like a weaver, Donald M'Gillavry;
Pack on your back an elwand o' steelary,
Gie them full measure, my Donald M'Gillavry!

[1] *Vide* pp. 38–9.

Donald has foughten wi' reif and roguery,
Donald has dinner'd wi' banes an' beggary;
Better it war for whigs an' whiggery
Meeting the deevil, than Donald M'Gillavry.
Come like a tailor, Donald M'Gillavry,
Come like a tailor, Donald M'Gillavry;
Push about, in and out, thimble them cleverly,
Here's to King James an' Donald M'Gillavry!

Donald's the callant that bruiks nae tangleness,
Whigging an' prigging an' a' newfangleness;
They maun be gane, he winna be baukit, man,
He maun hae justice, or rarely he'll tak it, man.
Come like a cobbler, Donald M'Gillavry,
Come like a cobbler, Donald M Gillavry;
Bore them, an' yerk them, an' lingel them cleverly—
Up wi' King James and Donald M'Gillavry!

Donald was mumpit wi' mirds and mockery,
Donald was blindit wi' bladds o' property;
Arles ran high, but makings war naething, man;
Gudeness! how Donald is flyting an' fretting, man!
Come like the deevil, Donald M'Gillavry,
Come like the deevil, Donald M'Gillavry;
Skelp them an' scadd them pruved sae unbritherly—
Up wi' King James an' Donald M'Gillavry!

Hogg had the wit not to repent of that, but for one other of his best songs, *The Village of Balmaquhapple*, he was unwise enough to suggest an apology. "I cannot conceive what could induce me to write a song like this. It must undoubtedly have some allusion to circumstances which I have quite forgot." Of course there were no circumstances.

D'ye ken the big village of Balmaquhapple,
The great muckle village of Balmaquhapple?
'Tis steeped in iniquity up to the thrapple,
An' what's to become o' poor Balmaquhapple?
Fling a' aff your bannets, an' kneel for your life, fo'ks,
And pray to St Andrew, the god o' the Fife fo'ks;
Gar a' the hills yout wi' sheer vociferation,
And thus you may cry on sic needfu' occasion:

"O blessed St Andrew, if e'er ye could pity fo'k,
Men fo'k or women fo'k, country or city fo'k,
Come for this aince wi' the auld thief to grapple,
An' save the great village of Balmaquhapple
Frae drinking an' leeing, an' flyting an' swearing,
An' sins that ye wad be affrontit at hearing,
An' cheatin' an' stealing; oh, grant them redemption,
All save an' except the few after to mention:

"There's Johnny the elder, wha hopes ne'er to need ye,
Sae pawky, sae holy, sae gruff, an' sae greedy;
Wha prays every hour as the wayfarer passes,
But aye at a hole where he watches the lasses:
He's cheated a thousand, an' e'en to this day yet
Can cheat a young lass, or they're leears that say it;
Then gie him his gate; he's sae slee an' sae civil,
Perhaps in the end he may wheedle the devil.

"There's Cappie the cobbler, an' Tammie the tinman,
An' Dickie the brewer, an' Peter the skinman,
An' Geordie our deacon for want of a better,
An' Bess, wha delights in the sins that beset her.
O worthy St Andrew, we canna compel ye,
But ye ken as weel as a body can tell ye,
If these gang to heaven, we'll a' be sae shockit,
Your garret o' blue will but thinly be stockit.

"But for a' the rest, for the women's sake, save them,
Their bodies at least, an' their sauls, if they have them;
But it puzzles Jock Lesly, an' sma' it avails,
If they dwell in their stamocks, their heads, or their tails.
An' save, without word of confession auricular,
The clerk's bonny daughters, an' Bell in particular;
For ye ken that their beauty's the pride an' the staple
Of the great wicked village of Balmaquhapple!"

There is something of the same gusto in *When Maggy gangs away:*

Oh, what will a' the lads do
When Maggy gangs away?
Oh, what will a' the lads do
When Maggy gangs away?

There's no a heart in a' the glen
  That disna dread the day:
Oh, what will a' the lads do
  When Maggy gangs away?

Young Jock has ta'en the hill for't—
  A waefu' wight is he;
Poor Harry's ta'en the bed for't,
  An' laid him down to dee;
An' Sandy's gane unto the kirk,
  An' learnin' fast to pray:
An' oh, what will the lads do
  When Maggy gangs away?

The young laird o' the Lang-Shaw
  Has drunk her health in wine;
The priest has said—in confidence—
  The lassie was divine,
And that is mair in maiden's praise
  Than ony priest should say:
But oh, what will the lads do
  When Maggy gangs away?

The wailing in our green glen
  That day will quaver high;
'Twill draw the redbreast frae the wood,
  The laverock frae the sky;
The fairies frae their beds o' dew
  Will rise an' join the lay:
An' hey! what a day will be
  When Maggy gangs away!

Hogg "heard a girl lilting over the first line" of that to his little daughter, and "forthwith went in and made a song of it." He did not often take more than a few words of an old song to make a new one; his version of *Charlie is my darling* has more of the old in it than he usually took and is not very successful; he had not made it sufficiently his own. But his rendering of *My Love she's but a*

Lassie yet is his own, and an odd contrast to the older versions:

My love she's but a lassie yet,
A lightsome lovely lassie yet;
    It scarce wad do
    To sit an' woo
Down by the stream sae glassy yet.
But there's a braw time coming yet,
When we may gang a-roaming yet;
    An' hint wi' glee
    O' joys to be,
When fa's the modest gloaming yet.

She's neither proud nor saucy yet,
She's neither plump nor gaucy yet;
    But just a jinking,
    Bonny blinking,
Hilty-skilty lassie yet.
But oh, her artless smile's mair sweet
Than hinny or than marmalete!
    An' right or wrang,
    Ere it be lang,
I'll bring her to a parley yet.

I'm jealous o' what blesses her,
The very breeze that kisses her,
    The flowery beds
    On which she treads,
Though wae for ane that misses her.
Then oh, to meet my lassie yet,
Up in yon glen sae grassy yet;
    For all I see
    Are nought to me,
Save her that's but a lassie yet!

This is far enough from the robustness of the old song. Hogg once expressed his opinion that Moore's notes were "far owre finely strung" and his own "just right," but he sometimes went rather near the border. Usually his songs are like this one, just sweet enough to be right, and fresh in spite of his frequently repeated tenderness for "the lasses" and what

Christopher North called his besetting imagery—a fondness for comparing the beauties of nature with the beauties of the lasses. The *Boy's Song* escapes both temptations:

Where the pools are bright and deep,
Where the gray trout lies asleep,
Up the river and o'er the lea,
That's the way for Billy and me.

Where the blackbird sings the latest,
Where the hawthorn blooms the sweetest,
Where the nestlings chirp and flee,
That's the way for Billy and me.

Where the mowers mow the cleanest,
Where the hay lies thick and greenest;
There to trace the homeward bee,
That's the way for Billy and me.

Where the hazel bank is steepest,
Where the shadow falls the deepest,
Where the clustering nuts fall free,
That's the way for Billy and me.

Why the boys should drive away
Little sweet maidens from the play,
Or love to banter and fight so well,
That's the thing I never could tell.

But this I know, I love to play,
Through the meadow, among the hay;
Up the water and o'er the lea,
That's the way for Billy and me.

There is the Shepherd piping with that touch of child-like innocence and simplicity which, however doubtful some of his actions may have been, never quite forsook him.

9. *THE LAST DAYS OF THE SHEPHERD*

BACK at Altrive after his visit to London, Hogg set to work again to produce stories, poems and articles. The most important of his later books is *The Domestic Manners and Private Life of Sir Walter Scott*—important in itself for its glimpses of Scott, and important also for its effect on the relations between Hogg and Lockhart.

It is unfortunate for the Shepherd that his friends have always shown themselves too eager in his defence. It is not enough for them that he should be on the whole a lovable person for whom anyone would make allowances; he must also be scrupulously honourable and blameless in all his transactions and at every moment of his life. No reader of Mrs Garden's *Memorials* of her father, or Thomson's *Memoir*, or the other Dr Thomson's Memoir prefacing the 1909 edition of the *Domestic Manners*, would be likely to suppose that Hogg had any faults except an amusing vanity and perhaps a slight tendency to envy. Of the three the earlier Thomson is the least partial, but even he goes so far in speaking of the *Domestic Manners* as to accuse Lockhart of a foolish jealousy which was not part of Lockhart's character. The argument appears to be that if Lockhart objected to the book, as we know he did, jealousy is the only explanation. Veitch in his introduction to the *Memorials* takes the same view. Mrs Garden prints a friendly letter of Lockhart's written early in 1833, before he had seen anything of the book, and then accuses him of persistent endeavours to blacken the reputation of a dead man to whom he had always professed a hypocritical friendship.

But is that the explanation? The tone of Lockhart's references to Hogg would not, as a matter of fact, strike any reader as cruel or malign, but rather as generous in recognition of the Shepherd's literary merits and tolerant, even if with a little contemptuous amusement, of his personal failings. But there is one strong sentence at the end of the *Life of Scott* on which all the accusations of malignity and the rest are based: "It had been better for his fame had his end been of earlier date, for he did not follow his best benefactor until he had insulted his dust."

The *Domestic Manners* was published in the summer of 1834; Hogg died in 1835; the *Life of Scott* was published a year later. Therefore Lockhart is accused of waiting until Hogg was dead to make cruel insinuations against him. It does not seem to have struck Mrs Garden that she too was accusing a dead man, with the difference that no one was left to defend Lockhart, while many might have defended Hogg in 1836 and later, if they had chosen or been able to defend him. But as a matter of fact Lockhart did not wait until Hogg was dead; he protested against the *Domestic Manners* before it was published, with such vigour and effect that it appeared in a weakened form and bears marks of a hasty but not thoroughgoing attempt to propitiate him. The story can be made out from two letters in Mrs Oliphant's *William Blackwood and His Sons*. The first (vol. II, pp. 119–20) was written by William Blackwood, who was then in London, to his son Alexander and is dated April 19, 1833—some weeks later than the friendly letter of Lockhart's which Mrs Garden quotes:

We sat nearly a couple of hours with Mr Lockhart, and had a great deal of talk with him. He is just the old man, as friendly and as satirical as ever. He gave us a most ludicrous account of some interviews he had had with this fellow Mr S.—Cochrane's partner. This worthy, you know, has announced a Life of Sir Walter Scott, and told Mr L. he had got a number of his (Sir Walter's) letters to Constable which he intended to incorporate in his work. Mr L. made him aware that the law would entitle Sir W.'s executors to get an injunction to prevent them being published without their consent. This, however, Mr S. did not at first believe, but he soon found Mr L. was right. Their next interview—and this is the best joke of all—was to consult Mr L. with respect to a large MS which he had received from his friend Hogg, containing anecdotes of Sir Walter. Mr L., knowing well what a bundle of lies it would be, at first declined to look at it, but Mr S. pressed him so much that he opened the scroll. The first page he glanced at contained such abominable things that he could not restrain his indignation, but poured it forth upon Hogg in such unmeasured terms that his poor auditor was dumbfoundered. He, however, left the manuscript for Mr L.'s consideration. He went over it, and filled with utter disgust not only at the lies on every page, but the bad feeling displayed in mentioning the three Dukes of Buccleuch, Scott of Harden, and many others, and speeches of Sir Walter and Lady Scott in the most offensive way possible[1]. He therefore returned the MS with a note saying he could give no opinion upon it. I had almost forgot to tell you a very curious part of the affair: though all in Hogg's handwriting, it is given as if it were written by Mr S., and he takes good care to speak of himself in the most laudatory way as the excellent Shepherd, the original genius, &c., &c., and Mr S. is supposed to write down the remarks of this son of genius[2]. One atrocious lie Mr L. was able to detect from his own personal knowledge. Hogg details to Mr S. at great length an interview he had with Sir Walter on his last return from Drumlanrig, when, he says, Sir Walter called on him with Miss Scott. He makes Sir Walter pay him the most extravagant compliments, and exalt him far above any poet of the age. And this is all pure fiction, except that Sir Walter did call, and Mr Lockhart was with him, not Miss Scott. What a fortunate escape we have made in not having anything more to do with Hogg, for he would have been an eternal torment.

[1] There is something missing here. Mrs Oliphant suggests that "concerning them" has dropped out after "Scott."

[2] Cf. Hogg's proposal to Scott of a life of himself done in the same way (Lockhart, II, p. 172, and here, p. 52).

What happened next is not very easy to make out. The *Domestic Manners*, as we have the book, is written in the first, not the third, person and is anxiously polite in most, though not all, of the references to Lockhart. In August 1833—that is, four months after Lockhart's outburst—an American tourist visited Hogg at Altrive Lake and was told by him[1] that he had some time before sent to two correspondents in Albany, "the Rev. Mr S—— and Mr S. De Witt B——," a manuscript entitled *Reminiscences of Sir Walter Scott*, which they had advised him would be published in the *Mirror*. The only paper of note of that name was, as the tourist told Hogg, the *New York Mirror*, but I have not found Hogg's *Reminiscences* in the files of that journal. But in the spring of 1834, in time to be reviewed in the May issue of the *American Monthly Magazine*, there appeared in New York, published by Harper and Brothers, *Familiar Anecdotes of Sir Walter Scott. By James Hogg, the Ettrick Shepherd; with a Sketch of the Life of the Shepherd, by S. De Witt Bloodgood*—evidently one of the Albany correspondents. This book I have not seen[2], but the extracts in the *American Monthly Magazine* prove that it is a version of the *Domestic Manners*, and as they are in the first, not the third, person, it would seem to be what may be called the revised version. Even so the reviewer, though admitting the liveliness and interest of much of the book and recommending it—as much for the Shepherd's pecuniary benefit as for any other reason —was unpleasantly struck by what he calls an "in-

[1] *A Visit to the Ettrick Shepherd* (*American Monthly Magazine*, April 1834, vol. III, pp. 85–91).

[2] For the particulars given in the *Bibliography*, I am indebted to a note by "C. D." in *Notes and Queries*, Eleventh Series, VI, p. 248.

delicate and ungenerous" reference to Lady Scott and by the fact that "in more instances than one, the Shepherd places Scott in a new light—and, we fear, aims to make him, in some respects, unamiable and jealous."

In the same summer the book appeared in Great Britain, not, I think, in a pirated edition but delayed naturally since the preceding spring by revision and the search for a publisher. Cochrane seems in the end to have declined to take the risk, and the book was actually published by Reid of Glasgow, Oliver and Boyd of Edinburgh, and Black, Young and Young of London. The memoir by Bloodgood remained in this edition. On August 18th, 1834, Lockhart wrote to Blackwood (Mrs Oliphant, vol. II, pp. 123–4):

> ...I was delighted with the last "Noctes." There was never a better or more lively and ludicrous picture drawn than in all the earlier part of it, and there is also a vast deal of real shrewd good sense, observation, and most biting sarcasm to boot. In Wilson's hands the Shepherd will always be delightful; but of the fellow himself I can scarcely express my contemptuous pity, now that his "Life of Sir W. Scott" is before the world. I believe it will, however, do Hogg more serious and lasting mischief than any of those whose feelings he has done his brutal best to lacerate would wish to be the result. He has drawn his own character, not that of his benevolent *creator*, and handed himself down to posterity—for the subject will keep *this* from being forgotten—as a mean blasphemer against all magnanimity. Poor Laidlaw will be mortified to the heart by this sad display. The bitterness against me which peeps out in many parts of Hogg's narrative is, of course, the fruit of certain rather hasty words spoken by me to Cochrane and MacCrone when they showed me the original MS, but nevertheless Hogg has *omitted* the only two passages which I had read when I so expressed myself,—one of them being a most flagrant assault on Scott's veracity, and the other a statement about poor Lady Scott, such as must have afflicted for ever her children, and especially her surviving daughter. Dr Maginn has handled Hogg in his own way in "Fraser's Mag."

As for the gossip about Lady Scott, there is enough of it even in this revised version; the Drumlanrig inaccuracy still remains, though with some modification, and Maginn in his review[1] pointed out certain passages which are not easy to reconcile with known dates. The persistent glorification of the Shepherd is merely amusing and probably amused Lockhart, but it is very hard to deny him, the man most nearly concerned after Scott's children, the right of indignation at such things as the accusations made against Scott of plagiary and jealousy, and the broad hint that Lady Scott was illegitimate; even if we suppose that his view of the book was not affected by his recollection of the suppressed passages. And yet, in spite of all its glaring faults, the *Domestic Manners* is a delight to read: the Shepherd is there, as Lockhart remarked, and Sir Walter, however Hogg may have distorted some of his features, is there also.

In the same year as the *Domestic Manners* appeared *A Series of Lay Sermons on Good Principles and Good Breeding*, which, although Hogg might not be supposed to be an authority on manners, contains much sound sense; and in the next year the last volume published in the Shepherd's lifetime, *Tales of the Wars of Montrose*. His health had been failing for some time, and he died on November 21st, 1835. After all his struggles his family was left almost destitute, and it was not until 1853 that a small pension from the Civil List was settled on his widow.

It is easy to find faults both in the Shepherd himself and in his work. He was shrewd enough to guard against the grosser physical temptations, he was good-humoured—except when an offence to his vanity called forth a sort of spitefulness—and a good husband and

[1] *Fraser's Magazine*, vol. x, pp. 125–56.

father, as well as a dutiful son, but in other ways he was not to be trusted. His friends helped him untiringly, but the greatest kindness they could have done him would have been to keep him free from any but a shepherd's responsibilities. He might have written less if he had remained the shepherd which he always called himself, but I doubt whether his best things would have been lost: *Kilmeny*, *The Confessions of a Justified Sinner* and the songs all belong to that side of him. There never was a writer who showed fewer signs of growth in his craft; you can find no essential difference of spirit or technique between *The Mountain Bard* and *A Queer Book*, or the early ghost-stories and the *Justified Sinner*. He lived as he wrote, in a casual, rather breathless fashion; he was a man less fitted than most for the world's business, and if he could have been kept out of it we might have been able to regard him with some of the affectionate veneration of his daughter. As things are he is a figure comic even in his iniquities.

The Bibliography appended to this study gives some idea of the number of the Shepherd's writings, yet of the verses comparatively few are still alive, and the prose, greater in actual bulk, has been almost entirely forgotten. A few people know *The Confessions of a Justified Sinner*, and a few with an appetite for Covenanters and bogles have read *The Brownie of Bodsbeck*, but most of the long list of stories which Hogg put together are resting in a sleep which it is kinder to him to leave undisturbed. As for his longer poems—*Mador of the Moor*, *The Pilgrims of the Sun*, *Queen Hynde*, even *The Queen's Wake*—they are in much the same case. Yet the fragments that remain, *Kilmeny* and *The Witch of Fife* and a passage or two more from *The Queen's Wake*, with some of the shorter poems and nearly all the songs, are enough to show how much there was in the Shepherd if he had only realised his own strength and used a little moderation. He had a fairy fantasy which he overworked; he could repeat the grotesqueness of *The Witch of Fife*, and he could do more with supernatural terrors than the people who made horrid mysteries their business, but in the gentler kind of faerie he was always trying to repeat *Kilmeny* with more and more wearying results. He came at last to the feebly pretty *Greek Pastoral*:

> Thus ends my yearly offering bland,
> The Laureate's Lay of the Fairy Land.

He could make excellent songs and very good ballads, but the ballads were nearly always too long. Scott could recite all seventy-four stanzas of *Gilmanscleuch* with enthusiasm, and it is good, but it would have been better if the half had been cut out. Worst of all, Hogg, who was what he called himself, the King of the mountain and fairy school, neglected his own dominions to make raids on those of other monarchs. He could write charming sketches of country life and gruesome ghost-stories, but he persisted in trying to develop elaborate plots and write fashionable historical romances. *The Poetic Mirror* shows that he was not without critical faculty, but he had very little power of criticising his own work, and it was too seldom that he listened to the advice of his friends.

But though Hogg's works need weeding out more than those of most writers, if the best of his verse and prose were rescued it would make a larger volume than might be supposed. And even if his achievement were less, he would still be, in his own person, one of the most amusing of untaught writers, more comic in actual life than the riotous and poetic Shepherd of the *Noctes Ambrosianae*, rich though that creation is. Peasant poets are sometimes rather insubstantial and ineffective figures, as if their strength went into their verse and left nothing in the man behind, but Hogg has no want of vitality: he is intensely interested in himself, easily snubbed and easily recovering an impudence which is so simple that it rouses rather kindly laughter than wrath, neither truthful nor altogether trustworthy, but as warm in his affections as in his vanity, and not undeserving, in spite of some lapses, of the affection which he received from better men.

APPENDIX

(*a*) AULD MAITLAND.

THE ballad of *Auld Maitland* was printed for the first time in the third volume of the *Minstrelsy*, published in 1803. Doubts of its authenticity arose even before its publication[1], and almost every later writer on ballads has had a fling at it. Child included it in 1861 but left it out of his later collection; unfortunately he never gave his reasons for finally rejecting it. The chief objections made to it are three:

1. The unlikeliness of a ballad on such a comparatively uninteresting story surviving from the thirteenth century in tradition, and with that its length and the difficulty of carrying it in mind for long.

2. The undeniable fact that the military terms, which Scott adduced as a proof of age, might have been learnt and inserted from Blind Harry's *Wallace*.

3. The possibility that Hogg learnt about Auld Maitland and his three sons from either Scott or Leyden—the conclusion being that Hogg forged the ballad, possibly with Scott's connivance.

The first objection does not matter very much; if the ballad is genuine, the unlikeliness of its survival is a minor detail. It should be noted, however, that Aytoun, who made this point in the first edition of his *Ballads*, in the second edition confessed that the discovery that first Laidlaw and afterwards Scott actually heard *Auld Maitland* from recitation had shaken his

[1] *Vide* Hogg's letter of June 30th, 1802, pp. 24–7; and his *Autobiography*.

doubts. The second objection makes the doubtful assumption that Hogg knew Blind Harry; but as far as we know, the only *Wallace* that he had read was the modernised version by Hamilton of Gilbertfield, in which the old terms do not appear. But the third, on which the second is dependent—for Hogg might have learnt the terms from someone who had read the original *Wallace*—is really serious. It has been worked out thoroughly by Colonel Fitzwilliam Elliot in his *Further Essays on the Border Ballads*, where he tries to prove that Hogg did get the historical background from Leyden and that Scott discovered the deception and helped it to win further currency. That this was not so was fairly proved by Lang in *Sir Walter Scott and the Border Minstrelsy*, and besides his arguments there are others in favour of Hogg's honesty.

The first and almost the most important thing to be remarked is that the ballad did not come in the first instance from Hogg. "I heard," writes Laidlaw[1], "from one of our servant-girls, who had all the turn and qualifications for a collector, of a ballad called *Auld Maitland* that a grandfather of Hogg's could repeat, and she herself had several of the first stanzas (which I took a note of and have still the copy). This greatly aroused my anxiety to procure the whole, for this was a ballad not even hinted at by Mercer in his list of desiderata received from Mr Scott. I forthwith wrote to Hogg himself, requesting him to endeavour to procure the whole ballad. In a week or two, I received his reply[2], containing *Auld Maitland* exactly as he had copied it from the recitation of his uncle, Will Laidlaw of Phawhope, corroborated by

[1] *Abbotsford Notanda*, p. 118.

[2] This is now in the Abbotsford MSS, in the possession of Mr Hugh Walpole.

his mother, who both said that they learned it from their father, a still older Will of Phawhope, and an old man called Andrew Muir, who had been servant to the famous Mr Boston, minister of Ettrick."

Hogg gives some information about this old man in his introduction to *Mess John* in *The Mountain Bard*:

> Andrew Moore, who died at Ettrick about twenty-six years ago, at a great age, often averred, that he had, in his youth, seen and conversed with many people who remembered every circumstance of it. . . . This singular old man could repeat by heart every old ballad which is now published in the "Minstrelsy of the Border," except three, with three times as many; and from him, "Auld Maitland," with many ancient songs and tales, still popular in that country, are derived.

The pedigree was carried a step further back by old Mrs Hogg—"My brothers an' me learned it frae auld Andrew Moor, an' he learned it, an' mony mae, frae auld Baby Mettlin, that was housekeeper to the first laird o' Tushilaw."[1]

It sounds plausible, and Lang has pointed out[2] that auld Baby Mettlin must have lived at the end of the seventeenth century and probably belonged to an impoverished branch of the Maitlands. It would therefore not be surprising if she knew some of the Maitland traditions.

Whether Laidlaw sent Scott the servant's fragment is not quite certain; he almost certainly did not send him Hogg's version but waited for his arrival in the district. Colonel Elliot quotes a passage from Scott's Memoir of Leyden and supposes that the reference

[1] *Vide* that form of the Memoir which is given by Thomson as Hogg's *Autobiography*, II, p. 461. So also in the *Domestic Manners*, where the name is given as Baubie Mettlin. Hogg refers to the ballad indifferently as Auld Maitland, Auld Maitlan, Auld Maitlen, Auld Mettlin, and Old Mettlin.

[2] *Sir Walter Scott and the Border Minstrelsy*, pp. 48–9; cf. Lang in ch. XV of Farrer's *Literary Forgeries*, pp. 254–8.

is to *Auld Maitland*—the story of how in 1802 "an interesting fragment had been obtained of an ancient historical ballad, but the remainder...was not to be recovered," and how Leyden "walked between forty and fifty miles and back again, for the sole purpose of visiting an old person who possessed this precious remnant of antiquity."[1] If this refers to *Auld Maitland*—there is nothing to prove that it does, and there are other ballads to which it might refer—Laidlaw may have sent Scott the first fragment and Leyden may have gone direct to old Will Laidlaw or Mrs Hogg. But if so, he can hardly have avoided meeting Laidlaw, to whom he needed letters of introduction when he went with Scott, or Hogg, whom he also did not know[2]. It seems very doubtful whether Laidlaw sent any part of *Auld Maitland* to Scott; he may have remarked that he had found a ballad about Auld Maitland, and Scott or Leyden, knowing of the passage about Maitland and his sons in the Maitland MSS to which Scott refers in the *Minstrelsy*, and not having met with any other tradition or ballad about them, felt a little doubtful about this ballad's authenticity. What is certain is that they took some pains to be sure of their sources before accepting the ballad.

Some confusion has been caused here by a mistake of Lockhart's[3], who knew that Scott visited Laidlaw in one of the vacations of 1802 and supposed it was in the autumn. As a matter of fact this visit was

[1] Leyden's *Poems and Ballads*, 1858, p. 29.

[2] Cf. *Sir Walter Scott and the Border Minstrelsy*, Preface, pp. ix–x, and also *Scottish Historical Review*, VIII, p. 221, a note by Lang: "To Mr Kennedy I also owe complete proof, from a MS of Laidlaw's, that Leyden did not know Hogg till the day after that on which Laidlaw gave to Scott, in Leyden's presence, Hogg's holograph MS of *Auld Maitland*."

[3] Followed by Carruthers in the *Abbotsford Notanda*, p. 113.

made in the spring, as Lang proves from letters which passed between Scott and Ritson, and Scott and Ellis. In the first, written just after his return to Edinburgh, Scott informs Ellis that he has found "a complete and perfect copy of 'Maitland with his Auld Berd Graie.' ...You may guess the surprise of Leyden and myself when this was presented to us, copied down from the recitation of an old shepherd, by a country farmer."[1] This, by the way, seems to argue against the sending of *Auld Maitland* to Scott in Edinburgh, since it was apparently new to him at Blackhouse. In the next letter to Ellis which Lockhart gives (pp. 100–1) Scott remarks, "I have lately had from (Ritson) *a copie* of 'Ye litel wee Mon,' of which I think I can make some use. In return, I have sent him a sight of Auld Maitland, the original MS. If you are curious, I dare say you may easily see it. Indeed, I might easily send you a transcribed copy,—but I wish him to see it *in puris naturalibus.*" This copy of *Ye litel wee Mon* was sent by Ritson to Scott on April 10th, 1802, and on June 10th, 1802, Ritson acknowledged the receipt of *Auld Maitland*, which was therefore probably sent off by Scott some time in May[2].

The spring vacation that year was from March 11th to May 12th, and some time between these dates Scott and Leyden arrived at Blackhouse, "carrying letters of introduction."[3] "After the party had explored the scenery of the burn, and inspected Douglas

[1] Lockhart, II, pp. 99–100.

[2] Ritson's *Letters*, II, pp. 217–20, 222–30.

[3] *Abbotsford Notanda*, p. 120. Colonel Elliot (*Further Essays*, pp. 175–6) considers it highly improbable that Scott should have been so much in the district for the past two years without meeting Laidlaw and Hogg, but all the evidence points to this. The very easiness of arranging a meeting may have led to its postponement.

Tower," writes Carruthers, "Laidlaw produced his treasure of *Auld Maitland*." This was Hogg's MS, which is still among the Abbotsford MSS, addressed to "Mr Laidlaw, Blackhouse." "Leyden seemed inclined to lay hands on the manuscript, but the sheriff said gravely that *he* would read it. Instantly both Scott and Leyden, from their knowledge of the subject, saw and felt that the ballad was undoubtedly ancient, and their eyes sparkled as they exchanged looks. Scott read with great fluency and emphasis. Leyden was like a roused lion. He paced the room from side to side, clapped his hands, and repeated such expressions as echoed the spirit of hatred to King Edward and the Southrons, or as otherwise struck his fancy. 'I had never before seen anything like this,' said the quiet Laidlaw; 'and though the sheriff kept his feelings under, he, too, was excited, so that his *burr* became very perceptible.'"

This enthusiasm was all very well, but it did not last long. Almost at once, Scott, or Leyden, seems to have seen or returned to the possibility of forgery. The two went out riding with Laidlaw, who tells in a passage omitted by Carruthers but quoted by Lang[1] of a conversation between himself and Leyden. "Near the Craigbents, Mr Scott and Leyden drew together in a close and seemingly private conversation. I, of course, fell back. After a minute or two, Leyden reined in his horse (a black horse that Mr Scott's servant used to ride) and let me come up. 'This Hogg,' said he, 'writes verses, I understand.' I assured him that he wrote very beautiful verses, and with great facility. 'But I trust,' he replied, 'that there is no fear of his passing off any of his own upon Scott for old ballads.' I again assured him that he would

[1] *Sir Walter Scott and the Border Minstrelsy*, Preface, pp. ix–x.

never think of such a thing; and neither would he at that period of his life. 'Let him beware of forgery,' cried Leyden with great force and energy, and in, I suppose, what Mr Scott used afterwards to call the *saw tones of his voice*."

Scott may have been thinking of Hogg's earlier offer to versify traditions, but for the moment the critics were satisfied, and the rest of the visit passed very pleasantly. Leyden met Hogg the next day, but it is not certain that Scott was there too, in spite of an ambiguous phrase of Laidlaw's in telling of this first visit to Blackhouse: "I felt the same sort of pleasure that I experienced when I found that Walter Scott was delighted with Hogg." Scott took Hogg's address and thereafter corresponded with him directly instead of through Laidlaw[1]. The evidence seems to show that the meeting of the Sheriff and the Shepherd came shortly afterwards, in the late spring or early summer; in the letter of June 30th, 1802, Hogg states that he has "seen and conversed with" Scott, and both Hogg and Carruthers remark that the meeting was on a fine summer day, though both are uncertain of the date[2]. The reason of the second visit to Blackhouse is also variously given. According to Carruthers, Scott became "curious to see the poetical Shepherd," while the Shepherd himself with unusual modesty takes Scott's desire to meet him not as a personal tribute but as arising from a spirit of scientific enquiry: "I thought Mr Scott had some dread of a part (of *Auld Maitland*) being forged; that had been the cause

[1] *Abbotsford Notanda*, p. 128.

[2] "In the summer of 1801," says Hogg, though it was certainly after the publication of the first two volumes of the *Minstrelsy*; Carruthers is more confused and inserts before his account of the meeting a letter of Scott's which, on internal evidence, was written in September 1802.

of his journey into the wilds of Ettrick." There may be some truth in both explanations, but it is doubtful whether Hogg really knew then of Scott's suspicions. In the letter of June 30th the suggestion of forgery seems to be new to him; and besides, Scott would not be likely to put the possible culprits on their guard. Who was the doubter this time cannot be told: certainly not Ellis or even the normally sceptical Ritson, both of whom accepted *Auld Maitland* unquestioningly; perhaps still Scott or Leyden, unable to escape from the feeling that a ballad coming down from the thirteenth century, in however corrupt and partially modernised a form, was too good to be true.

Externally, then, the evidence for Hogg's honesty and the authenticity of *Auld Maitland* is fairly strong.

1. The mere argument of improbability is not enough by itself.

2. The ballad came in the first instance not from Hogg but from Laidlaw's maidservant. If Hogg forged it, he must have taught it to his mother and his uncle, both old people, in order to get it recited to the girl—an exceedingly roundabout and difficult way of managing a deception.

3. Hogg cannot have forged it without being first informed of the story of Auld Maitland and his three sons, and the evidence for their existence is to be found in a manuscript which he could not have heard of except from Leyden or Scott. He did not meet them until after he had sent the ballad, and there is not the slightest evidence that Scott ever gave permission for even such mild pieces of editing and adaptation as Hogg suggested in his letter of July 20th, 1801. Imitations of ballads by various hands were included frankly in the *Minstrelsy*, and Hogg thought so poorly of them that he made others himself to show how

it should be done. But none of his ballads is like *Auld Maitland*.

Internally the evidence for the honesty of Hogg and Scott is no weaker, and here Hogg has suffered from the repeated modernisation and regularisation of the spelling when the ballad has been printed. The form of his original manuscript has been followed by Lang (*Sir Walter Scott and the Border Minstrelsy*, pp. 32–9), and one or two curious points are worth noting. In the first place, Hogg has been accused of taking the names of mediaeval engines of war from Blind Harry; if he did—though he probably did not know the real *Wallace* of Blind Harry—it is very odd that one of them should appear in the form of

> springs: wall stanes, and good of ern

—which gives no sense at all. Wall stones are a most unlikely kind of projectile to be thrown from a besieged castle; "good of ern" is mere nonsense. Again Billopgrace, for which Scott suggested Ville-de-Grace, is not a corruption that would be made deliberately. The most obvious and most probable explanation is that Hogg really did not understand what he heard, but wrote it down in the hope that Scott would be able to make sense of it, just as he had done with the "Soudan Turk" in *The Outlaw Murray*.

In the second place there are certain peculiarities of vocabulary which are not Hogg's own and not in the least the kind of thing which he invented when he wanted to be archaic. Nor would anyone be likely to invent them. The most important is the curious reduplicative preposition "inon"[1]

> But sic a gloom inon ae browhead (st. 26)

[1] Professor W. P. Ker pointed this out in the *Scottish Historical Review*, VIII, pp. 191–2.

and earlier:

> Met themen on (i.e. them inon) a day (st. 15)[1].

Miss Beatrice Allen has kindly pointed out to me another instance of the same doubled preposition, in the *Buke of the Howlat* (c. 1450), II, 321–3:

> He ruschit in the gret rowte, the kyncht to reskewe,
> Feile of the fals folk, that fled of befor,
> Relevit in on thir twa, for to tell trewe,
> That thai war samyn ourset[2].

In the *Minstrelsy* both lines are changed: st. 15, which needs two syllables, reads, "Met them upon a day," and st. 26 drops the "in."

There is another much less important word, on which I would not lay too much stress. Stanza 6 in Hogg's MS reads:

> King Edward rade King Edward ran—
> I wish him dool and pain!
> Till he had fifteen hundred men
> Assembled on the Tyne.
> And twice as many at North Berwick
> Was a' for battle bound.

Hogg thought that something was needed here, and accordingly he suggested two lines, which were duly acknowledged in the *Minstrelsy*:

> And marching south with curst Dunbar
> A ready welcome found.

In the *Minstrelsy* there are slight verbal alterations, but the main fact is that the six-lined stanza has become two four-lined stanzas. The change may very well be unnecessary: it may be that the original stanza was six-lined, ending not in *bound* but in *boun*. The rhyme is not good, but neither is the rhyme of *pain*

[1] In Hogg's MS these are stanzas 25 and 14.

[2] "Relieve," II, b, To return or rally in battle. . . . Const. *on*, *upon*, *to*. Obs.—N. E. D., which gives this quotation.

and *Tyne*—Scott changed *pain* to *pine*. It is worth noticing that *boun*, not an unfamiliar word, seems to have been unfamiliar to Hogg; when he wanted it for a rhyme in *Earl Walter* he spelt it with an apostrophe as a shortened form of *bound*:

> Earl Walter rose ere it was day,
> For battle made him boun';
> Earl Walter mounted his bonny gray,
> And rode to Stirling town.

Lang's earlier theory, given in his preface to Farrer's *Literary Forgeries*, was that a seventeenth century Maitland forged the ballad. That would offer commentators one way out of the difficulty, but it would not account for *inon*, and I do not think it is the right solution. The only certain date is that of Babby Maitland who served the first Anderson laird of Tushilaw, and he reigned from 1688 to 1721 or 1724, so that "if a manuscript copy ever existed, and was Babby's ultimate source, it would be of the late seventeenth century. That is the ascertained date of the oldest known MS of *The Outlaw Murray*....Granting a MS of *Auld Maitland* existing in any branch of the Maitland family in 1680–1700, Babby Mettlin's knowledge of the ballad, and its few modernisms, are explained."[1] As a matter of fact, *Auld Maitland* is very much the same sort of thing as *The Outlaw Murray*, a really old ballad which has suffered from keeping bad company. Child's words about the one apply with some modification to the other: "The story gained a place in oral tradition...and I prefer to err by including rather than by excluding." He included *The Outlaw Murray*, and it is to be regretted that he finally excluded *Auld Maitland*.

[1] *Sir Walter Scott and the Border Minstrelsy*, p. 49.

(b) OTTERBURN.

Hogg seems to have taken a great deal of trouble over *Otterburn*. Scott had used Herd's version in the first edition of the *Minstrelsy*, but he was not very well satisfied with it, and for the second edition he was trying to find a better and more complete version. That which he received from Hogg differed from Herd's considerably. There is a letter from Scott to Laidlaw in the *Notanda*[1], acknowledging the receipt of several ballads and continuing, "I am so anxious to have a complete Scottish *Otterburn*, that I will omit the ballad entirely in the first volume, hoping to recover it in time for insertion in the third." Hogg's letter containing the ballad must have arrived almost immediately afterwards, in time for *Otterburn* to keep its place. The letter itself throws so much light on Hogg's method of collecting and dealing with his material that it deserves quoting in full, as Lang quoted it in *Sir Walter Scott and the Border Minstrelsy*[2]:

Ettrick House, Sept. 10.

Dear Sir,—Though I have used all diligence in my power to recover the old song about which you seemed anxious, I am afraid it will arrive too late to be of any use. I cannot at this time have Grame and Bewick; the only person who hath it being absent at a harvest; and as for the scraps of Otterburn which you

[1] Pp. 126–7. Undated, and from the mention in it of "the Tushilaw lines" Lang supposed that it was written in Dec. 1802 or Jan. 1803; Hogg sent these lines on January 7th, 1803. But *The Laird of Logie* and *The Border Widow*, acknowledged in Scott's letter, were received in September 1802. Hogg had offered to send *Graham and Bewick* on June 30th, 1802, and his *Otterburn* letter, which refers again to it, may well have been sent in September 1802. "1805" in Lang's dating of Hogg's letter is probably a misprint for 1803, but there is much more reason for putting it in 1802.

[2] Pp. 79–80.

have got, they seem to have been some confused jumble made by some person who had learned both the songs you have[1], and in time had been straitened to make one out of them both. But you shall have it as I had it, saving that, as usual, I have sometimes helped the metre without altering one original word.

That is a frank confession which accounts for the excellence of most of the ballads which Hogg sent to Scott. Then follow in the letter stanzas 1–24, and then:

The ballad, which I have collected from two different people, a crazy old man[2] and a woman deranged in her mind, seems hitherto considerably entire; but now, when it becomes most interesting, they have both failed me, and I have been obliged to take much of it in plain prose. However, as none of them seemed to know anything of the history save what they had learned from the song, I took it the more kindly. Any few verses which follow are to me unintelligible.

He told Sir Hugh that he was dying, and ordered him to conceal his body, and neither let his own men nor Piercy's know; which he did, and the battle went on headed by Sir Hugh Montgomery, and at length—

Here follow stanzas 35–38 ("But I will yield to Lord Douglas, Or Sir Hugh Montgomery"), on which Hogg comments:

Piercy seems to have been fighting devilishly in the dark. Indeed my narrators added no more, but told me that Sir Hugh died on the field, but that

> He left not an Englishman on the field,
>
> . . . .
>
> That he hadna either killed or ta'en
> Ere his heart's blood was cauld.

Almonshire (Stanza iii) may probably be a corruption of Bamburghshire, but as both my narrators called it so I thought

1 *The Hunting of the Cheviot* and Herd's *Otterburn* (Lang).

2 Lang suggests that this may have been the half-daft John Scott who first recited *Tam o' Shanter* to Hogg, v. *Autobiography*, p. 444.

proper to preserve it[1]. The towers in Roxburgh fells (Stanza iii) may not be so improper as we were thinking, there may have been some strength[2] on the very borders.—I remain, Dear Sir, your most faithful and affectionate servant, JAMES HOGG.

Not being able to get the letter away to the post, I have taken the opportunity of again pumping my old friend's memory, and have recovered some more lines and half lines of Otterburn, of which I am becoming somewhat enamoured. These I have been obliged to arrange somewhat myself, as you will see below, but so mixed are they with original lines and sentences that I think, if you pleased, they might pass without any acknowledgement. Sure no man will like an old song the worse of being somewhat harmonious. After stanza xxiv. you may read stanzas xxv. to xxxiv. Then after xxxviii. read xxxix.

Child prints these stanzas accordingly within brackets. How much of them is Hogg's it is impossible to make out; he himself would probably have found it difficult to say. He has been accused of making stanzas 8 and 9 as well, but there is not much evidence in support of the accusation, and the verses are bad enough to be genuine. What is noteworthy is again Hogg's honesty in putting down what he heard, however unintelligible to him, and his frankness in declaring his own work. Colonel Fitzwilliam Elliot would have it that in *Auld Maitland* this frankness is the deepest guile and designed to conceal thorough-going forgery[3], but when the same thing appears so frequently—in *The Outlaw Murray* and *Otterburn*, where Hogg's statements can be verified, as well as in *Auld Maitland*, where they have mostly to be taken on trust or rejected without further evidence—the presumption is that he spoke the truth.

[1] Scott changed it to Bambroughshire, but Lang considers that it may have been a corruption of Alnwickshire. It may be so, if the term Alnwickshire was ever used. Professor W. P. Ker suggested to me in conversation that it might be connected with Almund, an earlier form of Almouth. That is possible etymologically, but again definite evidence of use is wanting.

[2] I.e. English strength, as Lang points out. Scott changed Roxburgh to Reidswire.

[3] *Further Essays*, pp. 225–6.

BIBLIOGRAPHY

The Mistakes of a Night. Unsigned. *Scots Magazine*, vol. LVI, Oct. 1794, p. 624.

Never reprinted.

SCOTTISH / PASTORALS, / POEMS, SONGS, ETC. / Mostly written in the / Dialect of the South. / By James Hogg. / Edinburgh: / Printed by John Taylor, Grassmarket. / 1801. / Price One Shilling. 8vo, pp. 62.

Contents:

Geordie Fa's Dirge.
Dusty; or Watie and Geordie's Review of Politics.
Willie an' Keatie.
A Dialogue in a country Church Yard.
The Death of Sir Niel Stuart and Donald M'Vane, Esq.
Song I.
Song II.

Song II was reprinted as The Constant Shepherd and ascribed to Burns in Seventeen Songs by Robert Burns.... Glasgow, 1809.

No others reprinted.

Sandy Tod, A Scottish Pastoral. To a Lady. Signed, A Shepherd. *Edinburgh Magazine*, New Series, vol. XIX, May 1802, pp. 368–70.

Reprinted in The Mountain Bard.

A Journey through the Highlands of Scotland in the months of July and August 1802, in a Series of Letters to ——, Esq. *Scots Magazine*, vol. LXIV, Oct. 1802, pp. 813–8; Dec., pp. 956–63; vol. LXV, Feb. 1803, pp. 89–95; April, pp. 251–4; May, pp. 312–4; June, pp. 382–6.

The first has an introductory letter signed S. W. The last is signed, "The Ettrick Shepherd. (To be continued.)"

Never reprinted.

A Song. (By a Bush.) Signed, A Shepherd. *Edinburgh Magazine*, New Series, vol. XXI, Jan. 1803, pp. 52–3.

Reprinted in The Forest Minstrel.

Bonny Jean. By a Scots Shepherd. *Scots Magazine*, vol. LXV, May 1803, p. 339.

Reprinted in The Mountain Bard, 1807, afterwards transferred to The Forest Minstrel. In this version there is an extra stanza, afterwards omitted, between the first and second.

Blythe an' Cheerie. Signed, A. Shepherd. *Scots Magazine*, vol. LXV, July 1803, pp. 479–80.

Reprinted with omission of refrain and verbal changes as On Ettrick Clear in The Forest Minstrel.

Scotia's Glens. A Song. By James Hogg. *Scots Magazine*, vol. LXV, Oct. 1803, p. 725.

Reprinted in The Mountain Bard, 1807, afterwards transferred to The Forest Minstrel.

Auld Ettrick John. A Scottish Ballad. Signed, A Shepherd. *Scots Magazine*, vol. LXVI, March 1804, p. 217.

Reprinted in The Mountain Bard, 1807, afterwards transferred to The Forest Minstrel; verbal changes in later appearances.

Jamie's Farewell to Ettrick. Signed, A Shepherd. *Scots Magazine*, vol. LXVI, May 1804, p. 377.

Reprinted with considerable changes in The Mountain Bard.

The Death of Douglas, Lord of Liddesdale; a Scottish Ballad, in Imitation of the Ancients. By James Hogg, the Ettrick Shepherd. *Scots Magazine*, vol. LXVI, May 1804, pp. 378–9.

The "old" stanzas are printed in italics; they are 2, the first half of 3, 10, 11, 12, first half of 14, 15. The end is different from the later version—the lady dies.

Reprinted in The Mountain Bard with considerable changes.

Song for the Earl of Dalkeith's Birthday. Written by James Hogg. *Scots Magazine*, vol. LXVI, July 1804, pp. 533–4.

Reprinted in The Forest Minstrel as Hap an' rowe the feetie o't.

The Bonnets o' Bonny Dundee. By the same . . . . p. 534.

Reprinted in The Mountain Bard, 1807, afterwards transferred to The Forest Minstrel.

The Pedlar. A Scottish Ballad in Imitation of the Ancients. By James Hogg. *Scots Magazine*, vol. LXVI, Nov. 1804, pp. 855–6.

First version, without discovery of the murderer.

Reprinted with changes in The Mountain Bard.

The Haymaking. By J. Hogg. *Scots Magazine*, vol. LXVII, Jan. 1805, p. 56.

Reprinted with verbal changes in The Mountain Bard, afterwards transferred to The Forest Minstrel.

Love Abused. Signed, A Shepherd. *Scots Magazine*, vol. LXVII, April 1805, p. 295.

Reprinted with changes in The Mountain Bard, 1807, afterwards transferred to The Forest Minstrel.

Bauldy Fraser's Description of the battle of Culloden. Signed, A Shepherd . . . . p. 295.
Lowland version, with extra final stanza.
Reprinted in The Forest Minstrel.

Letters on Poetry, by the Ettrick Shepherd. Forwarded by S. L. *Scots Magazine*, vol. LXVII, May 1805, pp. 352–4; vol. LXVIII, Jan. 1806, pp. 17–20.
Never reprinted.

To Mr T. M. C., London. Signed, A Shepherd. *Scots Magazine*, Vol. LXVII, Aug. 1805, pp. 621–2.
Reprinted in The Mountain Bard, 1807 and 1840.

Journal of an Excursion into the Counties of Stirling, Perth, and Kinross. Signed, H. *Scots Magazine*, vol. LXVII, Sept. 1805, pp. 664–8; Oct., pp. 757–60; Nov., pp. 835–8.
Never reprinted.

Sir David Graham. A Border Ballad. Signed, A Shepherd . . . . pp. 701–3. First version. Reprinted in The Mountain Bard, 1807.

The Drinkin' O. A Sang for the Edinburgh Ladies. Signed, A Shepherd. *Scots Magazine*, vol. LXVII, Nov. 1805, p. 864.
Reprinted in The Forest Minstrel.

A Shepherd's Address to his auld Dog Hector. Signed, A Shepherd. *Scots Magazine*, vol. LXVII, Dec. 1805, pp. 943–4.
Reprinted with changes in The Mountain Bard.

Jock an' Samuel. A Scots Pastoral. Signed, A Shepherd. *Scots Magazine*, vol. LXVIII, Jan. 1806, pp. 53–5.
Never reprinted.

Mary's Lament. Signed, A Shepherd . . . . p. 55.
Reprinted as Mary at her Lover's Grave in The Forest Minstrel.

THE / SHEPHERD'S GUIDE: / being / a Practical Treatise / on / the Diseases of Sheep, / Their Causes, and the Best Means of / Preventing Them; / with observations on / the most suitable farm-stocking / for the various climates of this country. / By / James Hogg, / the Ettrick Shepherd. / Edinburgh: / Printed by J. Ballantyne and Co. / for Archibald Constable and Co. Edinburgh; and / John Murray, 32, Fleet-street, London. / 1807. / 8vo, pp. vi, 338.
(Dedication) To / Brigadier General Dirom / of Mount Annan; / as a small testimony of esteem / for a gentleman who has the welfare and / improvement of his country / so much at heart, / the following treatise is respectfully / inscribed by his obliged / humble servant, / The Author.
Never reprinted.

THE / MOUNTAIN BARD; / consisting of / Ballads and Songs, / founded on / Facts and Legendary Tales. / By / James Hogg, / the Ettrick Shepherd. /

> Fain would I hear our mountains ring
> With blasts which former minstrels blew;
> Drive slumber hence on viewless wing,
> And tales of other times renew.

Edinburgh: / Printed by J. Ballantyne and Co. / for Arch. Constable and Co. Edinburgh, / and John Murray, London. / 1807. 12mo, pp. (8) xxiii, 202.

(Dedication) To / Walter Scott, Esq. / Sheriff of Ettrick Forest, / and / Minstrel of the Scottish Border, / the following / Tales / are respectfully inscribed / by his friend and humble servant, / The Author.

Contents:

Memoir of the Life of James Hogg (in the form of a letter to Scott, dated Mitchell-Slack, Nov. 1806, preceded by a note written by Scott)

Sir David Graeme (first version).
The Pedlar (first version).
Gilmanscleuch.
The Fray of Elibank.
Mess John.
The Death of Douglas.
Willie Wilkin.
Thirlestane.
Lord Derwent.
The Laird of Lairistan.
Sandy Tod.
Farewell to Ettrick.
Love Abused.
Epistle to Mr T. M. C., London.
Scotia's Glens.
Donald MacDonald.
The Author's Address to his auld dog Hector.
The Bonnets o' Bonny Dundee.
Auld Ettrick John.
The Haymaking.
Bonny Jean.

THE / MOUNTAIN BARD; / consisting of / Legendary Ballads and Tales. / By James Hogg, / the Ettrick Shepherd. / The third edition, greatly enlarged. / To which is prefixed / A Memoir of the Author's Life, / written by himself. / Edinburgh; / Oliver and Boyd, High-street: / sold also by / G. and W. B. Whittaker, Ave-Maria Lane, London; /and William Turnbull, Glasgow. / 1821.

12mo, pp. lxxvii, 350.

Dedication as before, with addition at foot, "Mitchelslack, Sept. 27, 1807."

Contents:

Memoir (much enlarged).
Sir David Graeme (second version).
The Pedlar (second version).
Gilmanscleuch.
The Fray of Elibank.
Mess John.
The Death of Douglas.
Willie Wilkin.
Thirlestane.
Lord Derwent.
The Laird of Lairistan.
The Wife of Crowle.
The Lairde of Kirkmabreeke.
The Tweeddale Raide (by Robert Hogg).
Robin an' Nanny.
Sandy Tod.
Farewell to Ettrick.
The Author's Address to his auld dog Hector.

The Mountain Bard was not included in the Poetical Works of 1822. In the edition of 1838–40 it has the form of 1821, with the exception of The Lairde of Kirkmabreeke and the addition of May of the Moril Glen. The Lairde of Kirkmabreeke was never reprinted.

THE / MOUNTAIN BARD, / AND / FOREST MINSTREL; / consisting of / Legendary Poems and Songs. / By James Hogg, / the Ettrick Shepherd. / Glasgow: / Published by George Love, / Nelson Street. / 1840.

24to, pp. 192.

The Mountain Bard ends at p. 130. No dedication or memoir. The text is that of 1807, but the contents agree with 1821, with the exception of The Tweeddale Raide and May of the Moril Glen, and the inclusion of the Epistle to Mr T. M. C.

Verses on the Earl of Dalkeith's Birthday. By the Ettrick Shepherd. *Scots Magazine*, vol. LXIX, Aug. 1807, p. 607.

Reprinted in The Forest Minstrel as Highland Harry back again.

The Bonny Lass of Deloraine. By the Ettrick Shepherd.... pp. 607–8.

Reprinted in The Forest Minstrel.

The Delight of Prince Owen Kyveliog. By the Ettrick Shepherd. *Scots Magazine*, vol. LXIX, Sept. 1807, p. 688.

Reprinted with repetitions as Prince Owen and the Seer in The Forest Minstrel.

The Braes of Bushby. By the Ettrick Shepherd. *Scots Magazine*, vol. LXIX, Oct. 1807, p. 768.

Reprinted in The Forest Minstrel.

An Evening Hymn. By the Ettrick Shepherd. *Scots Magazine*, vol. LXX, May 1808, p. 365.

Never reprinted.

A Journey through the Highlands and Western Isles, in the Summer of 1804.—In a Series of Letters to a Friend. By the Ettrick Shepherd. *Scots Magazine*, vol. LXX, June 1808, pp. 423–6; Aug., pp. 569–72; Sept., pp. 672–4; Oct., pp. 735–8; Nov., pp. 809–11; Dec., pp. 889–92; vol. LXXI, Jan. 1809, pp. 14–17; Feb., pp. 99–101; March, pp. 181–4.

Never reprinted.

The Guardian Angel. By the Ettrick Shepherd. *Scots Magazine*, vol. LXX, Oct. 1808, pp. 766–7.

Reprinted in The Forest Minstrel.

Epitaphs on Living Characters. By the Ettrick Shepherd. *Scots Magazine*, vol. LXXII, June 1810, p. 447.

Never reprinted.

(THE FOREST MINSTREL; a Selection of Songs, adapted to the most favourite Scottish Airs; few of them ever before published. By James Hogg, the Ettrick Shepherd, and Others. Small 8vo. 5s. Constable and Co.)

Title from review in *Scots Magazine*, vol. LXXII, Aug. 1810, pp. 604–9. *Vide*. pp. 63–4 here.

THE / MOUNTAIN BARD, / AND / FOREST MINSTREL; / consisting of Legendary Poems and Songs. / By James Hogg, / the Ettrick Shepherd. / Glasgow: / Published by George Love, / Nelson Street. / 1840.

24to, pp. 192.

The Forest Minstrel begins at p. 131

Contents:

The Soldier's Widow. The Flower. The moon was a-waning.	} Pathetic Songs.

Mary at her Lover's Grave.	Pathetic Songs.
Bonny Dundee.	
My Peggy an' I.	
The Minstrel Boy.	
The Gloamin'.	
Lord Eglinton's auld man.	
The Guardian Angel.	
Cauld is the Blast.	
The Skylark.	
Bonny Mary.	Love Songs.
My blythe an' bonny lassie.	
The Braes of Bushby.	
Blythe an' Cheerie.	
To Miss Jane S——f (I wasna sae soon to my bed).	
I hae lost my Jeanie, O.	
I'm gane a' wrang, Jamie.	
The Bonny Lass of Deloraine.	
Here fix'd by choice.	
The Bogles.	
The Haymakers.	
Bonny Jean.	
Bonny Leezy.	
Now well may I.	
The Sheep Shearing.	
How foolish are mankind.	
My dear little Jeanie.	
When the kye come hame.	
O Jeanie, there's naething to fear ye.	
Doctor Monro.	Humorous Songs.
Love's like a Dizziness.	
Auld Ettrick John.	
The Drinkin' O.	
Jack and his Mother.	
Willie Wastle.	
When Maggy gangs away.	
Auld John Borthick.	
Scotia's Glens.	National Songs.
The Jubilee.	
My Native Isle.	
Highland Harry back again.	
Hap an' rowe the feetie.	
Born, laddie.	

By a Bush.
The Emigrant.
Honest Duncan.
Prince Owen and the Seer.
The Wee House.
} National Songs.

THE SPY. / A Periodical Paper, / of / Literary Amusement and Instruction. / Published Weekly, / in / 1810 and 1811. / Edinburgh: / Printed for the Proprietors and Sold by Archibald Constable & Co. Edinburgh, / and by all the principal booksellers. / 1811.

4to, pp. (2) iv, 1–183, 148–384, 335–416.

There are two mistakes in the numbering of the pages. The following are Hogg's contributions, as far as they can be ascertained. Owing to the confusion in the numbering of the pages, the numbers of the papers are given. Items marked * were never reprinted.

No. I. Introductory.

No. II. *The Scottish Muses, Continued in Nos. V and X.
*Epitaphs on Living Characters.

No. III. On Instability in one's calling. Continued in No. IV.
Revised and reprinted as Basil Lee in Winter Evening Tales.

No. V. Epitaphs on Living Characters. (Whose headstone is this that's so fretted and airy.)
Reprinted in 1822, in *Edinburgh Literary Journal*, vol. VI, p. 273, and in 1838–40.

No. VI. *Life of a Profligate Student—Two Living Characters drawn in his Parents. Continued in Nos. VIII, IX, XI.

No. VII. The Fall of the Leaf.
Reprinted in 1822.

No. X. A Fragment—Lord Huntley's sheets were like the milk.
Reprinted in 1822.
Epitaph on a Living Character (Warrior, when the battle's o'er).
Reprinted in 1822.

No. XII. *John Miller the Shepherd.
A Peasant's Funeral.
Reprinted in Winter Evening Tales.
Poor little Jessy. A Scottish Song, by John Miller.
Reprinted in 1838–40.

A Fragment.
Reprinted as The Wife of Crowle in The Mountain Bard, 1821.

No. XIII. *John Miller on the Play and Actors.
Letter on the death of Major Macpherson
Reprinted in Winter Evening Tales.

No. XIV. The Dawn of July, 1810.
Reprinted in 1822.
Scotch Song—What gars the parting day-beam blush.
Reprinted in 1822.

No. XV. Scotch Song—Mischievous Woman.
Reprinted in Friendship's Offering, 1830, and in 1838–40.

No. XVI. Autobiography of the Spy.
Expanded into The Love Adventures of Mr George Cochrane, in Winter Evening Tales.

No. XVII. Story of Two Highlanders.
Reprinted in Winter Evening Tales.
*Maria, A Highland Legend.

No. XVIII. Story of the Ghost of Lochmaben. By John Miller.
Reprinted in Winter Evening Tales.

No. XX. King Edward's Dream.
Reprinted as the 15th bard's song in The Queen's Wake.

No. XXII. *The Country Girl.
Will and Davy. A Scotch Pastoral.
Reprinted in 1822.

No. XXIII. *The Twa Craws.

No. XXIV. The Country Laird. A Tale by John Miller.
Continued in Nos. XXV and XXVI.
Revised and reprinted as The Woolgatherer in 1818.
The Battle of Busaco.
Reprinted in 1822.

No. XXVII. *Glencoe.

No. XXVIII. *Story of Helen Maxwell (Melvile).

No. XXIX. The Auld Man's Farewell to his Little House.
Revised and reprinted in 1822.

No. XXX. The Lady's Dream.
Reprinted in 1822.

No. XXXI. Border Song (Lock the door, Lariston).
Reprinted in 1822.

No. XXXV. Love of Fame.
Reprinted as Adam Bell in Winter Evening Tales.
No. XXXVI. The bittern's quavering trump on high.
Reprinted in 1822.
? *The Harper of Mull.
No. XXXVII. *Belief in Providence.
Scottish Song (Ah Peggy! since thou'rt gane away).
Reprinted in 1822.
No. XXXVIII. *The Scots Tutor. Continued in Nos. XLII and XLVI.
Morning.
Reprinted in 1822.
No. XXXIX. Elegy. (Fair was thy blossom.)
Reprinted in *Blackwood's*, vol. II, p. 47, and in 1822.
No. XL. Malise's Tour. Continued in No. XLIV.
Reprinted as Highland Adventures in Winter Evening Tales.
Macgregor. A Highland Tale.
Reprinted as the 11th Bard's song in The Queen's Wake.
No. XLI. *Story of the youth who might not marry until he was twenty-eight.
No. XLIII. Regret.
Reprinted in 1822.
No. XLIV. The Admonition.
Reprinted in 1822.
No. XLV. *Jessy Murray and Elen Inglis.
No. XLVIII. *Antient Fragment, Copied from an old MS book in the possession of Adam Hunter, Esq.
No. XLIX. Duncan Campbell. Continued in No. LI.
Reprinted in Winter Evening Tales.
Hymn to the Evening Star.
Reprinted in 1822.
No. L.? *On the advantages of literary societies.
No. LII. *Farewell paper.
Alas! alas! the time draws nigh. Reprinted as To Mary at Parting, in 1822.

The History of Rose Selby. By the Ettrick Shepherd. *Scots Magazine*, vol. LXXIV, March 1812, pp. 179–83.
Never reprinted.
Love Pastoral . . . . p. 216.
Never reprinted.

The / Queen's Wake: / a / Legendary Poem. / By / James Hogg. /

> Be mine to read the visions old,
> Which thy awakening Bards have told,
> And whilst they meet thy tranced view,
> Hold each strange tale devoutly true.
>
> Collins.

Edinburgh: / Printed by Andrew Balfour, / for George Goldie, 34, Prince's Street, Edinburgh; / and / Longman, Hurst, Rees, Orme, and Brown, / London. / 1813. 8vo, pp. (8) 354.

(Dedication) To / Her Royal Highness / Princess Charlotte of Wales, / a Shepherd / among / the Mountains of Scotland, / dedicates / This Poem.

The remaining copies were re-issued with a fresh title-page as the Second Edition, with the poem by Bernard Barton, also in later editions, added.

Third Edition in 1814.

Fourth (really remains of third) Edition in 1815.

. . .Fifth Edition / Edinburgh; / William Blackwood, Prince's street: / and John Murray, Albemarle-street, London. / 1819. 8vo, pp. (8) 384.

With portrait of Queen Mary. Subscription edition.

Sixth edition, in form a duplicate of the fifth, 1819.

The / Queen's Wake: / a / Legendary Poem. / By / James Hogg, / the Ettrick Shepherd. / (Motto as above) Edinburgh: Thomas Nelson. / MDCCC.XLII.

16mo, pp. 236.

The Queen's Wake / a / Legendary Poem. / By James Hogg. / (Motto) / William and Robert Chambers / London and Edinburgh. (1867) 16mo, pp. 188.

Portrait of Hogg and 13-page memoir.

Blackie's School Classics. / Selections / from / The Queen's Wake. / By / James Hogg, the Ettrick Shepherd. / The Summons, The Contest, The Award. / Kilmeny. / With Prefatory and Explanatory Notes. . . . 1880. 16mo, pp. 32.

Kilmeny has also been printed as No. 9 of the London Booklets (Foulis, 1912) with illustrations by Jessie M. King; and as No. 33 of Flowers of Parnassus (John Lane, 1905) with illustrations by Mary Corbett.

The / Hunting of Badlewe, / a / Dramatic Tale. / By / J. H. Craig, of Douglas, Esq. / London: / Printed for Henry Colburn, 50, Conduit Street, / and / George Goldie, 34, Prince's Street, / Edinburgh. / 1814. 8vo, pp. (2) viii, 132.

(Dedication) To / John Wilson, Esq. / author of The Isle of Palms, &c. &c. / as a small testimony of esteem / for native genius, / A Stranger / respectfully inscribes / the following / dramatic poem.

Reprinted as The Profligate Princes in Dramatic Tales.

Tam Wilson. By the Ettrick Shepherd. *Scots Magazine*, vol. LXXVI, April 1814, p. 296.

Reprinted as Tam Nelson in *Blackwood's*, vol. XX, Oct. 1826. Not again reprinted.

THE / PILGRIMS OF THE SUN; / a Poem. / By James Hogg, / author of The Queen's Wake, &c.

A Pupil in the many chambered school
Where Superstition weaves her airy dreams.
Wordsworth.

Edinburgh: / Printed for William Blackwood, South Bridge / Street; / and sold by J. Murray, London. / 1815. 8vo, pp. (12) 148.

Contents:

The Pilgrims of the Sun, Superstition.

Included in 1822.

THE / ETTRICKE GARLAND; / being / Two Excellent New Songs / on / The Lifting of the Banner / of the / House of Buccleuch, / at the great foot-ball match on Carterhaugh, / Dec. 4, 1815. / Edinburgh: / Printed by James Ballantyne and Co. / 1815.

8vo, pp. 8, with portrait of Scott at beginning and Hogg at end. To the Ancient Banner of the House of Buccleuch occupies pp. 6–8 and ends, "Quoth the Ettrick Shepherd. Altrive Lake, Dec. 1, 1815," which looks as if the poem anticipated its occasion. Scott's is also dated Dec. 1st.

The Ettricke Garland. *Scots Magazine*, vol. LXXVII, December 1815, pp. 935–6.

Both poems.

Hogg's reprinted in 1822.

THE / POETIC MIRROR, / or / The Living Bards of Britain. /

Mopsa.—Is it true think you?
Auti.—Very true, and but a month old.
Shakespeare.

London: / printed for Longman, Hurst, Rees, Orme, and Brown; / and John Ballantyne, Edinburgh, / 1816. 12mo, pp. vi, 276.

MADOR OF THE MOOR; / a Poem. / By James Hogg, / author of The Queen's Wake, &c.

Wild mirth of the desart! fit pastime for Kings,
Which still the rude Bard in his solitude sings. Wilson.

Edinburgh: / printed for William Blackwood: / and John Murray, Albermarle-street, London. / 1816. 8vo, pp. (8) 140.

DRAMATIC TALES; / by the / author of "The Poetic Mirror." / In two volumes. / Vol. I. (Vol. II.)

Turn in and taste this sharpe preparative
For our intended feaste; but no restraynt
Fetter thy free imaginatioune;
If it not likes thee, curse it, and walke forth.

Edinburgh: / Printed by James Ballantyne and Co. / For Longman, Hurst, Rees, Orme, and Brown, / London; and John Ballantyne, Hanover-street, / Edinburgh. / 1817. 12mo.

Vol. I, pp. (2) 274.

All-Hallow Eve.

Sir Anthony Moore.

Vol. II, pp. (2) 272.

The Profligate Princes.

The Haunted Glen.

The Haunted Glen was reprinted in 1822. The others have never been reprinted.

Tales and Anecdotes of the Pastoral Life. No. I. Signed H. *Blackwood's Magazine*, vol. I, April 1817, pp. 22–5; No. II in May, pp. 143–7; No. III in June, pp. 247–50.

No. I never reprinted. Nos. II and III reprinted as A Country Wedding in Winter Evening Tales.

Verses. Recited by the Author, in a Party of his Countrymen, on the Day that the News arrived of our final Victory over the French. Signed H. (Now, Britain, let thy cliffs o' snaw) . . . . p. 72.

Reprinted in 1822.

A Last Adieu. Signed H. *Blackwood's Magazine*, vol. I, May 1817, p. 169.

Reprinted in 1822.

Elegy by the Ettrick Shepherd. (Fair was thy blossom.) *Blackwood's Magazine*, vol. II, Oct. 1817, p. 47.

Reprinted in 1822.

Translation from an Ancient Chaldee Manuscript . . . . pp. 89–96.

Only in part by Hogg, v. pp. 94–5 here.

Not reprinted in Hogg's works.

A Hebrew Melody. By the Ettrick Shepherd. *Blackwood's Magazine*, vol. II, Jan. 1818, p. 400.

Reprinted in 1822.

Sonnet to the Publisher. *Blackwood's Magazine*, vol. II, March 1818, on inserted leaf before first article of magazine.

Of very doubtful authenticity, v. p. 97 here.

Never reprinted.

Further Anecdotes of the Shepherd's Dog. Letter, signed James Hogg. . . . pp. 621–6.

Reprinted with slight changes in The Shepherd's Calendar.

On Carmel's Brow. A Hebrew Melody, by the Ettrick Shepherd. *Blackwood's Magazine*, vol. III, April 1818, p. 90.

Reprinted in 1822.

To the Editor of the Glasgow Chronicle. 4to, p. 1.

Reprinted from the Glasgow Chronicle. A Letter confirming one written by William Blackwood, dated 13th May, 1818.

Never reprinted.

Verses, addressed to the Right Hon. Lady Anne Scott of Buccleuch. Signed J. H. *Blackwood's Magazine*, vol. IV, Oct. 1818, pp. 74–6.

Dedication to The Brownie of Bodsbeck.

Reprinted in 1822.

The / Long Pack. / A / Northumbrian Tale, / An Hundred Years old. /

In winter nights, when gossips old,
With youthful list'ners draw around the fire,
Who 'tentive hear the legend told,
Of some fell waugh of an old murther'd sire,
'Tis then in anxious hope and fear,
The pelting hail is dreaded as a sprite;
And, cruddling round, their youthful ear
Marks to the memory a tale of some poor hapless wight.

Printed for / John Bell / on the Quay, / Newcastle. / MDCCCXVII. 12mo, pp. 24.

Reprinted in Winter Evening Tales, and separately.

The / Long Pack. / An interesting / Northumberland Tale, / for / a Winter's Evening. / (Verse) Newcastle upon Tyne: / Printed by William Hall, / in the Groat Market. / 1818. 12mo, pp. 24.

The / Long Pack; / or, the / Robbers Discovered: / A Scottish Story. / By the Ettrick Shepherd. / (Cut) / Glasgow: / Printed for the Booksellers. 24.

No date. 12mo, pp. 24.

The / Long Pack. / (Cut) / Newcastle-on-Tyne: / Bowman, Publisher, Nuns' Lane.

No date. 12mo, pp. 24.

THE HISTORY / OF THE LONG PACK: / A NORTHUMBERLAND LEGEND. / By the Ettrick Shepherd. / Newcastle-on-Tyne: / T. Arthur, Percy St.; A. Everatt, Newgate St. / Sunderland: T. Huntley. / And all booksellers. No date. 8vo, pp. 16.

Olde ffrendes / wyth / newe Faces. / Adorn'd with sutable SCVLPTVRES. / CIↃ.IↃ.CCC.LXXXIII / London: / Field & Tuer. Simpkin, Marshall & Co. / Hamilton, Adams & Co. / New York: Scribner & Welford. 8vo.

No. III is The / Long Pack: / A Northumbrian Tale / about / an Hundred & Sixty Year / OLD.

THE / BROWNIE OF BODSBECK; / AND / OTHER TALES. / By / James Hogg, / author of "The Queen's Wake," &c. &c. / "What, has this thing appeared again to-night?" / In two volumes. / Vol. I (vol. II) / Edinburgh; / printed for William Blackwood, Prince's-street: / and / John Murray, Albemarle-street, London. / 1818. 12mo.

Vol. I, pp. (2) xii, 296.

Verses addressed to the Right Hon. Lady Anne Scott of Buccleuch.

The Brownie of Bodsbeck.

Vol. II, pp. (4) 346.

The Woolgatherer.

The Hunt of Eildon.

Verses reprinted in *Blackwood's*, vol. IV, Oct. 1818, pp. 74–6, and in 1822.

All the stories reprinted in 1837.

Selkirkshire Edition. / THE / BROWNIE OF BODSBECK / by / the Ettrick Shepherd / with preface by the / Rev. R. Borland, F.S.A. / Revised and edited by George Lewis. / Illustrated. / Selkirk: James Lewis, 13 High Street / 1903.

8vo, pp. (4) ix, 262.

Spelling revised to agree with Ettrick pronunciation.

(The Border Garland, containing Nine New Songs by James Hogg; the Music partly old, partly composed by himself and friends, and arranged with Symphonies and Accompaniments for the Piano Forte, No. 1. 3s.—Advertisement in *Blackwood's Magazine*, vol. V, May 1819.)

THE / JACOBITE RELICS / OF / SCOTLAND; / being / the Songs, Airs, and Legends, / of the / Adherents to the House of Stuart. / Collected and illustrated / by / James Hogg, / author of "The Queen's Wake," &c. &c. / Edinburgh: / Printed for William Blackwood, Prince's Street; / and / T. Cadell and W. Davies, Strand, London. / MDCCCXIX. 8vo, pp. xx, 424.

THE / JACOBITE RELICS....Second Series. / Edinburgh: / Printed for William Blackwood, Prince's Street: / and / T. Cadell and W. Davies, Strand, London. / MDCCCXXI. 8vo, pp. viii, 480.

The / Jacobite Relics....Reprinted from the Original Edition (First and Second Series) Paisley: Alex. Gardner. / 1874.

The Shepherd's Calendar. Storms. Signed James Hogg. *Blackwood's Magazine*, vol. V, April 1819, pp. 75–81; May, pp. 210–6.
Reprinted in 1837.

The Mermaid. A Scottish Ballad. By James Hogg. *Scots Magazine*, New Series, vol. IV, May 1819, pp. 400–1.
Reprinted in 1822.

Stanzas addressed to a Comet. A Night Piece. By James Hogg. *Scots Magazine*, New Series, vol. V, July 1819, p. 30.
Reprinted in 1822.

(The Song to a Salmon and Tent verses, which appeared in *Blackwood's*, vol. V, Aug. and Sept. 1819, pp. 610 and 640, are not Hogg's.)

Letter from the Ettrick Shepherd. *Blackwood's Magazine*, vol. VI, Jan. 1820, pp. 390–3.

Sonnet, by the Ettrick Shepherd; addressed to Christopher North, Esq....p. 464.
Both probably spurious, v. p. 97 here.
Never reprinted.

Letter from the Ettrick Shepherd, enclosing one from James Laidlaw. *Blackwood's Magazine*, vol. VI, March 1820, pp. 630–1.
Part ("Cow Wat") printed in Mrs Oliphant's William Blackwood and his Sons, vol. I, pp. 327–9, with some verbal differences. Not elsewhere reprinted.

Letter from James Hogg to his (Edinburgh) Reviewer. *Blackwood's Magazine*, vol. VIII, Oct. 1820, pp. 67–75. Followed by

Letter to Christopher North, pp. 75–6.
Never reprinted. It owns the authorship of Donald M'Gillavry.

WINTER EVENING TALES, / collected among / the Cottagers / in the / South of Scotland. / By James Hogg, / author of "The Queen's Wake," &c. &c. / In two volumes. / Vol. I. (Vol. II.) /

"In rangles round afore the ingle's lowe,
Frae Gudame's mouth auld-warld Tales they hear,
O' Warlocks loupin' round the Wirrikow,
O' Ghaists that won in glen and kirk-yard drear,
Whilk touzles a' their tap, an' gars them shake wi' fear."

— *Fergusson*. / Edinburgh; / printed for Oliver and Boyd, High-street; and / G. & W. B. Whittaker, Ave-Maria-Lane, / London. / 1820. 12mo.

Vol. I, pp. (4) 340.

The Renowned Adventures of Basil Lee.
Adam Bell.
Duncan Campbell.
An Old Soldier's Tale.
*Highland Adventures.
*Halbert of Lyne.
The Long Pack.
A Peasant's Funeral.
*Dreadful Story of Macpherson.
Story of Two Highlanders.
*Maria's Tale, written by herself.
*Singular Dream, by a correspondent.
*Love Adventures of Mr George Cochrane.
*Country Dreams and Apparitions. No. I. John Gray o' Middleholm.

Vol. II, pp. (4) 336.

The Bridal of Polmood.
*King Gregory.
The Shepherd's Calendar (Storms and Country Wedding).
Country Dreams and Apparitions. No. II. Connel of Dee.
No. III. The Wife of Lochmaben.
No. IV. Cousin Mattie.
No. V. Welldean Hall.
No. VI. Tibby Johnston's Wraith.

Connel of Dee was reprinted in 1822, the rest in 1837, with the exception of those marked *, which were never reprinted.

The History / of / Duncan Campbell / and his / Dog Oscar. / From Hogg's Evening Tales. / Glasgow: / Published and Sold, Wholesale and Retail by / Robert Hutchison, Bookseller, / No. 19, Saltmarket. / 1821. 12mo, pp. 24.

The History / of / Duncan Campbell, / and his / Dog, Oscar. / From Hogg's Evening Tales. / Glasgow: / Printed for the booksellers. / 1824. 12mo, pp. 24.

The Powris of Moseke, ane rychte plesant Ballaunt, maide by Maistere Jamis Hougge. *Scots Magazine*, New Series, vol. IX, Oct. 1821, pp. 356–61.

Reprinted in 1822.

Jacobite Relics, not published in Mr Hogg's Collection, *Scots*

Magazine, New Series, vol. IX, Nov. 1821, pp. 439–43; vol. X, Jan. 1822, pp. 49–52; April 1822, pp. 460–3.

Red Clan-Ronald's Men; reprinted in 1831.

A New Ballad; never reprinted.

The Farce; never reprinted.

The Two Men of Colston; reprinted in 1831.

Up and rin awa, Geordie; reprinted in 1831.

A New Ballad; never reprinted.

A Toast; never reprinted.

It is just possible that those which were not reprinted were not written by Hogg; v. pp. 41–2 here.

Cary O'Kean, A Poem. By James Hogg. *Scots Magazine*, New Series, vol. IX, Dec. 1821, pp. 575–81.

Reprinted in 1822.

O sairly may I rue the day. *Blackwood's Magazine*, vol. XII, Dec. 1822, *Noctes Ambrosianae*, VI, pp. 705–6.

This is Hogg's first appearance in the *Noctes*.

Reprinted as The Women Fo'k in 1831.

THE / POETICAL WORKS / OF / JAMES HOGG. / In four volumes. / (Vol. I) / Edinburgh: / Printed for Arch. Constable & Co. Edinburgh; / and Hurst, Robinson & Co. London. / 1822. 12mo.

Vol. I, pp. (6) 382.

The Queen's Wake.

Vol. II, pp. (6) 352.

Midsummer Night Dreams (v. p. 78 here).

Vol. III, pp. (8) 384.

The Poetic Mirror, Miscellanies, Songs.

Vol. IV, pp. viii, (6), 360.

Mador of the Moor, Sacred Melodies, Miscellaneous Poems, Songs.

All reprinted in 1838–40.

THE ROYAL JUBILEE. / A SCOTTISH MASK. / By the Ettrick Shepherd. / But I will sing a rantin' sang / That day our King comes o'er the Water. / Jacobite Relics. / William Blackwood, Edinburgh; and / T. Cadell, Strand, London. / MDCCCXXII. 8vo, pp. 42.

Never reprinted.

THE / THREE PERILS OF MAN; / or, / War, Women, and Witchcraft. / A Border Romance. / By James Hogg, / author of "Winter Evening Tales," "Brownie of / Bodsbeck," "Queen's Wake," &c. &c. / In three volumes. / (vol. I) / Beshrew me if I dare open it. / Fletcher. / London: / Longman, Hurst,

Rees, Orme and Brown, / Paternoster Row. / 1822. 12mo, vol. I, pp. (4) 342; vol. II, pp. 354; vol. III, pp. 450.

Revised and reprinted as The Siege of Roxburgh in 1837.

The Hon. Captain Napier and Ettrick Forest. An Ettrick Shepherd. *Blackwood's Magazine*, vol. XIII, Feb. 1823, pp. 175–88. Hogg in part, revised by one of his colleagues.

Never reprinted.

The Shepherd's Calendar. Class Second. Deaths, Judgments, and Providences. Unsigned. *Blackwood's Magazine*, vol. XIII, March 1823, pp. 311–20.

Reprinted in The Shepherd's Calendar, vol. I, ch. I.

On the Head of George Buchanan, *Noctes Ambrosianae*, VII, p. 384.

Never reprinted.

THE / THREE PERILS OF WOMAN; / or, / Love, Leasing, and Jealousy. / A Series of / Domestic Scottish Tales. / By James Hogg, / author of "The Three Perils of Man," / "Queen's Wake," &c. &c. / In three volumes. / (vol. I) /

The fam'ly sit beside the blaze,
But O, a seat is empty now!

John Gibson.

London: / Longman, Hurst, Rees, Orme, Brown, and Green, / Paternoster Row. / 1823. / 12mo, vol. I, pp. 336; vol. II, pp. 334; vol. III, pp. 374.

Never reprinted.

Les / Trois Ecueils / des Femmes; / roman traduit de l'anglais / Par M...., / Auteur de plusieurs ouvrages, et traducteur de / *l'Incendie de Moscou; les Bohémiens*, etc. / (Tome premier) / A Paris, / chez Haut-Coeur et Gayet, Libraires, / Rue Dauphine, No. 20. / 1825. 12mo, vol. I, pp. 226; vol. II, pp. 226; vol. III, pp. 240; vol. IV, pp. 208.

Les Trois Ecueils ends at p. 62 of vol. IV, the rest of which is taken up with three "nouvelles."

When the Kye come hame. *Blackwood's Magazine*, vol. XIII, May 1823, *Noctes Ambrosianae*, VIII, p. 598.

This version does not agree exactly either with that of The Three Perils of Man or with that of 1831.

The Shepherd's Calendar. Class Second. Deaths, Judgments, and Providences. Signed H. *Blackwood's Magazine*, vol. XIII, June 1823, pp. 629–40.

Reprinted in The Shepherd's Calendar, vol. I, ch. II.

A Scots Mummy. To Sir Christopher North. Signed James Hogg. *Blackwood's Magazine*, vol. XIV, Aug. 1823, pp. 188–90.

Reprinted almost verbatim in The Confessions of a Justified Sinner.

THE PRIVATE MEMOIRS / AND CONFESSIONS / OF A JUSTIFIED SINNER: / written by himself: / with a detail of curious traditionary facts, and / other evidence, by the editor. / London: / printed for Longman, Hurst, Rees, Orme, Brown, / and Green, Paternoster Row. / MDCCCXXIV. 8vo, pp. 390.

Facing title-page is facsimile of "original" of part of p. 366.

Reprinted as THE SUICIDE'S GRAVE and acknowledged by Hogg, 1828.

Reprinted with omissions and alterations as THE CONFESSIONS OF A FANATIC in 1837.

James Hogg. / THE SUICIDE'S GRAVE / BEING THE PRIVATE / MEMOIRS & CONFESSIONS / OF A JUSTIFIED SINNER / WRITTEN BY HIMSELF / with a detail of curious / traditionary facts / & other evidence / by the editor / Photogravures by R. Easton Stuart / London MDCCCXCV / J. SHIELS & Co. 8vo, pp. (6) 266.

7 Illustrations, one being the facsimile. The Publishers' Note, p. (3), gives the history of the book. The text is that of the first edition.

The Campion Reprints. No. I / THE PRIVATE MEMOIRS / AND CONFESSIONS OF / A JUSTIFIED SINNER / By James Hogg / With an Introduction by / T. Earle Welby / A. M. Philpot, Ltd. / 69 Great Russell Street / London: MDCCCCXXIV. 8vo, pp. 288.

Text of first edition.

The Shepherd's Calendar. Class IV. Dogs. Signed H. *Blackwood's Magazine*, vol. XV, Feb. 1824, pp. 177–83.

Reprinted in The Shepherd's Calendar, vol. II, ch. X.

The Shepherd's Calendar, Class V. The Lasses. Unsigned. *Blackwood's Magazine*, vol. XV, March 1824, pp. 296–304; vol. XVII, Feb. 1825, pp. 180–6.

Reprinted in The Shepherd's Calendar, vol. II, ch. I.

The Left-Handed Fiddler. By the Ettrick Shepherd. *Blackwood's Magazine*, vol. XVI, Nov. 1824, pp. 528–9.

Never reprinted.

New Christmas Carol. By the Ettrick Shepherd. *Blackwood's Magazine*, vol. XVI, Dec. 1824, p. 680.

Reprinted as The March of Intellect in 1838–40.

QUEEN HYNDE. / A Poem, / in six books. / By James Hogg, / author of The Queen's Wake; Poetic Mirror; / Pilgrims of the Sun, &c. &c. / London: / Printed for Longman, Hurst,

Rees, Orme, Brown, / and Green, Paternoster-row, London and / William Blackwood, Edinburgh. / M.DCCC.XXV. 8vo. pp. (4) 444.
Reprinted in 1838–40.

The Grousome Caryl. Ane most Treuthful Ballant, Compilit by Mr Hougge. *Blackwood's Magazine*, vol. XVII, Jan. 1825, pp. 78–85.
Reprinted in A Queer Book.

To O'Doherty, in Answer to Farewell.... *Noctes Ambrosianae*, XVIII, p. 120.
Reprinted in 1838–40.

Hymn to the Devil. *Blackwood's Magazine*, vol. XVII, March 1825, *Noctes Ambrosianae*, XIX, pp. 367–9.
From The Three Perils of Man; not again printed.

If e'er you would be a brave fellow.... pp. 383–4.
Reprinted in 1831 as The Blue and the Yellow.

The Laird o' Lamington. *Blackwood's Magazine*, vol. XVII, May 1825, *Noctes Ambrosianae*, XX, p. 620.
Reprinted in 1838–40.

Ringan and May. Ane richt mournfulle ditty, Maide be Mr Hougge. *Blackwood's Magazine*, vol. XVII, June 1825, pp. 712–4.
Reprinted in A Queer Book.

The Witch of the Gray Thorn. By James Hogg the Ettrick Shepherd.... pp. 714–6.
Reprinted in A Queer Book.

Some Passages in the Life of Colonel Cloud. In a Letter by the Ettrick Shepherd, to the Hon. Mrs H-r-y. *Blackwood's Magazine*, vol. XVIII, July 1825, pp. 32–40.
Never reprinted.

There's naught sae sweet. *Blackwood's Magazine*, vol. XVIII, Sept. 1825, *Noctes Ambrosianae*, XXI, pp. 391–2.
Never reprinted.

The Brakens wi' me. *Blackwood's Magazine*, vol. XVIII, Dec. 1825, *Noctes Ambrosianae*, XXIII, pp. 753–4.
Reprinted in 1831.

Rejoice, ye wan and wilder'd glens; Wat o' Buccleuch. *Blackwood's Magazine*, vol. XIX, Feb. 1826, *Noctes Ambrosianae*, XXIV, pp. 217–9.
Never reprinted.

The Great Muckle Village of Balmaquhapple; Meg o' Marley. *Blackwood's Magazine*, vol. XIX, June 1826, *Noctes Ambrosianae*, XXIV, pp. 739–40, 756.
Reprinted in 1831.

My Bonny Mary. *Blackwood's Magazine*, vol. XX, July 1826, *Noctes Ambrosianae*, XXVII, pp. 93–4.

Reprinted in 1831.

O Weel Befa' . . . .p. 108.

From The Haunted Glen. Reprinted in 1831 and again in *Noctes Ambrosianae*, LV, vol. XXIX, pp. 546–7.

I lookit east. *Blackwood's Magazine*, vol. XX, Oct. 1826, *Noctes Ambrosianae*, XXVIII, pp. 622–3.

Tam Nelson . . . .p. 623.

There's some souls 'll yammer and cheep . . . .pp. 630–1.

First reprinted with extra verse at beginning as The Soldier's Widow, 1831. Others never reprinted.

The Shepherd's Calendar. By the Ettrick Shepherd. General Anecdotes. Sheep, Prayers, Odd Characters. *Blackwood's Magazine*, vol. XXI, April 1827, pp. 434–48.

Reprinted in The Shepherd's Calendar, vol. II, chs. V, VI, VII.

Ode for Music. On the Death of Lord Byron. By the Ettrick Shepherd. *Blackwood's Magazine*, vol. XXI, May 1827, pp. 520–1.

Never reprinted.

The Shepherd's Calendar. By the Ettrick Shepherd. Dreams and Apparitions, Containing George Dobson's Expedition to Hell, and The Souters of Selkirk . . . .pp. 549–62.

Reprinted in The Shepherd's Calendar, vol. I, chs. V, VI.

The Shepherd's Calendar. Dreams and Apparitions. Part II. Containing Tibby Hislop's Dream, and the Sequel. Unsigned. *Blackwood's Magazine*, vol. XXI, June 1827, pp. 664–76.

Reprinted in The Shepherd's Calendar, vol. I, ch. VIII.

The Shepherd's Calendar. Dreams and Apparitions, containing Smithy Cracks, &c. Part III. Unsigned. *Blackwood's Magazine*, vol. XXII, July 1827, pp. 64–73.

Reprinted as The Laird of Wineholm in The Shepherd's Calendar, vol. I, ch. II.

The Shepherd's Calendar. By the Ettrick Shepherd. Dreams and Apparitions. Part IV. *Blackwood's Magazine*, vol. XXII, Aug. 1827, pp. 173–85.

Reprinted as The Laird of Cassway in The Shepherd's Calendar, vol. I, ch. VII.

The Perilis of Wemyng. Ane moste woeful Tragedye. Compilit be Maister Hougge . . . .pp. 214–21.

Reprinted as May of the Moril Glen in A Queer Book.

The Marvellous Doctor. By the Ettrick Shepherd. *Blackwood's Magazine*, vol. XXII, Sept. 1827, pp. 349–61.

Reprinted in The Shepherd's Calendar, vol. I, ch. III.

Ane Pastorale of the Rocke. Maide be Maister Hougge. *Blackwood's Magazine*, vol. XXII, Dec. 1827, pp. 675–84.

Never reprinted.

Trials of Temper. By the Ettrick Shepherd. *Blackwood's Magazine*, vol. XXIII, Jan. 1828, pp. 40–6.

Reprinted in 1837.

Moralitas . . . . p. 47.

Reprinted in 1838–40.

I'll no wake wi' Annie. *Noctes Ambrosianae*, XXXV, pp. 113–4.

Reprinted in 1831.

The Shepherd's Calendar. Class IX. Fairies, Brownies, and Witches. By the Ettrick Shepherd. *Blackwood's Magazine*, vol. XXIII, Feb. 1828, pp. 214–27.

Reprinted as Mary Burnet in The Shepherd's Calendar, vol. I, ch. IX.

The Shepherd's Calendar. Class IX. Fairies, Deils, and Witches. By the Ettrick Shepherd. *Blackwood's Magazine*, vol. XXIII, April 1828, pp. 509–19.

Reprinted as The Witches of Traquair in The Shepherd's Calendar, vol. II, ch. IV.

In Embro town they made a law. *Blackwood's Magazine*, vol. XXIII, May 1828, *Noctes Ambrosianae*, XXXVI, p. 782.

Chalk! chalk! . . . . p. 794.

Good night and Joy . . . . p. 802.

Good night reprinted in 1831; others never reprinted.

A Strange Secret. Related in a Letter from the Ettrick Shepherd. *Blackwood's Magazine*, vol. XXIII, June 1828, pp. 822–6.

Enlarged and reprinted in The Shepherd's Calendar, vol. II, ch. II.

Ane rychte gude and pretious ballande. Compylit be Mr Hougge. *Blackwood's Magazine*, vol. XXIV, Aug. 1828, pp. 177–83.

Reprinted as The Spirit of the Glen in A Queer Book.

The Brownie of the Black Haggs. By the Ettrick Shepherd. *Blackwood's Magazine*, vol. XXIV, Oct. 1828, pp. 489–96.

Reprinted in The Shepherd's Calendar, vol. I, ch. X.

The Stuarts of Appin . . . . *Noctes Ambrosianae*, XXXVIII, pp. 535–6.

Reprinted in 1831.

The Goode Manne of Allowa. Ane most strainge and treuthfulle Ballande, Made be Mr Hougge. *Blackwood's Magazine*, vol. XXIV, Nov. 1828, pp. 561–9.

Reprinted in A Queer Book.

A Letter from Yarrow. The Ettrick Shepherd to the Editor of the *Edinburgh Literary Journal*. *Edinburgh Literary Journal*, vol. I, Nov. 15, 1828, pp. 9–10.

Never reprinted.

A Pastoral Sang. By the Ettrick Shepherd . . . p. 12.

Reprinted as Marion Graham in 1831.

John Nicholson's Daughter. *Blackwood's Magazine*, vol. XXIV, Dec. 1828, *Noctes Ambrosianae*, XL, p. 688.

Reprinted in *Friendship's Offering*, 1829, and in 1831.

Noctes Bengerianae. By the Ettrick Shepherd. *Edinburgh Literary Journal*, vol. I, Dec. 27, 1828, pp. 87–90.

Prose never reprinted. Verses, i.e. Mary is my only joy, What tongue can speak, and Auld John Nicol (only two verses here), reprinted in 1831.

SELECT AND RARE / SCOTISH MELODIES. / The Poetry by / the Celebrated / Ettrick Shepherd / The / Symphonies and Accompaniments / Composed and the Whole Adapted and Arranged / By Henry R. Bishop. / London Published by Goulding and D'Almaine, 20, Soho Square. / Manufacturers of Cabinet, Harmonic & Square Piano Fortes, / where an elegant assortment for Sale or Hire may be seen. (1829.)

Four of the songs were quoted in the *Edinburgh Literary Journal*, vol. I, pp. 101–3; and all were reprinted in 1831.

THE / SHEPHERD'S CALENDAR. / By James Hogg, / author of "The Queen's Wake," &c. &c. / In two volumes. / (vol. I) / William Blackwood, Edinburgh; / and T. Cadell, London. / MDCCCXXIX. 12mo.

(Advertisement. The greater number of the Tales contained in these volumes appeared originally in Blackwood's Edinburgh Magazine. They have been revised with care; and to complete the Collection, several Tales hitherto unpublished have been added.)

Vol. I, pp. 326.

Rob Dodds.
Mr Adamson of Laverhope.
The Prodigal Son.
The School of Misfortune.
George Dobson's Expedition to Hell.
The Souters of Selkirk.
The Laird of Cassway.
Tibby Hyslop's Dream.

Vol. II, pp. 326.

Window Wat's Courtship.
A Strange Secret.
The Marvellous Doctor.
The Witches of Traquair.
Sheep.
Prayers.
Odd Characters.
Nancy Chisholm.
Snow-Storms.

Vol. I (*contd.*)	Vol. II (*contd.*)
Mary Burnet.	The Shepherd's Dog.
The Brownie of the Black Haggs.	
The Laird of Wineholm.	

Reprinted in 1837.

Tales of / the Ettrick Shepherd / Edited by / George C. Pringle, M.A. / Rector of Peebles High School. / London / Blackie & Son....1909. 8vo, p. 96.

Shortened versions of The Souters of Selkirk, Sheep, The Shepherd's Dog, Storms.

The Wanderer's Tale. By the Ettrick Shepherd. *Edinburgh Literary Journal*, vol. I, Jan. 3, 1829, pp. 109–10.

Really part of the *Noctes Bengerianae*.

Never reprinted.

1828. By the Ettrick Shepherd...pp. 113–4.

Reprinted 1838–40.

A Scots Sang. By the Ettrick Shepherd. *Edinburgh Literary Journal*, vol. I, Jan. 17, 1829, p. 140.

Reprinted in 1831 as I hae lost my love.

Jock Johnstone the Tinkler. By the Ettrick Shepherd. *Blackwood's Magazine*, vol. xxv, Feb. 1829, pp. 173–8.

Reprinted in A Queer Book.

Noctes Bengerianae, No. II. By the Ettrick Shepherd. *Edinburgh Literary Journal*, vol. I, March 21, 1829, pp. 258–60.

Prose never reprinted. Songs reprinted, i.e. O saw ye this sweet bonny lassie (but v. pp. 102–3 here); Auld John Nicol (in full); Dennis Delany; There's a bonny, bonny laddie.

Mary Melrose. By the Ettrick Shepherd. *Blackwood's Magazine*, vol. xxv, April 1829, pp. 411–20.

Never reprinted.

An Eskdale Anecdote. Extract of a Letter from the Ettrick Shepherd. *Edinburgh Literary Journal*, vol. I, April 25, 1829, pp. 337–8.

Never reprinted.

A Real Love Sang. By the Ettrick Shepherd. *Edinburgh Literary Journal*, vol. I, May 2, 1829, p. 352.

Reprinted in 1831 as Love came to the door.

Reminiscences of Former Days. My first interview with Allan Cunningham. By the Ettrick Shepherd. *Edinburgh Literary Journal*, vol. I, May 16, 1829, pp. 374–5.

....My first interview with Sir Walter Scott....Vol. II, June 27, 1829, pp. 51–2.

Both included in later issues of the Memoir.

Sound Morality. By the Ettrick Shepherd. *Blackwood's Magazine*, vol. xxv, June 1829, pp. 741–7.
Reprinted in 1837.

Will and Sandy. A Scots Pastoral. By the Ettrick Shepherd.... pp. 748–51.
Reprinted in A Queer Book.

A Tale of the Martyrs. By the Ettrick Shepherd. *Blackwood's Magazine*, vol. xxvi, July 1829, pp. 48–51.
Reprinted in 1837.

O Love's a bitter thing....*Noctes Ambrosianae*, XLV, p. 135.
Reprinted in 1838–40.

A Letter about Men and Women. From the Ettrick Shepherd. *Blackwood's Magazine*, vol. xxvi, Aug. 1829, pp. 245–50.
Never reprinted.

? The Bards of Britain. By David Tweedie. *Edinburgh Literary Journal*, vol. II, Aug. 1, 1829, pp. 127–8.
Possibly by Hogg. Never reprinted.

Elen of Reigh. By the Ettrick Shepherd. *Blackwood's Magazine*, vol. xxvi, Sept. 1829, pp. 271–7.
Reprinted in A Queer Book.

Let them cant about Adam and Eve....*Noctes Ambrosianae*, XLVI, pp. 403–4.
Never reprinted.

A New Poetic Mirror. By the Ettrick Shepherd. No. I.—Mr W. W. Ode to a Highland Bee. *Edinburgh Literary Journal*, vol. II, Sept. 5, 1829, p. 199.
....No. II, Mr T. M....Oct. 24, 1829, pp. 297–8.
Never reprinted.

Wat the Prophet. By the Ettrick Shepherd. *Edinburgh Literary Journal*, vol. II, Sept. 12, 1829, pp. 207–10.

The Auld Man's Wife's Dead. A Parody. By the Ettrick Shepherd....pp. 212–3.
Neither reprinted.

The P and the Q; or, the Adventures of Jock M'Pherson. By the Ettrick Shepherd. *Blackwood's Magazine*, vol. xxvi, Oct. 1829, pp. 693–5.
Reprinted in 1838–40.

Anecdotes of Highlanders. By the Ettrick Shepherd. *Edinburgh Literary Journal*, vol. II, Oct. 24, 1829, pp. 293–5.
Never reprinted.

A Singular Letter from Southern Africa. Communicated by Mr Hogg, the Ettrick Shepherd. *Blackwood's Magazine*, vol. xxvi, Nov. 1829, pp. 809–16.

Reprinted as The Pongos in Altrive Tales.

A Song. By the Ettrick Shepherd. *Edinburgh Literary Journal*, vol. II, Nov. 14, 1829, p. 346.
Reprinted in 1831 as Row on, row on, thou cauldrife wave.

A Ballad about Love. By the Ettrick Shepherd. *Edinburgh Literary Journal*, vol. II, Nov. 28, 1829, p. 375.
Reprinted in 1838–40.

A Story of the Forty-Six. By the Ettrick Shepherd. *Edinburgh Literary Journal*, vol. II, Dec. 26, 1829, pp. 421–2.
Reprinted in 1837.

Aughteen Hunder an' Twanty-Nine. By the Ettrick Shepherd. . . .pp. 432–3.
Never reprinted.

The Carle of Invertime. By the author of The Queen's Wake. *The Anniversary*, 1829, pp. 100–7.
Reprinted in A Queer Book.

The Cameronian Preacher's Tale. By the author of The Queen's Wake. . . .pp. 170–91.
Reprinted in 1837.

The Minstrel Boy. By the Ettrick Shepherd. *Friendship's Offering*, 1829, pp. 209–13. (Tread light this haunted grove.)
Never reprinted.

Auld Joe Nicholson's Bonny Nannie. A Scotch Sang. By the Ettrick Shepherd. . . .pp. 263–4.
Reprinted from *Blackwood's*, v. p. 206 here.
Reprinted in 1831.

Ballad. By the Ettrick Shepherd. . . .pp. 415–6. (The Broken Heart.)
Reprinted in 1831.

Verses to a Beloved Young Friend. By the Ettrick Shepherd. . . . pp. 417–8.
Never reprinted.

Dr David Dale's Account of a Grand Aerial Voyage. By the Ettrick Shepherd. *Edinburgh Literary Journal*, vol. III, Jan. 23, 1830, pp. 50–4.
Never reprinted in full. Two of the songs, The Moon and The Witch of Fife, reprinted in 1831.

The Last Stork. By the Ettrick Shepherd. *Blackwood's Magazine*, vol. XXVII, Feb. 1830, pp. 217–22.
Reprinted in A Queer Book.

My Love she's but a lassie yet. By the Ettrick Shepherd. *Edinburgh Literary Journal*, vol. III, March 6, 1830, pp. 147–8.
Reprinted in 1831.

A Letter from Yarrow. The Scottish Psalmody Defended. Signed, James Hogg. *Edinburgh Literary Journal*, vol. III, March 13, 1830, pp. 162–3.
Never reprinted.

Andrew the Packman; After the manner of Wordsworth. By the Ettrick Shepherd. *Edinburgh Literary Journal*, vol. III, March 20, 1830, pp. 179–80.
Never reprinted.

The Lairde of Lonne. Ane Rychte Breiffe and Wyttie Ballande, compilit by Maister Hougge. *Blackwood's Magazine*, vol. XXVII, April 1830, pp. 571–7.
Reprinted in A Queer Book.

The Flower of Annisley. By the Ettrick Shepherd. *Fraser's Magazine*, vol. I, April 1830, pp. 308–9.
Reprinted in 1831.

A Greek Pastoral. By the Ettrick Shepherd. *Blackwood's Magazine*, vol. XXVII, May 1830, pp. 766–71.
Reprinted in A Queer Book.

I hae naebody now. By the Ettrick Shepherd. *Fraser's Magazine*, vol. I, May 1830, p. 398.
Reprinted in 1831.

Verses for the Eye of Mr David Tweedie of that Ilk. By the Ettrick Shepherd. *Edinburgh Literary Journal*, vol. III, May 8, 1830, pp. 276–7.
Never reprinted.

The Meeting of Anglers, or, The St Ronan's Muster Roll. *Edinburgh Literary Journal*, vol. III, May 15, 1830, p. 290.
Almost certainly by Hogg.
Never reprinted.

A Grand New Blacking Sang. By the Ettrick Shepherd.... p. 290.
Never reprinted.

Song. By the Ettrick Shepherd. *Edinburgh Literary Journal*, vol. III, May 29, 1830, p. 319. (Afore the moorcock begin.)
Reprinted in 1838–40.

The First Sermon. By the Ettrick Shepherd. *Blackwood's Magazine*, vol. XXVII, June 1830, pp. 879–80.
Reprinted in 1838–40.

Some Remarkable Passages in the Remarkable Life of the Baron St Gio. By the Ettrick Shepherd....pp. 891–905.
Reprinted in 1837.

Story of Adam Scott. By the Ettrick Shepherd. *Blackwood's Magazine*, vol. XXVIII, July 1830, pp. 41–6.

Reprinted in 1837.

A Real Vision. By the Ettrick Shepherd....pp. 63–5.

Never reprinted.

The Lass o' Carlisle. An Excellent New Song. By the Ettrick Shepherd. *Fraser's Magazine*, vol. I, July 1830, p. 654.

Reprinted in 1831.

A Ballad from the Gaelic. By the Ettrick Shepherd. *Edinburgh Literary Journal*, vol. IV, July 10, 1830, p. 30. (Balloch.)

Reprinted in 1838–40.

The Origin of the Fairies. By the Ettrick Shepherd. *Blackwood's Magazine*, vol. XXVIII, Aug. 1830, pp. 209–17.

Reprinted in A Queer Book.

When Bawdrons, wi' her mousin' paw; The Cutting o' my hair; Maga at No. 45....*Noctes Ambrosianae*, LI, pp. 385, 406, 422–3.

First and third never reprinted; second reprinted in 1838–40.

Lines for the Eye of the beautiful Miss E. B. By the Ettrick Shepherd. *Fraser's Magazine*, vol. II, Aug. 1830, pp. 31–2.

Never reprinted.

Jocke Taittis Expeditioune till Hell. Compilit bee Maister Hougge. *Blackwood's Magazine*, vol. XXVIII, Sept. 1830, pp. 512–7.

Reprinted in A Queer Book.

The Unearthly Witness. By the Ettrick Shepherd. *Fraser's Magazine*, vol. II, Sept. 1830, pp. 171–8.

Never reprinted.

A Horrible Instance of the Effects of Clanship. By the Ettrick Shepherd. *Blackwood's Magazine*, vol. XXVIII, Oct. 1830, pp. 680–7.

Reprinted as Julia M'Kenzie in Tales of the Wars of Montrose.

Allen Dhu. A Love Song. By the Ettrick Shepherd. *Edinburgh Literary Journal*, vol. IV, Oct. 9, 1830, p. 232.

Reprinted in 1831.

A Genuine Love Letter. By the Ettrick Shepherd. *Edinburgh Literary Journal*, vol. IV, Oct. 23, 1830, p. 262.

Reprinted in 1838–40.

Some Remarks on the Life of Sandy Elshinder. By the Ettrick Shepherd. *Edinburgh Literary Journal*, vol. IV, Oct. 30, 1830, pp. 280–2.

Never reprinted.

A Sunday Pastoral. By the Ettrick Shepherd. *Blackwood's Magazine*, vol. XXVIII, Nov. 1830, pp. 737–41.

Reprinted in A Queer Book.

The Raid of the Kers. By the Ettrick Shepherd. *Blackwood's Magazine*, vol. XXVIII, Dec. 1830, pp. 895–9.

Reprinted in A Queer Book.

The Mysterious Bride. By the Ettrick Shepherd....pp. 943–50.
Reprinted in 1837.

Strange Letter of a Lunatic. To Mr James Hogg of Mount Benger. *Fraser's Magazine*, vol. II, Dec. 1830, pp. 526–32.
Never reprinted.

I dinna blame thy bonny face. A Song. By the Ettrick Shepherd. *Edinburgh Literary Journal*, vol. IV, Dec. 17, 1830, p. 379.
Reprinted in 1838–40.

A Highland Song of Triumph for King William's Birthday. By the Ettrick Shepherd. *Edinburgh Literary Journal*, vol. IV, Dec. 25, 1830, p. 385.
Reprinted in 1838–40.

A Story of the Black Art. Part I. By the Ettrick Shepherd.... pp. 396–9;....Part II....vol. V, Jan. 1, 1831, pp. 10–2.
Never reprinted.

A Scots Luve Sang. By the Ettrick Shepherd. *Friendship's Offering*, 1830, pp. 185–6.
Reprinted from The Spy; reprinted in 1831 as Mischievous Woman.

The Fords of Callum. An Ower True Tale....pp. 187–96.
Reprinted in 1837; and in *The Sphere* Christmas Number, 1926, pp. 8, 9, 46.

A Bard's Address to his Youngest Daughter....pp. 312–4.
Reprinted in A Queer Book.

A Child's Prayer. By the Ettrick Shepherd. *Juvenile Forget Me Not*, 1830, pp. 114–5.
Never reprinted.

A Cameronian Ballad. By James Hogg. *Annual Register*, 1830, pp. 529–32.
Reprinted as Bothwell Brig in A Queer Book.

The Club Book, / being / Original Tales, / &c. / by various authors. / Edited by the author of "The Dominie's Legacy." / In Three Volumes. / (Vol. I) / London: / printed for / Cochrane and Pickersgill, / 11, Waterloo-place, Pall-Mall. / 1831. 12mo.
The Laidlaws and the Scotts. A Border Tradition. By the Ettrick Shepherd. Vol. III, pp. 143–64.
Never reprinted.
The Bogle o' the Brae; a Queer Courting Story....pp. 231–64.
Reprinted on pp. 107–21 of Ascanius, or The Young Adventurer....Cameron & Ferguson (1876).

SONGS, / by / the Ettrick Shepherd. / Now first collected. / William Blackwood, Edinburgh: / and T. Cadell, London. / MDCCCXXXI.

All reprinted in 1838–40, with the exception of Oh-hon, oh righ! there's something wanting.

King Willie. *Blackwood's Magazine*, vol. XXIX, Jan. 1831, *Noctes Ambrosianae*, LIII, pp. 17–8.
Reprinted in 1838–40.

Geordie Scott. A Hamely Pastoral. By the Ettrick Shepherd. *Fraser's Magazine*, vol. III, Feb. 1831, pp. 39–43.
Never reprinted.

O weel befa', *Blackwood's Magazine*, vol. XXIX, March 1831, *Noctes Ambrosianae*, LV, pp. 546–7.
Quoted from the Songs.

The Barber of Duncow. A ghost story. By the Ettrick Shepherd. *Fraser's Magazine*, vol. III, March 1831, pp. 174–80.
Never reprinted.

The Bogle. A Song. By the Ettrick Shepherd. *Edinburgh Literary Journal*, vol. V, March 12, 1831, pp. 171–2.
Never reprinted.

The Minister's Annie. Communicated by the Ettrick Shepherd. *Edinburgh Literary Journal*, vol. V, March 26, 1831, pp. 189–92.

The Dominie. By the Ettrick Shepherd . . . . p. 199.
Neither reprinted.

A Story of Good Queen Bess. By the Ettrick Shepherd. *Blackwood's Magazine*, vol. XXIX, April 1831, pp. 579–93.
Reprinted in 1837.

Johnee Graimis Eckspeditioun till Hevin. Compilit be Mr Hougge . . . . pp. 641–4.
Reprinted as The Miser's Warning in A Queer Book.

The Miser's Grave. By the Ettrick Shepherd. *Blackwood's Magazine*, vol. XXIX, June 1831, pp. 915–8.
Never reprinted.

Disagreeables. By the Ettrick Shepherd. *Fraser's Magazine*, vol. III, June 1831, pp. 567–9.
Never reprinted.

The Flower o' Glendale. By the Ettrick Shepherd. *Edinburgh Literary Journal*, vol. V, June 4, 1831, pp. 361–2.
Never reprinted.

Aunt Susan. By the Ettrick Shepherd. *Fraser's Magazine*, vol. III, July 1831, pp. 720–6.
Never reprinted.

I'm a' gane wrang. A Song. By the Ettrick Shepherd. *Edinburgh Literary Journal*, vol. VI, July 2, 1831, p. 15.
Reprinted in 1838–40.

An Awfu' Leein'-Like Story. By the Ettrick Shepherd. *Blackwood's Magazine*, vol. xxx, Sept. 1831, pp. 448–56

Never reprinted.

The Magic Mirror. By the Ettrick Shepherd. *Blackwood's Magazine*, vol. xxx, Oct. 1831, pp. 650–4.

Never reprinted.

Lyttil Pynkie. By the Ettrick Shepherd. *Blackwood's Magazine*, vol. xxx, Nov. 1831, pp. 782–9.

Reprinted in A Queer Book.

The Monitors . . . . *Noctes Ambrosianae*, LIX, pp. 843–4.

Reprinted in 1838–40.

Crawford John. By the Ettrick Shepherd. *Fraser's Magazine*, vol. IV, Nov. 1831, pp. 422–8.

Never reprinted.

An Epitaph on two living characters. Supposed by the Ettrick Shepherd. *Edinburgh Literary Journal*, vol. VI, Nov. 5, 1831, p. 273.

Reprinted from The Spy. Reprinted in 1838–40.

On the Separate Existence of the Soul. By the Ettrick Shepherd. *Fraser's Magazine*, vol. IV, Dec. 1831, pp. 529–37.

Never reprinted.

Grizel Graham. By the Ettrick Shepherd. *Edinburgh Literary Journal*, vol. VI, Dec. 24, 1831; Dec. 31, 1831; pp. 374–7, 385–7.

Never reprinted.

A Child's Hymn for the Close of the Week. By the Ettrick Shepherd. *Juvenile Forget-me-not*, 1831, pp. 78–80.

Never reprinted.

A / QUEER BOOK. / By / the Ettrick Shepherd. / William Blackwood, Edinburgh; and / T. Cadell, Strand, London. / MDCCCXXXII. 12mo, pp. (4) ii, 380.

Dedication to Christopher North and Timothy Tickler.

Contents:

*Wife of Ezdel-More.
*Robin Reid.
Elen of Reigh.
The Good Man of Alloa.
Jock Johnstone the Tinkler.
A Lay of the Martyrs.
Bothwell Brig.
The Carle of Invertime.
*The Laird of Lun.
Ringan and May.
*The Grousome Carle.
Love's Jubilee.
The Spirit of the Glen.
*Jock Tait's Expedition to Hell.
A Bard's Address to his youngest Daughter.
The Miser's Warning.
St Mary of the Lowes.
The Origin of the Fairies.
Allan of Dale.
*Will and Sandy. A Scots Pastoral.

The Last Stork. A Greek Pastoral.
Superstition and Grace. *A Sunday Pastoral.
*The Witch of the Gray Thorn. May of the Moril Glen.

Those marked * were never reprinted; the rest were reprinted in 1838–40.

ALTRIVE TALES: / collected / among the peasantry of Scotland, / and / from foreign adventurers. / By / the Ettrick Shepherd. / With illustrations by George Cruikshank. / Vol. I. / London: / James Cochrane and Co. / 11 Waterloo Place, Pall Mall. / 1832. 8vo, pp. cli, 190.

Twelve volumes were planned, to be printed "uniformly with the Waverley Novels," but owing to the publisher's failure no more were published.

Pp. i–cli are occupied by the Dedication to the Right Hon. Lady Anne Scott of Buccleuch (verses as in The Brownie of Bodsbeck), the Memoir of the Author's Life, and Reminiscences of Former Days; all reprinted in 1838–40.

Adventures of Captain John Lochy, written by himself.
The Pongos: a letter from Southern Africa.
Marion's Jock.
None of the three stories reprinted.

The Twa Burdies. By the Ettrick Shepherd. *Fraser's Magazine*, vol. v, Feb. 1832, pp. 20–2.

One Thousand Eight Hundred and Thirty-One. By the Ettrick Shepherd . . . .p. 84.

Neither reprinted.

A Tale of an Old Highlander. By the Ettrick Shepherd. *The Metropolitan*, vol. III, Feb. 1832, pp. 112–20.

Never reprinted.

The Elder in Love. By the Ettrick Shepherd. *Fraser's Magazine*, vol. v, March 1832, pp. 234–7.

Never reprinted.

Some Terrible Letters from Scotland. Communicated by the Ettrick Shepherd. *The Metropolitan*, vol. III, April 1832, pp. 422–31.

Never reprinted.

The Mountain Dew Men. By the Ettrick Shepherd. *Fraser's Magazine*, vol. VI, Sept. 1832, pp. 161–70.

Never reprinted.

This Warld's an unco Bonny Place. By the Ettrick Shepherd. *Fraser's Magazine*, vol. VI, Oct. 1832, pp. 359–61.

Never reprinted.

Gallery of Literary Characters. No. XXX. Sir David Brewster,

K.H. Signed, James Hogg. *Fraser's Magazine*, vol. VI, Nov. 1832, p. 416.
Never reprinted.

Ewan M'Gabhar. By the Ettrick Shepherd . . . . pp. 450–9.
Reprinted in 1837.

Letter to Oliver Yorke. Signed. *Fraser's Magazine*, vol. VII, Jan. 1833, p. 16.

An Auld Wife's Dream. By the Ettrick Shepherd . . . . pp. 68–72.
Neither reprinted.

A Remarkable Egyptian Story. Written by Barek, a learned Jew of Egypt, about the latter end of the reign of Cambyses the Persian. (Discovered and Communicated by the Ettrick Shepherd.) *Fraser's Magazine*, vol. VII, Feb. 1833, pp. 147–58.
Never reprinted.

(The Shepherd's Noctes, and the Reason why they do not appear in Fraser's Magazine.) *Fraser's Magazine*, vol. VIII, July 1833, pp. 49–54. Part of the dialogue and seven songs quoted.
Dialogue never reprinted. All the songs except the first—Awa, Whigs! awa, Whigs!—reprinted in 1838–40, i.e. King Willie; Hey, then up go we; M'Kimmon; Gin ye meet a bonny lassie; Me an' my Moggy; Rise, rise.
For the authorship of the songs, v. pp. 102–3 here.

Letter from Hogg. *Fraser's Magazine*, vol. VIII, Nov. 1833, p. 635.
Never reprinted.

A Series of Lay Sermons / on Good Principles / and Good Breeding. / By the Ettrick Shepherd. / London / James Fraser Regent Street / MDCCCXXXIV. 12mo, pp. xii, 330.
Never reprinted.

(Familiar Anecdotes of Sir Walter Scott. By James Hogg, the Ettrick Shepherd; with a Sketch of the Life of the Shepherd, by S. De Witt Bloodgood. 'A man's a man for a' that." New York: published by Harper and Brothers, No. 82 Cliff-Street. And sold by the principal Booksellers throughout the United States. MDCCCXXXIV. Post 8vo, pp. vi, 251.)
Published in Great Britain as:

The Domestic Manners / and / Private Life / of / Sir Walter Scott. / By James Hogg. / With a memoir of the author, notes, &c. / MDCCCXXXIV. / Glasgow:—John Reid & Co.; / Edinburgh:—Oliver and Boyd; / London:—Black, Young and Young. 12mo, pp. iv, 136. The memoir is Bloodgood's Sketch.
Reprinted, without memoir or footnotes, by William Brown, 149 Prince's Street, Edinburgh, 1882. 8vo, pp. viii, 102.
Reprinted, with old footnotes but new memoir by the Rev.

J. E. H. Thomson, D.D., by Eneas Mackay, Stirling. 1909. 8vo, pp. 124.

Extraordinary History of a Border Beauty. By the Ettrick Shepherd. *Fraser's Magazine*, vol. IX, Jan. 1834, pp. 97–110.

More promised but not given.

Never reprinted.

The Frasers in the Correi. By the Ettrick Shepherd. *Fraser's Magazine*, vol. IX, March 1834, pp. 273–8.

Prose never reprinted. Verses already printed in 1831 and reprinted in 1838–40.

Mora Campbell. By the Ettrick Shepherd. *Blackwood's Magazine*, vol. XXXV, June 1834, pp. 947–54.

Reprinted in 1838–40.

Love's Legacy. By the Ettrick Shepherd. Canto I. *Fraser's Magazine*, vol. X, Oct. 1834, pp. 403–8; .... Canto II.... Nov. 1834, pp. 556–60; .... Canto III.... Dec. 1834, pp. 639–44.

Never reprinted.

TALES / OF THE / WARS OF MONTROSE. / By James Hogg, Esq., / author of "The Queen's Wake," / In three volumes. / (Vol. I) / London: / James Cochrane and Co. / 11 Waterloo Place. / 1835. 12mo.

Vol. I, pp. (2) 298.

Some remarkable passages in the Life of an Edinburgh Baillie.

Vol. II, pp. (2) 274.

The Adventures of Colonel Peter Aston.

Julia M'Kenzie.

The Remarkable Adventures of Sir Simon Brodie.

Vol. III, pp. (2) 258.

Wat Pringle o' the Yair.

Mary Montgomery.

All except Sir Simon Brodie reprinted in 1837.

(Sketches by HB. From the Portfolio of the Ettrick Shepherd. *Blackwood's Magazine*, vol. XXXVII, Jan. 1835, pp. 72–5; .... Feb. 1835, pp. 410–2.)

Not Hogg's in the main, though he may have had a hand in the production. It is really an extension of the *Noctes Ambrosianae*; cf. vol. XXXVI, Dec. 1834, *Noctes Ambrosianae*, LXIX, p. 857.

Never reprinted.

Anecdotes of Ghosts and Apparitions. By the Ettrick Shepherd. I. David Hunter and Phemie. II. Robert Armstrong and Kennedy. *Fraser's Magazine*, vol. XI, Jan. 1835, pp. 103–12.

Never reprinted.

A very ridiculous sermon. By the Ettrick Shepherd. *Fraser's Magazine*, vol. XI, Feb. 1835, pp. 226–31.

Never reprinted.

The Hunter of Comar. By the Ettrick Shepherd. *Fraser's Magazine*, vol. XI, March 1835, pp. 357–9.

Never reprinted.

A Screed on Politics. By the Ettrick Shepherd. *Blackwood's Magazine*, vol. XXXVII, April 1835, pp. 634–42.

Never reprinted.

A Dream. By the Ettrick Shepherd. *Fraser's Magazine*, vol. XI, May 1835, pp. 516–7.

Never reprinted.

The Three Sisters. By the Ettrick Shepherd. *Fraser's Magazine*, vol. XI, June 1835, pp. 666–79.

Revised and reprinted from The Three Perils of Man.

Never reprinted.

The Chickens in the Corn. By the Ettrick Shepherd. *Fraser's Magazine*, vol. XII, Sept. 1835, pp. 281–2.

Never reprinted.

Hymn to the Redeemer. By the Ettrick Shepherd. *The Amulet*, 1835, pp. 118–20.

Reprinted with slight changes from The Three Perils of Man.

Never reprinted.

The Turners. By the Ettrick Shepherd. *Fraser's Magazine*, vol. XIII, May 1836, pp. 609–19.

Never reprinted.

The Ettrick Shepherd's Last Tale, Helen Crocket, with an Introduction by Oliver Yorke. *Fraser's Magazine*, vol. XIV, Oct. 1836, pp. 425–40.

Never reprinted.

THE / WORKS / OF / ROBERT BURNS. / Edited by / the Ettrick Shepherd, / and / William Motherwell, Esq. / (vol. I) / Glasgow: / Archibald Fullarton, and Co. / 110, Brunswick Street; / and 6, Roxburgh Place, Edinburgh. / 1840. (Really 1838–41.)

Hogg was responsible only for the Memoir in vol. V; two of his songs are in vol. V, pp. 28–9—What can ane say—and pp. 287–8—Robin's Awa! Never reprinted.

TALES AND SKETCHES, / by / the Ettrick Shepherd. / Including / The Brownie of Bodsbeck, Winter Evening Tales, / Shepherd's Calendar, &c. &c. / and several pieces not before printed, / with illustrative engravings, / chiefly from real scenes. / By

D. O. Hill, Esq., S.A. / (vol. I) / Blackie & Son, Queen Street, Glasgow; / South College Street, Edinburgh; / and Warwick Square, London. / MDCCCXXXVII.

12mo, vol. I, pp. (6) 352; vol. II, pp. (4) 354; vol. III, pp. (4) 360; vol. IV, pp. (4) 360; vol. V, pp. (4) 360; vol. VI, pp. (4) 360.

The "pieces not before printed" are:

Vol. I. Allan Gordon.
A Tale of Pentland.
Vol. II. The Bush aboon Traquhair; or The Rural Philosophers. A Pastoral Drama with Songs.
Vol. III. Katie Cheyne.
Vol. IV. Emigration.
The Watchmaker.
Nature's Magic Lantern.
Vol. VI. Gordon the Gipsey.

Reprinted in 1852 with a new title-page.

THE TALES / OF JAMES HOGG, / THE ETTRICK SHEPHERD. / Library Edition.—In two volumes. / (Vol. I) / London: Hamilton, Adams & Co. / Glasgow: Thomas D. Morison. / 1880. 8vo, vol. I, pp. xvi, 496; vol. II, pp. viii, 502.

Follows the text of 1837. Life in vol. I, by J. T. B.

THE / POETICAL WORKS / OF THE / ETTRICK SHEPHERD, / including / The Queen's Wake, Pilgrims of the Sun, Mador of / the Moor, Mountain Bard, &c. &c. / With a life of the author, / by / Professor Wilson, / University of Edinburgh; / and Illustrative Engravings, / from original drawings, / by D. O. Hill, Esq., S.A. / (vol. I) / Blackie & Son, Queen Street, Glasgow; / South College Street, Edinburgh: / and Warwick Square, London. / MDCCCXXXVIII. 12mo.

Vol. I, pp. viii, 352; vol. II, pp. iv, 356; vol. III, pp. (2) 356; vol. IV, MDCCCXXXIX, pp. iv, 356; vol. V, MDCCCXL, pp. cxxvi, 234.

Vol. V has facsimile of autograph announcement by Wilson—"Messrs. Blackie inform the subscribers to this work that a Memoir of Mr Hogg, on a more extensive scale than was at first contemplated, is in preparation by Professor Wilson, and will be published by them, within a few months, in the same type and form as these volumes."

Hogg's Autobiography, as in Altrive Tales, was therefore included instead (pp. ix–cxxvi).

Wilson's Life never appeared.

(A rhymed epistle to John Morrison, land-surveyor, and a rhymed epitaph, both by Hogg, are included in the introduction to

Morrison's Random Reminiscences, *Tait's Magazine*, vol. x, Sept. 1843. They are dated July 18th, 1810, and were never reprinted.)

Song written in album (Alone in the mountains poor Mona reclined) sent to *Notes & Queries*, 3rd Series, vol. II, pp. 430–1, 1863.

Never reprinted.

THE WORKS / OF / THE ETTRICK SHEPHERD. / A New Edition, / Revised at the instance of the author's family, / by the / Rev. Thomas Thomson, / author of "The Comprehensive History of England," "History of Scotland," Supplement to / "Lives of Eminent Scotsmen," etc. etc. / Tales and Sketches. / With illustrative engravings. / (Blackie's device) / London: / Blackie and Son, Paternoster Row; / and Glasgow and Edinburgh. / 1865. 8vo, pp. vi, 712. . . . Poems and Life. . . . 8vo, pp. lvi, 468.

Reprinted with new title-page in 1869.

Vol. I follows the 1837 edition of Tales and Sketches with some changes in the text and the omission of Allan Gordon, Cousin Mattie, The Bush aboon Traquhair, and The Prodigal Son.

Vol. II contains Biographical Sketch of the Ettrick Shepherd, by the Editor; The Poetical Works of the Ettrick Shepherd; with introductions by the Editor to the longer poems; and Hogg's Autobiography, Reminiscences of Former Days, and Reminiscences of Some of my Contemporaries, as in the 1838–40 edition. In contents and arrangement Thomson follows this edition, but there are some slight verbal differences.

This is the most complete edition of Hogg, but the text is not always trustworthy.

A TOUR IN THE HIGHLANDS / IN 1803: / A Series of Letters / by / James Hogg, the Ettrick Shepherd, / addressed to / Sir Walter Scott, Bart. / Reprinted from "The Scottish Review." / Alexander Gardner, / Paisley; and Paternoster Row, London. / 1888. 4to, pp. 118.

Introductory Note, explaining that letters were discovered by Mrs Garden among Hogg's papers, and had not been previously printed.

The Poems / of / James Hogg / the Ettrick Shepherd / (Selected) / with introduction by / Mrs Garden. / London: / Walter Scott, 24 Warwick Lane, Paternoster Row. / And Newcastle-on-Tyne. / 1887. 8vo, pp. 288.

The / Poets / and the / Poetry / of the / Century / George Crabbe / to / Samuel Taylor Coleridge / Edited by / Alfred

H. Miles / Hutchinson & Co. / 25, Paternoster Square, London (1891), 8vo, pp. xvi, 556.

Memoir of Hogg & Selections, pp. 173–210.

The / Story of James Hogg, / the "Ettrick Shepherd." / With selections from his / poetical works. / Edited by / J. Cuthbert Hadden. / Glasgow: / David Bryce and Son. (1897) 32mo, pp. 128.

The Poems of / James Hogg / the Ettrick Shepherd / selected and edited with / an introduction / by / William Wallace, LL.D. / London / Isbister and Company, Limited / 15 Tavistock Street, Covent Garden / 1903. 8vo, pp. 274.

The Songs of / The Ettrick Shepherd. / By James Hogg / With illustrations by Jessie M. King.

Pub. T. N. Foulis, 1912.

Scottish Fairy Tales / Selected and edited by / Sir George Douglas, Bart. / Seven illustrations by James Torrance.

Pub. Walter Scott Publishing Co. (n.d.) 8vo, pp. xxxi, 302.

Contains:

Adam Bell, pp. 201–7.

Cousin Mattie, pp. 278–90.

LIST OF AUTHORITIES

Review of The Jacobite Relics. *Edinburgh Review*, vol. XXXIV, 1819, pp. 148–60.

Review of 3rd edition of The Mountain Bard and Memoir. *Blackwood's Magazine*, vol. x, Aug. 1821, Part II, pp. 43–52.

Review of Familiar Anecdotes of Sir Walter Scott. *American Monthly Magazine*, vol. III, May 1834, pp. 177–84.

Review of The Domestic Manners of Sir Walter Scott. *Fraser's Magazine*, vol. x, Aug. 1834, pp. 125–56.

"A. H. B." (and another?) on the Ettrick Shepherd's career. *Scots Magazine*, vol. LVI, Oct. 1804, and vol. LVII, Jan. 1805. The earliest articles on the Shepherd, containing hardly any real information.

"An American Tourist." A Visit to the Ettrick Shepherd (*American Monthly Magazine*, vol. III, pp. 85–91). 1834.

Aytoun, W. E. Ballads of Scotland. 1858. (2nd Edition.) 1859.

"C. D." Note on Familiar Anecdotes of Sir Walter Scott (*Notes and Queries*, 11th Series, VI, p. 248). 1912.

Carlyle, T. Letters, 1826–36. 1888.

Carruthers, R., *see* Chambers, R.

Chambers, E. K., and Sidgwick, F. Early English Lyrics. 1907.

Chambers, R. Life of Sir Walter Scott (including Carruthers, Abbotsford Notanda). 1871.

Chambers, W. Memoir of Robert Chambers with Autobiographical Reminiscences of William Chambers. 1872.

Child, F. English and Scottish Popular Ballads. 1857–9. 1882–98.

"Dissector, An Old" (i.e. Dr J. Browne). Life of the Ettrick Shepherd Anatomised. 1832.

Douglas, Sir G. B. S. The Blackwood Group. 1897.

„ James Hogg. 1899.

Dyboski, R. Songs, Carols and other Miscellaneous Poems from Balliol MS 354. 1907.

Elliot, Colonel the Hon. W. Fitzwilliam. The Trustworthiness of the Border Ballads. 1906.

„ „ „ Further Essays on the Border Ballads. 1910.

"ε.τ.κ." Christmas Carol (*Notes and Queries*, 3rd Series, II, p. 103). 1862.
Farrer, J. A., and Lang, A. Literary Forgeries. 1907.
Flügel, E. Neuenglisches Lesebuch. 1895.
" Balliol MS 354, The Commonplace Book of Richard Hill (*Anglia*, XXVI, neue Folge XIV). 1903.
"G." Some Particulars relative to the Ettrick Shepherd. *New Monthly Magazine*, vol. XLVI, pp. 194–203; 335–42; 443–6.
Garden, Mrs. Memorials of James Hogg, the Ettrick Shepherd. (3rd edition.) 1903.
Gilchrist, Annie G. Note on Over Yonder's a Park (*Journal of Folk-Song Society*, vol. IV, pp. 52–66).
Gillies, R. P. Recollections of Sir Walter Scott. 1837.
" Memoirs of a Literary Veteran. 1851.
Goldie, G. Letter to a Friend in London. 1821.
Gordon, Mrs. "Christopher North." 1862.
Grundtvig, S. Danmarks gamle Folkeviser. 1853, etc.
Hall, S. C., and Mrs. Memories of the Authors of the Age. James Hogg. (*Eclectic Magazine of Foreign Literature*, n.s. vol. IV, pp. 696–705.) 1866.
Hunt, R. Popular Romances of the West of England. 1865.
James Hogg, the Ettrick Shepherd, Memorial Volume. 1898.
Johnson, J. Scots Musical Museum. 1787–1803.
Ker, W. P. Review of Lang, Sir Walter Scott and the Border Minstrelsy (*Scottish Hist. Review*, vol. VIII, pp. 100–3). 1911.
Lang, A. Life and Letters of J. G. Lockhart. 1897.
" Sir Walter Scott and the Border Minstrelsy. 1910.
" Note (*Scottish Hist. Review*, vol. VIII, p. 221). 1911.
Leyden, J. Poems and Ballads (with Scott's Memoir). 1858.
Lockhart, J. G. Life of Sir Walter Scott. (2nd edition.) 1839.
MacCunn, Mrs. Sir Walter Scott's Friends. 1909.
Manuel, J. Letter of James Hogg. (Communicated to *Notes and Queries*, 5th Series, XI, pp. 432–3.) 1879.
Moore, T. Irish Melodies (collected). 1821.
Morrison, J. Random Reminiscences of Sir Walter Scott, of the Ettrick Shepherd, Sir Henry Raeburn, &c. &c. (Tait's *Edinburgh Magazine*, n.s. vol. X, pp. 569–78, 626–8, 780–6).
"N." Note on Hogg, Wordsworth and Byron (*Notes and Queries*, 5th Series, II, pp. 157–8).
Oliphant, Mrs. William Blackwood and His Sons. (2nd edition.) 1897.
Percy, T. Reliques of Ancient English Poetry. 1765.
Quarles, F. The Shepheards Oracles. 1646.

"R.G." The Ettrick Shepherd's First Song (*Edinburgh Literary Journal*, vol. III, pp. 275–6). 1830.

Ritson, J. Letters. 1833.

Rogers, C. The Modern Scottish Minstrel. 1855, etc.

Russell, Dr J. Reminiscences of Yarrow. 1894.

Saintsbury, G. E. B. Essays in English Literature. 1890.

Scott, Sir W. Minstrelsy of the Scottish Border. 1803–4. (Ed. T. Henderson.) 1902.

„ Journals (ed. Douglas). 1890.

„ Familiar Letters (ed. Douglas). 1894.

Sidgwick, F. A Christmas Carol (*Notes and Queries*, 10th Series, IV, p. 181). 1905.

Smiles, S. A Publisher and his Friends. 1891.

Stephenson, H. T. The Ettrick Shepherd: A Biography. 1922.

Veitch, J. Border Essays. 1890.

„ History and Poetry of the Scottish Border. 1893.

Wilson, J., and others. Noctes Ambrosianae (*Blackwood's Magazine*, and several times reprinted). 1822, etc.

"Z." Further Particulars of the Life of James Hogg, the Ettrick Shepherd. *Scots Magazine*, vol. LVII, July and Nov. 1805.

These articles follow the phrasing of the 1807 Memoir so closely that it is safe to conclude that they were written either by Hogg or by one of his intimate friends under his supervision.

INDEX

GLOSSARY

arles, earnest-money

bauchle, shambler, poor creature
biel', *bield*, refuge
bieldy, affording shelter
biggin', building, esp. out-building
bizz (v.), bustle, hustle
bladd, fragment, lump
bourock, small heap of stones
bourtree, elder-tree
bouzy, *bowzy*, bushy, large
buggen (p.p.), built
bught, sheepfold, esp. pen for confining ewes at milking-time

canty, lively
catwuddied, "cat-witted," small-minded, obstinate and spiteful
cauldrife, chilly
creeshy, greasy

dadd, firm and shaking blow, knock or thump
doof, dull, heavy blow with a softish body
dung (p.p.), overcome

eiry, *eerisome*, gloomy, dismal, rather than weird
elwand, "yardstick"
ether, adder

flakes, wattled hurdles
fley away, frighten away, scare off
flyting, contention
foul flaip, unbroken fall; sometimes conveying the idea of one falling flat on moist or soft ground

gair, isolated strip of tender grass
gaucy, jolly-looking
gaw, wash away
gird, v. *laiggen gird*
gloffe, sudden start
gouk, cuckoo

hained, fenced, enclosed
hallan, partition wall in a cottage, esp. that between door and fireplace, sheltering the room from the draught
heff, holding, place of rest
heftit, (p.p.), A cow's milk is said to be *heftit* when it is not drawn off for some time
hirsel, flock of sheep under charge of a shepherd
hurkle-backit, crook-backed

ingle-cheek, jamb of a fireplace
izel, ash, ember

jurmummled, crushed

killiecoup, somersault
kipple, rafters

laibies, lappets
laiggen gird, hoop securing the bottom of a tub or wooden vessel

lingel, bind with cobbler's thread
lint-swingling, operation of separating the flax from the core by beating it
loan, open uncultivated piece of land, near farmhouse or village, on which the cows are milked
lum, chimney

meinging, mingling, mixture
mumpit, cheated

nailstring, nailstrip, strip of hot iron from which nails are cut out
neb, nose
neicher, laugh loudly

oord (p. def.), became

paik, firm, stiff blow, esp. on body
pawl, make an ineffective attempt to catch
prossing, arrogance

scadd, scald
scouder, scald, scorch
shedding, sheds (collective)
shott, worthless animal
skelp, beat, slap, smack
slogie riddles, wide riddles, used for onions, potatoes or any large produce
smeddum, spirit, energy
snell, sharp, bitter
sourick, common sorrel
stanged (p.p.), stung
swap, resounding blow
swirl, be dizzy

tangleness, indecision
theeking, covering
torfell, "Hogg's use of the word is vague" (N.E.D.). He himself explains it as "roll over," which agrees with one sense given in Wright
towzy, touzled, shaggy

unco (adj.), strange
upsetting, undue assumption

weigh-bauk, balance
whinge, whine
wort (p.p.), become
wud, furious, mad
wyse in to, allow to go in by removing any impediment, as by opening a door

For EU product safety concerns, contact us at Calle de José Abascal, 56–1°, 28003 Madrid, Spain or eugpsr@cambridge.org.

www.ingramcontent.com/pod-product-compliance
Ingram Content Group UK Ltd.
Pitfield, Milton Keynes, MK11 3LW, UK
UKHW012331130625
459647UK00009B/197

* 9 7 8 1 1 0 7 6 3 8 4 3 3 *